Integration of
Human Services

Sheldon P. Gans
Marshall Kaplan, Gans, and Kahn
Gerald T. Horton
The Research Group, Inc.

The study on which this book is based was funded
by the Department of Health, Education, and Welfare,
Social and Rehabilitation Services-Contract
(SRS) 73-02012

Integration of Human Services
The State and Municipal Levels

PRAEGER SPECIAL STUDIES IN U.S. ECONOMIC, SOCIAL, AND POLITICAL ISSUES

Praeger Publishers   New York   Washington   London

Library of Congress Cataloging in Publication Data

Gans, Sheldon P
    Integration of human services.

    (Praeger special studies in U.S. economic, social,
and political issues)
    1. Public welfare—United States.   I. Horton,
Gerald T., joint author.   II. Title.
HV95.G34   1975   361.6'2'0973   75-2030
ISBN 0-275-09970-9

361.6
Y 199i

PRAEGER PUBLISHERS
111 Fourth Avenue, New York, N.Y. 10003, U.S.A.

Published in the United States of America in 1975
by Praeger Publishers, Inc.

75-4253

Printed in the United States of America

This book is an evaluation of services integration—its nature, progress, and federal actions most conducive to this effort. The evaluation describes methods, organizational arrangements, and management techniques to improve the accessibility, continuity, and efficiency of the delivery of human services. Particular attention was also given to the status of human resources planning as it relates to the Allied Services Act of 1972 (reintroduced in 1974) and its implications for state and local planning.

During 1972, the firms of Marshall Kaplan, Gans, and Kahn of San Francisco, California and The Research Group, Inc. of Atlanta, Georgia examined more than 30 projects to determine the factors that lead to integration of social services. The study was commissioned by the Social and Rehabilitation Service, U.S. Department of Health, Education, and Welfare in order to understand more clearly the nature and progress of ongoing efforts in services integration and to identify among possible federal actions, those most conducive to this effort.

The basic approach to the study was the development of case studies based on reviews of documents and structured interviews with major participants in and observers of the projects' history and development. For the most part the field work was undertaken in the first quarter of 1972. A case study was developed for each project by the field teams. These reports provided the basic information for conducting the study analysis.

Part I contains a description of the study methodology, a summary of the study findings, study recommendations, comparative analyses of the projects according to a number of different dimensions, and summaries of the interesting features of selected projects. Part II contains a critique of the Allied Services Act of 1972 based on the experience of six states including the case studies that provide the material for the Part.

This evaluation was financed by a grant from the Social and Rehabilitation Service, Department of Health, Education, and Welfare, under Contract No. SRS 71-37. Acknowledgment must be given to the assistance of HEW staff, especially Mr. Kendrick Lee, in his capacity as project officer, and Mr. Paul J. Fiore as contract officer.

Staff, officials, and citizens involved in each of the services integration efforts provided unlimited cooperation and support to the project staff. The responsibility for this study rests with Marshall Kaplan, Gans, and Kahn (MKGK) and The Research Group,

Inc. (TRG) with their subcontractor, Linton, Mields and Costen.
MKGK was represented by Sheldon P. Gans, partner-in-charge;
George A. Williams, Jr., project director; and Dona Hoard, central
analytical staff. The Research Group provided Gerald T. Horton as
principal-in-charge, and Steven Carlson, state government analyst.

CONTENTS

PART I
INTEGRATION OF HUMAN SERVICES IN HEW:
AN EVALUATION OF SERVICES INTEGRATION PROJECTS

Chapter

PART II
HUMAN RESOURCE SERVICES IN THE STATES: AN ANALYSIS
OF STATE HUMAN RESOURCE AGENCIES
AND THE ALLIED SERVICES ACT OF 1972

LIST OF TABLES AND FIGURES

GLOSSARY

The terms used in this study to refer to various integrating linkages are defined as follows:

Administrative Linkages

1. Fiscal
    a. Joint budgeting: a process in which the integrator sits with all service providers together or individually to develop a budget.
    b. Joint funding: a process by which two or more service providers give funds to support service.
    c. Fund transfer: instances in which funds originally to be used to one service are shifted to be used for another service.
    d. Purchase of service: formal agreements that may or may not involve a written contract between the integrator and autonomous service providers to obtain service.
2. Personal practices
    a. Consolidated personnel administration: the centralized provision of some or all of the following: hiring, firing, promoting, placing, classifying, training, and so on.
    b. Joint use of staff: the case in which two different agencies deliver service by using the same staff.
    c. Staff transfers: the case in which an employee is on the payroll of one agency but is under the administrative control of another.
    d. Staff outstationing: the placement of a service provider in the facility of another service provider.
    e. Colocation: the stationing of staff by autonomous service providers in a common facility.
3. Planning and programing
    a. Joint planning: the joint determination of total service delivery system needs and priorities through a structured planning process.
    b. Joint development of operating policies: a structured process in which the policies, procedures, regulations, and guidelines governing the administration of a project are jointly established.
    c. Joint programing: the joint development of programmatic solutions to defined problems in relation to existing resources.
    d. Information-sharing: an exchange of information regarding resources, procedures, and legal requirements (but not individual clients) between the project integrator and various service providers.
    e. Joint evaluation: the joint determination of effectiveness of service in meeting client needs.

4. Administrative support services
    a. Record-keeping: the gathering, storing, and dissemination of information about clients, including (1) standardized and/or centralized case information and (2) procedures for flow of information.
    b. Grants-management: the servicing of grants.
    c. Central support services: the consolidated or centralized provision of services such as auditing, purchasing, exchange of material and equipment, and consultative services.

Direct Service Linkages

1. Core services
    a. Outreach: the systematic recruitment of clients.
    b. Intake: the process (including determination of eligibility) resulting in the admission of a client to direct service.
    c. Diagnosis: The assessment of a client's overall service needs.
    d. Referral: the process by which a client is directed to another provider for services.
    e. Follow-up: the process used to determine that clients receive the services to which they have been referred and, in general, help them negotiate the service delivery system.
2. Modes of case coordination
    a. Case conference: a meeting between the integrator's staff and staff of agencies that provide service to a given family for the purpose of discussing that family in general or a specific problem, possibly determining a course of action and assigning responsibility among the agencies for implementing the solution.
    b. Case coordinator: the designated staff member having prime responsibility to ensure the provision of service by multiple autonomous providers to a given client.
    c. Case team: the arrangement in which a number of staff members, either representing different disciplines or working with different members of a given family, work together to relate a range of services of autonomous providers to a given client. The primary difference between case conferences and case teams is that the former may be ad hoc while the latter involves continuous and systematic interaction between the members of the team.

xix

I

INTEGRATION OF
HUMAN SERVICES IN HEW:
AN EVALUATION
OF SERVICES
INTEGRATION PROJECTS

1

EXECUTIVE SUMMARY

This report presents in summary form the analytical framework, findings, conclusions, and recommendations contained in Part I. The purpose of Part I is to determine the factors that lead to the integration of social services based on the experience of 30 projects. In particular, its purposes are as follows:

1. To define services integration in workable terms;

2. To develop a methodology for examining critical characteristics of services integration in a large number of differing environments;

3. To assess the impact of integration of services on accessibility, continuity, and efficiency of service delivery;

4. To identify the critical factors that inhibit or facilitate the integration of services;

5. To evaluate the significance and impact of various linkages leading to services integration and the factors contributing to their development; and

6. To isolate those activities and actions that could be undertaken by HEW to foster services integration.

Analytical Framework

The working definition of social services integration utilized during the course of this study has been ''the linking together by various means of the services of two or more service providers to allow treatment of an individual's or family's needs in a more coordinated and comprehensive manner.''

3

Thirty projects meeting this definition were selected for study.[1]
The study sample was designed to provide examples of the wide
variety of projects fitting this definition. The sample was selected
to provide examples of projects with varying project characteristics
including the following:

- Organizing principle for service clustering—age group; problem group; geographic area; and program function.
- Organizational sponsorship—general-purpose government;
  special-purpose public agency; private voluntary council; and
  private non-profit corporation.
- Mode of coordination—voluntary coordination; mediated coordination; and directed coordination.

In the study, services integration projects were viewed as consisting of the integrator (who may also be a provider of direct
services) and autonomous services providers, which are organizationally independent of the integrator but which are tied to it by
various integrating linkages. (In the case of consolidated human
resource agencies, the term autonomous service providers refers
to those departments that previously were organizationally separate
and that have been made a part of the "super-agency.")

The integrator refers to the organizational entity, and more
particularly the board, staff, or person within the entity, responsible
for coordinating the services of autonomous service providers (and
its own services if the integrator should be a deliverer of services
as well) through the development of integrating linkages.

Integrating linkages are the mechanisms that maintain the coordination of the service providers in a services integration project
by tying together or consolidating the various administrative, fiscal,
and service delivery functions each provider ordinarily performs
separately.

There are two distinct types of linkages—direct service linkages
and administrative linkages. Direct services linkages—consisting of
core services (outreach, intake, diagnosis, referral, and follow-up)*
and modes of case coordination (case conference, case coordinator,
case team)—tie together the provision of services to specific clients.
They have immediate, direct results and focus on a client and his
specific needs.

Administrative linkages tie together or consolidate the management of service providers. These linkages are as follows:

Fiscal*	Planning and Programing*
• joint budgeting	• joint planning
• joint funding	• joint development of operating
• fund transfer	policies
• purchase of service	• joint programing
	• information-sharing
	• joint evaluation

---

*These terms are defined in the Glossary.

4

Personnel Practices[*]	Administrative Support[*]
● consolidated personnel administration	● record-keeping
● joint use of staff	● grants management
● staff transfer	● central support services
● staff outstationing	
● colocation	

These linkages focus on developing an apparatus to serve a
whole class of clients and their needs. Thus, the impact of these
linkages on service delivery is more indirect and may have little
initial effect because of the time required to develop them effectively.
However, though the benefits from these linkages may not be realized until sometime in the future, their eventual impact will be
generalized over the entire class of clients.

In order to compare the integrators with respect to the development of linkages in the various projects and, in turn, the impact of
the projects on service delivery to clients, three key factors were
identified. These factors were authority over service providers, the
intent or perceived role of the integrator (both in terms of project
objectives and the objectives and/or philosophy of the integrator),
and the resources or incentives under the control of the integrator.
Functioning within the framework of certain authority relationships
between integrator and provider, the integrator is guided by his
intent to parlay the resources and incentives under his control into
the development of integrating linkages.

The study assesses the effectiveness of services integration
efforts in terms of accessibility—that is, the ease with which the
client can initially enter the service delivery system; continuity—
that is, the ability of a multiproblem family or individual to move
through the service delivery system in order to receive the necessary range of services; and efficiency based on a qualitative esti-
mation of (1) reduction of duplication, (2) economies of scale, and
(3) impact on problem solution.

Findings

The Integration of Services Is Not Extensive

The study reveals that integration of services is not extensive
even in the projects recommended as being successful projects.
(Information within the Department of Health, Education, and Welfare
[HEW] about HEW-funded projects is frequently deficient. What was

---

[*]These terms are defined in the Glossary.

seen in the field was often much different from what HEW officials indicated was there. This was in part due to the fact that within HEW there was no consensus about what a successful services integration project was and in part due to a faulty information system in the department.) No project had fully developed a majority of the linkages. In general, progress in developing linkages had been slow, and internal difficulties had complicated many of the projects. Many of the projects had not been in operation long enough to have developed many linkages, and others were focusing primarily on service delivery and not integration. Other inhibiting factors are indicated in succeeding pages.

Services Integration Is an Evolutionary Process

The study indicates that services integration is an evolutionary process. It takes time for services integration to occur—time for organization and implementation of a project, time for a project to attain legitimacy in the eyes of service providers, and time for participating agencies to develop a comfortable working relationship, often a necessary prerequisite to the coordination or consolidation of agencies' functions. It is difficult to implement a services integration agenda. Once linkages have been made, they need continued attention and support in order that gains be protected and further progress be made.

There Is a Wide Range of Factors That Facilitate and Inhibit Services Integration

Facilitators and inhibitors to services integration cover a wide range of factors. The study disclosed no single factor that was either beneficial to, or impeded, a majority of the projects. Rather, there were eight distinct categories of facilitators and inhibitors, and each category was comprised of many constituent elements.

In summary, services integration has a better chance of occurring when the sociopolitical leadership in the locality wants it to happen; when integration is a high-priority objective of the project; when the project director aggressively pursues coordination and has good contacts with important actors in the process; and when service providers have strong incentives to cooperate.

Conversely, services integration is less likely to occur even given the already unreceptive environment in which services integration must take place: when the local leadership opposes change; when the integrator is so burdened by service delivery responsibilities and internal operations that he has no time to pursue coordination; when the project fails to define its mission as the development of integrative linkages; when service providers actively protect the status quo, jealously guarding their prerogatives; and when the project is poorly administered.

Superimposed on the local environment are the policies and procedures related to federal grant administration. These policies and procedures are beneficial when the integrator has control over service providers' funds, and when guidelines suggest or require that the project coordinate its efforts with other service providers. However, these policies and procedures can be critical impediments when projects are buffeted by unclear and conflicting guidelines and funding uncertainties. These issues relate to project survival and must command priority at the sacrifice of coordination.

The more significant facilitators and inhibitors, each of which is susceptible to change by actions of HEW, are described below.

The Environment. The sociopolitical environment in which the projects function is an important factor, both positive and negative, in services integration. Support from government, community, and public and private funding sources—in terms of need for service delivery changes in general, and by means of the project in particular—often enhances integrative efforts, while opposition exerts an important negative influence.

The local environment was found to be susceptible to change. If national leaders stress the need to overcome problems in the delivery system, and if services integration truly becomes part of the national agenda, a local environment can be created that is more responsible to it. Those sectors of the community that are interested in, or have a stake in, improving the service delivery system are able to surface and unite for action. If adequate resources are available to local entities to encourage change, community consensus and support can be developed. If some emphasis is given to the desirability of a role in services integration for those bodies most able to affect the environment (for example, local general-purpose governments, influential citizens acting through health and welfare planning councils, and consumer groups), those entities are more likely to undertake such roles and are better able to justify their initiatives.

Project Objectives and Priorities. A critical inhibitor to services integration is the lack of attention given to integrative efforts by the projects. This results from a variety of factors, most salient being an emphasis on service delivery responsibility and internal operations and a definition of project objectives that does not recognize the establishment of integrative linkages as a central part of project mission.

Project objectives and priorities are susceptible to change. Clear emphasis in program guidelines and/or in technical assistance on the desirability of coordination can affect priorities and legitimize coordination efforts. In some projects it is clear that the integrator has developed linkages with other service providers only in response to federal requirements.

7

Project Director. The study provides support for the "great man" theory that the personality of the project director is one of the most important factors in services integration. In many of the projects, the director played the critical role in services integration. Leadership, persuasiveness, commitment, and personal contacts with political sources, staff of service providers, and the community appeared to be those attributes which had the greatest positive impact. On the other hand, the absence of administrative capability of some project directors had a negative effect on services integration.

Professional credentials were not essential. While there were some directors whose recognition and respect in their specialized profession made them more effective as integrators, there were other generalists who were equally effective.

Project Staff. A critical facilitator of service integration is the existence of a capable project staff whose mission is the coordination of providers and not service delivery. The expertise of such staff is important because the ability to help providers in programing, training, grantsmanship, meeting federal requirements, and so on reinforces the providers' ties to the project.

Service Provider Objectives and Attitudes. The attitudes of service providers have great impact on services integration efforts. Where providers want to retain absolute control of funds, functions, and internal procedures and where they vie for control of the delivery system (which is probably normal organizational behavior), services integration is critically impeded. If, in addition, providers have their own power and influence with funding sources, attempts to overcome attitudinal obstacles are particularly hindered.

Provider attitudes can be changed or overridden if the authority and resources of the integrator are adequate. In addition, to the extent that the sociopolitical environment is changed, as previously outlined, the factions pressuring for change within these service providers can be assisted and reinforced. Service providers, most of which operate with public funds, can also be induced through guideline provisions and grant conditions to develop linkages with other providers.

Grant Administration Policies and Procedures. Grant administration policies and procedures can have a positive impact on services integration in the following ways:

1. Integrator control of service provider access to funds: Services integration is facilitated to the extent the project integrator has control over service provider access to funding. This control enables the integrator to require provider participation in linkages as a prerequisite to receiving funds.

8

Single-point funding is a powerful tool for integration. The integrator, through whom funds flow to providers, can link services more closely if he is paying for them. In super-agencies, the director can obtain greater cooperation from department heads if he is their funding source.

2. Open-ended funding and the availability of flexible funds: The study indicated that the integrator's ability to integrate services is enhanced if the project is operating within the framework of an open-ended funding source such as Title IVA. In such a project, the integrator could hold out the promise of nearly unlimited, constantly available funds for providers.

Conversely, projects functioning on grants of limited duration and fixed amounts encountered a variety of obstacles to linkage development as a result of their short-term expiration. Similarly, projects funded with demonstration grants (such as Section 1115) had difficulty in obtaining support from the community, developing linkages with providers, and making permanent changes in the delivery system.

Some linkages such as planning could not be accomplished with a short-term grant since they were continuous, long-range processes. Once linkages were developed, they had to be sustained—an effort a one-time grant cannot support.

3. In-kind contributions for federal funds. The opportunity to provide in-kind services instead of cash for local share can and in some cases has acted as an incentive to the integrator to seek out and involve provider agencies in services integration efforts. However, in many other cases, the making of the in-kind contribution has not resulted in a more closely-linked relationship between the donor and the integrator beyond the in-kind contribution itself.

On the other hand, grant administration policies and procedures can also act as an important impediment to services integration efforts. Unclear guidelines and funding delays and uncertainties can make the funding source part of the hostile environment in which the project must operate and can effectively cause projects to focus on internal operations to the detriment of coordination. These kinds of problems absorbed time of project staff, turned their attention to survival rather than coordination, and in some cases encouraged continued separation of potentially integrative processes.

Services Integration Results in Improved Accessibility, Continuity, and Efficiency

The divergent nature of the projects and the lack of baseline data coupled with the exploratory nature of the study made it infeasible to develop quantitative measures by which to assess impact on accessibility and continuity. The absence of data precluded the development of rigorous quantitative measures of the efficiency

9

or cost effectiveness of services integration. Before and after cost figures are unavailable; the accounting systems employed prevent accurate isolation of costs attributable to integrative activities; several of the projects studied were too new to have developed reliable figures. Therefore, the findings offered here can be characterized as trends, evidence gained from partial success, and projections of probable longer-term impacts rather than rigid, quantifiable results.

With these qualifications it can be said that services integration has a positive impact on accessibility, continuity, and efficiency of service delivery to clients. The direct economies achieved through integration did not appear to outweigh the costs of achieving integration, at least in the short run. However, if impact on problem solution is considered as a measure of efficiency, a stronger efficiency argument can be made for services integration.

Accessibility. Integrative linkages among service providers in many of the projects have begun not only to make new services available to clients but also to expand the clientele receiving existing services. For example, integration has brought services to clients' neighborhoods and improved attitudes of traditional service provider staff, thus enhancing their ability and willingness to serve new client groups. It has also increased the number and effectiveness of outreach personnel to find and admit clients for service, and led to systematic review of service requirements and resources resulting in development of needed services.

Continuity. Integrative linkages have affected continuity both by manipulating the fragmented service delivery system on a client-by-client basis and by administratively and programmatically rationalizing the system on behalf of all clients. Some projects have emphasized the core services of intake, diagnosis, referral, and follow-up supplemented by a variety of modes of case coordination (for example, case conference, case coordinator). These approaches have ensured that client acceptance into one service results in acceptance to other services, minimizing red tape and delay. Furthermore, they have facilitated initial assessment of overall service need and the delivery of specific services in a complementary, orderly, and timely manner. These approaches have also prevented client loss within the service delivery system.

Projects have also affected continuity by concentrating on administrative linkages to identify service gaps and augment the resources of the delivery system to assure that the range of client needs can be met. These administrative linkages (such as joint planning or programing, purchase of service, and joint funding) enabled projects to commit agencies to provide a specific amount of service and to plan and deliver their service in a manner that complements the service of other providers. In addition, they have facilitated increased communication among service providers. Finally, a few projects have begun to utilize administrative linkages to weld providers into a tight-knit system that can plan, program, budget, and evaluate across a broad range of client needs.

Efficiency. Fieldwork indicates that it may not be possible to justify services integration strictly in terms of total dollar savings. Centralized/consolidated operation of core services, record-keeping, joint programing, joint funding, joint training, and/or central purchase of service arrangements on behalf of a number of service providers promote economies of scale, and coordinated staff utilization, funding, planning and programing, and evaluation help reduce duplication.

Although there are some cost savings resulting from economies of scale and reduction of duplication, they do not appear (at least in the short run) to equal the input costs of administrative and core service staff required to support integrative efforts. However, if one includes protection of public investment in services as a measure of efficiency, then a stronger case can be made for service integration on grounds of efficiency. If the public investment in one service (job training, for example) is to have lasting benefit only if another service (a job placement service, for example) is also provided, the cost involved in assuring that the client gets the job placement services as well as job training may be justified in terms of protecting the investment in job training. (This measure is referred to as impact on problem solution.)

There Is No One Best Services Integration Model

Services integration can occur at various government levels with diverse sponsors, contexts, and activities. For example, the study included examples of services integration: (1) by state/local government/private agencies; (2) with a variety of organizational modes; (3) providing functional services ranging from child care to health care; (4) focused on target groups, target areas, age groups; and (5) occurring in hostile and favorable environments.

This study indicates that there is no one best services integration model. There were no indications of any significant difference in the impact that various project characteristics had on accessibility, continuity, and efficiency, with the exception of "mode of coordination."

(On the basis of the information analyzed, it is not possible to assert that other project characteristics have no difference in impact. Because of the present state of the service integration art, isolating and measuring difference is exceedingly difficult, particularly in a small sample. It is particularly difficult to determine

11

in precise, quantitative terms the impact any individual project had on accessibility and continuity and efficiency and is virtually impossible to compare in precise quantitative terms the relative impact of different kinds of projects on those measures.)

Impact Varies According to Mode of Coordination. The projects studied fell into three general categories of coordination:

1. In voluntary coordination, the integrator is responsible for administering the provision of direct service as well as developing linkages between autonomous service providers: for example, Head Start central staff are responsible for activities such as child development, nutrition, as well as involving such other service providers as health practitioners and social service agencies in the implementation of a comprehensive Head Start program.

2. In mediated coordination, the primary mission of the integrator is the development of linkages between autonomous service providers rather than the provision of direct service: for example, staff of a 4-C Committee, which, rather than providing day care services, relates the services of health providers, early childhood education specialists, and social agencies to the activities of day care centers in order to establish a network with the capability to plan, program, budget, implement, and evaluate comprehensive child development programs.

3. In directed coordination, the integrator has the authority to mandate the development of linkages between legally subordinate service providers: for example, the office of the administrator of a human resource agency has the authority to compel the division heads to participate in joint planning, budgeting, evaluation, and so on.

The impact of the project on accessibility, continuity, and efficiency appeared to vary according to the mode of coordination being employed.

● Voluntary coordination. In the projects studied that relied on voluntary coordination, the direct service provided was not previously available in the locality. Therefore, it is difficult to determine how much difference in accessibility is attributable to the fact that services are integrated as opposed to the mere fact that new services are available. It appears that when linkages have been developed, more clients receive the service because the linked service providers are more aware of and more readily make referrals to the service.

Positive impact on continuity occurs because the specific group of clients recruited for the project is guaranteed some services by external providers through such linkages as joint funding, purchase of service, joint programing, and staff outstationing. In addition, clients individually receive other services because of core services that negotiate access to external services, coordinate service needs with the providers, and follow up receipt of services. The provision of functional and supportive services by the project also increases client readiness to accept service from other providers.

With respect to efficiency, some economies of scale accrue from the assembly of a group of clients for service by a given provider. In addition, there is some reduction of duplication since the project provides core services, thus eliminating the need for services providers to engage in similar activities. However, the greatest impact on efficiency of these types of projects is their impact on problem solution by the provision of multiple services.

● Mediated coordination. Services integration implemented within the framework of mediated coordination utilizes administrative linkages (for example, joint programing, purchase of services, administrative support services) to impact accessibility and continuity. This occurs as a part of project efforts to rationalize the service delivery system by filling service gaps, increasing service relevance, developing complementary service, and standardizing eligibility and intake procedures. These projects have significant impact on efficiency because arrangements are developed simultaneously for all clients rather than on a client-by-client basis.

Focus on the delivery system enables the integrator to disclose service duplication and overlap, and assess total needs. Moreover, the provision of staff expertise to providers has resulted in a redirection of existing service resources and a modification of delivery methods. In addition, the availability of staff to act on behalf of each provider to support cooperative efforts, act as grantsmen, negotiate with various funding sources, and so on can free the resources of the providers for service delivery.

Finally, this type of coordination has greater impact on problem solution than does voluntary coordination from the point of view of both numbers of clients affected by the project and efforts to make services more complementary in content and delivery procedures.

● Directed coordination. Review of services integration efforts within the framework of directed coordination was limited to general purpose government human resource agencies. Each agency studied was currently in the throes of a horizontal administrative reorganization and/or consolidation. Their efforts to develop integrative linkages (for example, consolidated planning, budgeting, evaluation) at the state level and to decentralize to the regional level through the development of single administrative structures in uniform regions are still in the formative stage. Presently, the state agencies are proceeding with limited tests of regional service delivery strategies through the use of demonstration projects. These efforts hold promise for future impact on accessibility, continuity, and efficiency of service delivery to clients.

The development of organizational structures to implement the formal authority of the human resource agency administrators should result in a planning capability to assess needs and resources, eliminate overlap and duplication, and fill service gaps, thereby promoting continuity in the delivery system and impacting efficiency. This planning capability is generally being aligned with budgeting, evaluation, and central record-keeping initiatives by these administrators.

Programing efforts and continued review of personnel utilization for the purposes of establishing joint use should produce cost savings and greater efficiency. Information-sharing and the availability of technical support services to agency divisions should promote both standardized and complementary service delivery, which will enhance continuity.

The development of integrated regional delivery systems should enhance service accessibility by using purchase of service arrangements to initiate information and referral, the establishment of multiservice centers, and so on.

However, these benefits for the most part have not yet been realized; in most cases, the payoffs for service delivery statewide will probably not be demonstrated for several years.

Impact Varies According to Project Objectives. The study revealed that project objectives affect the impact of a project on accessibility, continuity, and efficiency. The implicit and explicit objectives of services integration projects have affected the allocation of resources (time, personnel, money) devoted to and the approach taken in developing integrating linkages. Accordingly, these projects differ in the extent of their impact on the success measures of accessibility, continuity, and efficiency according to their objectives.

Where the objectives are limited to the manipulation of the service delivery system on a case-by-case basis, there is less impact on continuity and on efficiency in terms of reduction of duplication since the delivery system itself remains the same.

Similarly, the single objective of bringing a variety of services into the clients' neighborhood (for example, most neighborhood service centers) limits impact on efficiency, largely because services are viewed by the integrator as discrete entities and not adapted to each other for maximum total effect. When these projects take a comprehensive approach to the identification and solution of client needs, continuity is enhanced. However, neighborhood services centers studied were typically limited in objective to providing core services and central record-keeping on a case-by-case basis with insufficient attention given to the coherence of the total delivery system.

Conversely, projects whose objectives emphasize the development of planning and coordinative arrangements between providers for the purpose of establishing a comprehensive and integrated service delivery system, may have little initial effect, primarily because of the amount of time required to develop effective linkages. However, they indicate capacity to produce, over time, more extensive and lasting impact on accessibility, continuity, and efficiency. There were ample indications that the more mature projects of this type were beginning to have such impacts. For example, in one project the integrator has used such linkages as joint development of operating policies, programing, purchase of service, and so on to develop a consortium of mental health providers in which intake by any one provider results in an immediate assignment for service by any other provider to which a client is referred.

Finally, approaches to integration that have begun with administrative consolidation (for example, conglomerate human resources agencies) were at too early a state of development to have had any discernible impact on the accessibility, continuity, or efficiency of service delivery to clients, although that was the objective of many of them.

Development of Different Linkages Requires Differing Resources and Incentives, Varying Periods of Time and Impacts on Accessibility, Continuity, and Efficiency in Differing Ways

The integrator's ability to circumvent and overcome the resistance of service providers to coordinate their efforts largely relates to the resources and incentives available to induce cooperation. Power resources such as direct line authority over service providers or control over providers' access to funds allowed the integrator to make fundamental inroads in overcoming agency autonomy for the purpose of services integration while the necessity to rely on persuasion generally resulted in more superficial gains.

Certain linkages can be made while still preserving organizational autonomy. Thus, direct service linkages and some administrative linkages (for example, information-sharing, joint programing, and so on) do not significantly encroach on agency independence and can be achieved when the integrator has few or no incentives beyond his persuasive ability. However, some administrative linkages lie close to the heart of agency governance—control over the organization's funds and personnel. These linkages can be achieved only when the integrator has substantial resources and incentives at its command.

Table 1.1 portrays an assessment of the kinds of resources and incentives needed to develop various linkages, the relative amount of time needed to develop them, and the importance of the linkage in terms of impact on accessibility, continuity, and efficiency. Given the small size of the sample, the short operational life of many of the projects, the difficulty of precisely measuring impact in general, and in particular of isolating the impact of individual linkages, these relationships can be presented only as working hypotheses based on the experience gained over the past year in analyzing 30 projects. It is suggested that these hypotheses continue to be tested by HEW over time and in additional projects and that modifications be made as additional experience indicates.

15

TABLE 1.1

Linkages: Their Impact and Resources and Incentives
and Time Needed to Develop Them

Linkage	Requirements		Impact on Accessibility, Continuity, and Efficiency
	Resources/Incentives	Time	
Joint budgeting	Formal authority; control over fund access; support staff	Long	High
Joint funding including in-kind	Cash; persuasion	Moderate	Medium-high
Purchase of service	Cash	Short	High
Consolidated personnel administration (excluding training)	Formal authority; control over fund access	Long	High[b]
Training	Persuasion; cash; expertise	Short	Medium-high
Joint use of staff	Formal authority; persuasion–shared objectives; control over fund access[a]	Moderate	Medium
Staff transfer	Shared objectives; formal authority;[a] control over fund access[a]	Long	Medium
Colocation	Formal authority; facility; control over fund access[a]	Short-moderate	High
Staff outstationing	Shared objectives; client bridge or buffer; formal authority	Short-moderate	High
Joint planning	Formal authority; control over fund access; support staff	Long	High
Joint development of operating policies	Formal authority; control over fund access; persuasion	Short	High
Information-sharing	Persuasion	Short	Medium
Joint programing	Support staff; access to funds; persuasion; formal authority; control over fund access	Short-moderate	Medium-high
Joint evaluation	Formal authority; control over fund access; support staff	Moderate-long	High
Record-keeping	Formal authority;[a] control over fund access; common facility	Moderate-long	Medium
Grants management	Control over fund access; limited number of grants	Short-moderate	Medium
Central support	Support staff	Short	High
Outreach	Staff; formal authority; control over fund access; common facility	Short	High
Intake	Staff; formal authority; control over fund access; common facility	Moderate-long	High
Diagnosis	Staff; formal authority; control over fund access;[a] common facility	Short-moderate	High
Referral	Staff; formal authority; control over fund access;[a] common facility	Short	High
Follow-up	Staff; formal authority; control over fund access;[a] common facility	Short	High
Modes of case coordination	Common facility; persuasion	Short-moderate	High

[a]Hypothesis not directly indicated by fieldwork.
[b]Impact probably confined to efficiency.

No significant correlation between the project characteristics and the successful development of various kinds of linkages could be discerned, the one exception again being the mode of coordination employed. This, in turn, reflects the differing resources and incentives available to the integrator.

As might be expected, there was a general correlation between the use of direct service linkages and voluntary projects and between the use of administrative linkages and mediated and directed projects. In voluntary projects, the integrator was responsible for providing direct service to a specific client group as well as developing linkages with service providers. Since there was little available time and no authority over service providers, emphasis was placed on establishing linkages that had immediate payoff in terms of getting services to clients. Integrators in voluntary projects related to providers only on a one-to-one basis as a general rule. Linkages were not consciously used to develop additional linkages.

On the other hand, the integrators in both mediated and directed projects were charged with the development of cooperative relationships between service providers rather than the provision of direct service and, in varying degrees, possessed the resources and incentives with which administrative linkages could be developed. Therefore, they placed their emphasis on the establishment of such linkages.

The integrators in mediated projects (except neighborhood service centers) also took an aggressive approach in developing linkages. Generally, they used one integrative linkage to involve service providers in others, parlaying the resources at their disposal into linkages to obtain wider participation by providers in project activities. Although the integrators did relate to providers on a one-to-one basis, this was generally a prelude to getting the providers to interact with each other.

However, in the mediated projects, there were two significant variables that affected the integrator's emphasis on, and ability to develop, particular linkages. These were cases where (1) the integrator controlled service providers' funds by virtue of single-point funding, and (2) the organizing principle of serving all the needs of clients within a specific geographic area resulted in development of a neighborhood service center.

The integrators in mediated projects with single-point funding were guided not only by objectives related to rationalizing the total delivery system but also had considerable leverage to involve service providers in integrative linkages. Neighborhood service centers tended to focus their attention on assuring that service was provided to individual clients and therefore initially used direct service linkages and only a few administrative linkages, such as colocation and central record-keeping. Therefore, in many respects, although neighborhood service centers generally conform to the definition of mediated coordination, the centers have more in common with voluntary coordination projects.

The types of resources and incentives under the control of the integrator under various project types are described below.

Voluntary Coordination Projects. In voluntary coordination projects, the major and almost sole resource available is the integrator's ability to persuade service providers to connect or to link their services with those of the prime service offered by the project. Only a few projects had as an additional resource the availability of funds to pay for some services if necessary. Given the lack of formal authority and the constant demands made on time and energy by direct service responsibilities, persuasion necessitated strong commitment and effort by the project director and staff.

Participation in the project was dependent on three related incentives acting on autonomous agencies; first was their perception that cooperation would assist or allow them to achieve their own organization's goals. A second incentive was the opportunity to expand clientele; projects gave service providers access to a concentrated target population, as well as making individual clients requiring specialized services easily available to them. A third incentive, in some projects, was the integrator's ability to be a bridge and buffer between the service provider (generally an established, traditional, and usually large service provider) and an unfamiliar client population. This was particularly important in instances where the client group involved was perceived as difficult or threatening by the service provider's administration or staff.

Mediated Coordination Projects. In mediated coordination projects, there was a staff whose primary mission was developing coordination among service providers. In a few other projects, the integrator also had control over service providers' access to funds.

Projects achieved their most significant leverage over service providers by virtue of their designation as the single conduit for certain federal funds. This single-point funding gave the integrator the capability to both deliver and control some or all of the service providers' financial resources. Service providers so urgently wanted funds to sustain or expand their direct service that they either actively solicited participation in the project or were willing to accept the integrator's coordination demands in return for new money.

In each project, the central staff could interrelate the activities of service providers partially because they were not competing to offer services to clients but instead assisted the agencies themselves. The integrative staff was a resource to service providers and, in the process of helping these agencies, affected their policies, procedures, and the ultimate delivery of services to clients.

Integrative staff was able to attain legitimacy in the view of service providers by demonstrating expertise useful to the agencies in accomplishing their own objectives and by relieving the agencies of administrative concerns, thus leaving them more time for service delivery.

The availability of expertise in a central coordinative staff was a major incentive to service providers to become involved in project activities and the integrative staffs implemented this linkage to pave the way for agencies' participation in other linkages.

Neighborhood Service Centers. The critical resource available to the integrator was the neighborhood service center facility itself, which enhanced the connection of the autonomous service providers with the clients. Use of center facilities provided some incentives to the service providers for participation in the project. First, the location of the facility in the target area provided ready access to a concentrated population as well as making individual clients requiring specialized services easily available to the service providers. Second, the service providers were not bound by an organizational framework that altered their roles, objectives, or programmatic policies to any appreciable extent.

In each case, the center as a facility was not utilized as a bargaining device to develop a single coherent delivery system but rather just as a shelter for service providers. The various service providers were more than happy to respond to the "invitation" to relocate. This colocation of providers generally resulted in staff meetings, which in turn led to the development of other linkages— but usually in an unstructured way. Many of the existing linkages in neighborhood service centers were inherent in the project design rather than the conscious agenda of the integrator.

Directed Coordination Projects (Human Resource Super Agencies). In the human resource super-agencies, there are diverse resources available to the integrator in the development of linkages among the previously separate service providers. First is the legislative mandate for reorganization. Typically this reflects a legislative intent to reduce service fragmentation, achieve administrative economies and establish unitary policy control over state human service agencies.

A second resource consists of the legal powers delegated to the integrator such as single-line authority over divisions of the agency, internal reorganization authority, budget and resource allocation authority, and comprehensive planning authority. (The extent to which the integrator has been given these powers varies from state to state.) Additionally, the integrator has access to a planning staff to review critically the existing systems of the service providers.

He also has special project or demonstration funds to test new systems.

Controlling these resources, the agency administrators tended to follow a pattern in which planning and programing linkages were established first, with fiscal linkages and administrative support service linkages following in that order. In those cases, the clear intent of the integrator was to pursue linkages between division heads systematically and as quickly as they could be accepted, reserving the use of line authority only as a last resort.

General Purpose Government Is an Important Facilitator of Services Integration

Local general purpose government played some role in many of the projects. Involvement ranged from direct project sponsorship, funding conduit, and general support of the project to a barrier to project activities.

Analysis of the case studies to test the hypothesis that general purpose government is better able to sponsor effective services integration than are other organizational auspices (for example, special purpose government, voluntary councils, private nonprofit corporations) yielded only a few tentative conclusions. Projects sponsored by general purpose government put somewhat more emphasis on the development of administrative linkages and less on direct service linkages and implemented linkages at a somewhat slower pace than do projects under other sponsorship.

However, the limited size of the sample and variations in the length of time projects under different sponsorship had been in operation make it impossible to ascribe the difference in type and timing of linkage development solely to the difference in organizational sponsorship. Other parts of the analysis indicated that projects vary not so much by type of organizational sponsorship as they do by mode of coordination.

Whether or not general purpose government is a more effective project sponsor, it is clear that support and aid to a project by general purpose government is an important facilitator of services integration.

The Client Can Be an Important Integrative Force

Although there was some degree of client participation in two-thirds of the projects studied, dramatic variations in the role of clients appeared, ranging from pro forma membership on committees prompted by funding source requirements to client control of policy-making and project operations.

The extent of client involvement does not seem to vary based on mode of coordination, except that the consolidated human resources

20

agencies (examples of directed coordination) have not yet determined, nor developed, organizational mechanisms to implement client involvement. The role of the client as integrator most nearly correlates with the extent to which clients initiated participation in the project, and this, in turn, primarily related to the level of organization and/or mobilization of client population at project inception. In some cases, this organization and/or mobilization was traceable to efforts by community action agencies; in others, to the experience derived from a shared problem (such as parents of mentally retarded children); and in a few cases, the efforts of project staff.

Clients have caused the integration of services by identifying problems, soliciting local contributions to finance remedies to the problem, supporting responsive agencies within the delivery systems, lobbying for the availability of existing service to new clientele, changing service provider attitudes, acting as a countervailing force to the establishment of a conservative consensus by participating agencies in the development of project policy, and establishing service legitimacy in the view of potential clients by virtue of their involvement. In many cases, unfettered by traditional definitions of feasibility, clients have achieved positive, creative solutions to service delivery problems.

Conclusion

The services integration projects studied were operating in extremely diffuse social service environments made up of a variety of public and private agencies with competing claims to funds and authority. Developing that structure into a unitary system, even if it were desirable, could probably not be done, for several reasons:

1. There are various approaches to designing systems—according to problem or age groups, geographic areas, or functions—each of which has some defensible rationale.

2. There are various funding sources, and they are not likely to agree on a single system. Although the trend is toward more public involvement, private charity will not be totally supplanted.

3. Organized constituencies with congressional supporters lobby for services organized around a lead function, such as vocational rehabilitation or mental health, as the prime service with other services as auxiliary.

4. There is no consumer group pressuring for a unitary system.

5. There are a variety of other obstacles to unity as suggested by the list of inhibitors uncovered by our fieldwork.

In summary, there is little support for a unified service delivery system either from service providers or from other sources.

While a unitary system may never be created, the study indicates that it would be feasible to create a more closely knit, although still pluralistic, system by getting providers to link services and enhancing the ability of certain agencies, such as general purpose government, to assume a leadership role in the pursuit of services integration. The study also indicates that such an effort has payoff to the client in terms of improved accessibility and continuity of service and to the taxpayer in terms of protecting his investment in services. This effort is the substance of services integration policy and necessitates certain actions by HEW.

Recommendations for a Comprehensive Strategy
to Promote Services Integration

There is the potential for services integration at all levels of HEW funding; however, to implement services integration, HEW must make a significantly greater effort.

There is no single approach to overcoming the obstacles to services integration. The effort must involve a variety of steps to facilitate the integration process and to shape the services integration product.

The study findings indicate that in order to achieve the greatest impact on accessibility, continuity, and efficiency, support should be focused on mediated and directed coordination projects since they pursue rationalization of the service delivery system on behalf of an entire class of clients rather than the manipulation of the delivery system for specific clients. Nevertheless, voluntary coordination projects should not be abandoned. While they currently rely on a coincidence of provider objectives to achieve services integration and concentrate on service delivery, a slightly greater investment of effort could produce effective services integration. Objectives and priorities of these projects can be expanded to include system change rather than being confined to system manipulation, and their capacity to implement these new directions can be enhanced by the availability of additional staff to focus on coordination among service providers rather than provision of direct services.

In sum, the study findings indicate a wide range of opportunities open to HEW to promote services integration. In order to take advantage of these opportunities, there must be a departmental commitment to services integration and the implementation of a comprehensive strategy to promote it. The major components of such a strategy are outlined below.

Creation of an Environment Receptive to Services Integration

There are a number of steps that HEW and other federal officials could take to create a local climate favorable to services integration. They include the whole range of activities that may be undertaken— such as speeches and national conferences—to establish in the minds of the public that the issue is a priority of the federal government.

This same climate must be established within the department in order for HEW to be able to undertake the rest of the program outlined below.

Study findings corroborate many of the recommendations of HEW's own task force on Administrative and Organizational Constraints to Services Integration. As emphasized in that report, many middle-level management staff are not in tune with the service integration policies of HEW. Likewise, service integration efforts have not reached many of the HEW program officials who make funding decisions and monitor grantee progress.

Provision of Support Services to Services Integration Projects

The level and manner in which HEW provides advocacy, technical assistance, and monitoring support services to projects should be reviewed to facilitate implementation of a services integration policy.

The HEW Regional Offices should be deeply involved in the development and operation of local service integration projects. The Regional Offices, given a staff capability in services integration, could undertake provision of technical assistance and program monitoring to local projects, rather than central office staff.

Projects analyzed in this study that received guidance from the HEW regional staff included several of the service integration concepts in their objectives. Although their initial objectives did not focus on service integration, they were altered when assistance was provided by the HEW regional officers.

Advocacy. HEW has demonstrated a reluctance to intervene at the state or local level in support of a project it has funded. While this reluctance is often predicated on a desire to permit localities to manage their own affairs, it may be detrimental to services integration efforts.

HEW needs to be more supportive of the projects it funds and to assume an advocacy role in their behalf to overcome impediments to services integration. HEW may particularly have to assume an advocacy role with intermediate funding sources, such as state departments that administer formula grant funds.

Also in an advocacy role, HEW should emphasize that all service providers receiving formula grant funds should coordinate their programs with local agencies that may be planning or operating an integrated delivery system in the providers' service area.

On-Site Technical Assistance and Training. In order to overcome the general lack of knowledge about services integration and its implementation and to alter the low priority given to coordination of delivery systems by service providers, HEW should provide sustained on-site technical assistance and training as necessary during the development and operation of a services integration project.

Technical assistance should include the following:

1. Information about linkages—what they are, how they can be and have been developed. Linkages should be defined with examples of how projects with similar environments and clientele have effectively linked services of autonomous providers.

2. Information about the use of purchase of services agreements for the development of linkages.

3. Information about the qualities that should be sought in a project director over and above a certain level of management expertise as guidance to those who will be selecting project directors.

4. Forums for directors and staff concerning services integration and linkage development.

5. Techniques for involving service providers and local general purpose governments in project development and the decision-making process.

Technical assistance should stress the following:

1. Services integration is an objective of major interest to HEW and should be a project objective.

2. Linkage development is a tool to achieve services integration and not a goal in itself.

3. Involvement of service providers and representatives of the local general purpose governments (state, city, and/or county) in initial project development can be very important to project success.

Indirect Technical Assistance. HEW should develop a capability to provide indirect technical assistance through the development of a services integration information clearinghouse either within the department or an independent organization. (There are some precedents that suggest that an independent entity might more readily make qualitative assessments about services integration efforts and be able more quickly to disseminate informational materials.) Indirect technical assistance can include such items as the outcomes and processes used in Section 1115 Research and Demonstration Projects

24

and Targets of Opportunity projects, model clauses for purchase of
service agreements, alternative strategies for linkage development
and instruments by which to identify, monitor, and evaluate services
integration progress.

Monitoring. The study found limited monitoring of services integration
projects. Much of the monitoring that did occur was counterproductive
and rarely focused on services integration. HEW should develop a
system for monitoring services integration projects that (1) focuses
on the achievement of services integration as well as the delivery of
services; (2) applies flexible performance standards to focus on
project objectives rather than preconceived objectives that do not
relate to the project's functions; and (3) relies on HEW staff visits
to project sites rather than on written reports by project staff.
    Monitoring and technical assistance to services integration
projects can be facilitated if it is based upon (1) reasonable expectations for linkage development; (2) determining which integrating
linkages are important to develop; and (3) determining what can be
done to enhance the development of these linkages.
    As part of this evaluation, a classification scheme and applied
analytical approach for analyzing services integration projects was
developed and tested. Application to the project sample studied
yielded some conclusions about relationships, which, because of the
size of the sample, can only be regarded as tentative. It is believed
that the classification system, or something similar to it, would be
a useful technique to be used by HEW in monitoring and evaluating
other services integration projects as a way of determining what
technical assistance needs might be and building up a broader base
of experience and insight into the process and results of linkage
development. It also would provide an organized system for interrelating the experience and insight gained from a variety of services
integration projects.

Elimination of Internal HEW Constraints to Services Integration

Many of the federal constraints to services integration disclosed
by the study are not so much related to the inherent limitations of
the categorical grant system per se as they are to the procedures,
policies, and organization of HEW. There is a clear need for a staff
within the department whose sole responsibility is coordinating
HEW's services integration efforts and reorienting existing HEW
staff to a services integration approach. (This recommendation supports that of the Task Force on Administrative and Organizational
Constraints to Services Integration.)
    This unit or staff should be organizationally placed in the office
of the secretary. There should be counterpart units or staffs in each
agency. This organization would be replicated in the regional offices

with units in the regional director's office and in each regional commissioner's office.

The focus of the Washington staff would be in developing general policy and technical assistance materials; the focus of the regional staff would be the provision of direct technical assistance and development of indirect technical assistance materials. These staffs could also be the focus of the implementation of the Allied Services Act, should it be enacted.[2]

There is also a need to experiment with alternative forms of organization that offer promise for a more integrated response by HEW to localities. For example, a single staff person might be authorized to represent all bureaus of the Social and Rehabilitation Service (SRS) in a geographic area (such as a large county or metropolitan area).

Building Services Integration into the HEW Grant System

A services integration policy should be built into a rationalized HEW grant system in which grant programs are coordinated, guidelines developed, and administrative procedures geared toward facilitating its implementation.

Development of Program Guidelines Reflecting a Services Integration Policy. HEW should write a services integration policy into program guidelines. Guidelines should make it clear that linkage development is a matter of significance to the funding source and that projects are expected to devote time and resources to it. This can occur if guidelines (1) indicate that linkage development is an eligible/required project expenditure; (2) encourage/require project reports to include the status of efforts to integrate services providers; (3) encourage/ require provider participation on project policymaking boards and committees and in project development (a facilitator uncovered by this study); and (4) encourage/require a project to take specific steps that will result in the development of specific linkages.

For example,

1. Guidelines could require the integrator to develop formal, structured mechanisms for the participation of providers in the planning and programing processes.

2. Guidelines could stimulate joint evaluation by indicating how purchase of service agreements might be used to implement this process.

3. Guidelines could stimulate the development of centralized record-keeping by indicating a variety of methods for the sharing of case information rather than by specifying that one method be used. (Too often the differing requirements of provider agencies' funding sources and agencies' small clientele make implementation of a single, mandated system untenable.)

Many of the discontinuities in regulations that make it difficult or impossible to use HEW programs jointly are administrative, not statutory, in origin. Administrative guidelines and regulations for formula grants and project grants should be thoroughly examined to determine what modifications will facilitate the joint use of HEW program funds.

HEW Funding Policy as a Means to Facilitate Services Integration.*
The case studies demonstrate that HEW policies and procedures concerning the allocation and use of grant funds can have either a positive or negative impact on services integration. They suggest ways in which HEW can use its funding authority to facilitate implementation of services integration projects.

• Integrator control of provider accessibility to funds—single-point funding. HEW should recognize that programs that might be set up through separate grants to individual service providers will result in greater integration if instead funds flow through a single local conduit. It should, therefore, consider single-point funding as a tool for services integration.

HEW might consider coupling this single-point funding procedure with a policy adopted by HUD in the Model Cities Program and stipulated in Title IV-A—a prohibition against the integrator itself providing the services if they can be obtained externally.

• Open-ended funding and the availability of flexible funds as facilitators of services integration. HEW should explore further the services integration potential of Title IV-A and the impediments of grants of limited duration. It might consider means of compensating for the lack of open-ended funding programs and the particular problems inherent in limited duration grants. One means of compensation might be the creation of a flexible pool of funds for services integration activities similar to those of the Target of Opportunity Program, but which would be implemented as a continuing support program rather than a research and demonstration program.

1. These flexible funds, perhaps from R and D programs, would be used to finance linkage development and services integration activities rather than service delivery. They might also be used in

---

*Some of these proposals could be implemented through the planning and capacity-building grants and the administrative cost grants under the proposed Allied Services Act if it is enacted. However, there is a whole range of opportunities at the local level for assisting services integration outside the context of the Allied Services Act that should be considered as well: (1) in communities that will not be developing local allied services plans; (2) in individually HEW-funded projects that will not be part of a local allied services plan; and (3) in activities not related to eligible uses of those grant funds.

a limited way for service delivery as an incentive for provider participation in a project.

2. The funds could be administered by a special HEW staff whose mission would be the coordination of HEW services integration activities and whose organizational placement would permit it to cut across agency and program lines.

● Funds for support services. HEW should consider the impact of support services on the service delivery system. Several projects relied on the provision of support services such as transportation to achieve continuity in service delivery. Funds for the provision of these services, however, were not readily available. HEW might (1) make it clear in guidelines that support services are eligible project expenditures; and (2) include in the funds awarded to a project sufficient amounts for the provision of support services.

● Planning grants to facilitate project implementation. HEW should consider the institution of planning grants to projects for initial start-up and operating costs. The plan produced with these funds could focus not just on service delivery but on the coordination process to be used in achieving services integration. The planning grants might come from the pool of flexible funds previously discussed. Technical assistance in linkage development should accompany these grants.

● Provision of funds for project staff to concentrate on services integration. HEW should facilitate acquisition of staff to concentrate on services integration either by making staff an eligible project cost or by providing special staffing grants. HEW should realize that coordination is evolutionary and requires time to develop; therefore, staffing funds must be provided on a long-term and sustained basis and not within the framework of a one-shot, short-term grant.

● In-kind contributions for federal funds as a services integration tool. HEW should consider in-kind contributions as a tool to encourage integrators to establish connections with providers (1) by requiring integrators to develop linkages with donors and (2) by providing technical assistance regarding the services integration potential of in-kind contributions.

● Purchase of service agreements as a services integration tool. HEW can enhance the efficacy of purchase of service agreements as a means to achieve services integration by (1) encouraging/ requiring integrators to make funding under purchase of service agreements contingent on provider participation in linkage development; (2) providing through technical assistance and guidelines information about the use of such agreements for linkage development, detailing what linkages can be developed at each stage of project implementation; and (3) indicating to state agencies administering formula grant funds (a) how purchase of service agreements may be used and developed to promote services integration through either program guidelines or technical assistance; and (b) the types of requirements that may be placed on project integrators who obtain formula grant funds through purchase of service agreements or enter into such agreements with other providers.

ORGANIZATION OF PART I

Part I contains a description of the study methodology (Chapter 3), a summary of the study findings (Chapter 4), study recommendations (Chapter 5), and comparative analyses of the projects according to a number of different dimensions (Chapters 6 through 12).

Chapter 6 describes the range of factors facilitating and inhibiting the integration of services, the frequency with which they occur, and the significance of their impact.

The range of integrating linkages that can be developed between separate agencies, the conditions under which the linkages appear to develop, and the significance of their development to services integration are discussed in detail in Chapter 7.

Much of the discussion about project integrators throughout the report regards the project director and his staff as the dominant forces acting as the integrator. However, in many projects the client was also a factor. Chapter 8 discusses the role of the client as integrator in the various projects studied.

The most significant variable among the projects in terms of project techniques for, and impacts of, services integration was the mode of coordination employed. Accordingly, projects employing the same mode of coordination are summarized and analyzed in separate chapters. Chapter 9 contains a comparative analysis of directed coordination projects; Chapter 10, a comparative analysis of mediated coordination projects; and Chapter 11, a comparative analysis of voluntary coordination projects. Neighborhood service centers, although they employed the mode of mediated coordination, did so in a way sufficiently different from other mediated projects; consequently, a separate discussion of these projects appears in Chapter 12.

The case reports for some of the more instructive projects have been summarized and their more interesting features highlighted in Chapter 13.

NOTES

1. Several additional projects, not discussed in this part, are described and analyzed in Part II.

2. See Chapter 19, pp.299-303, for more specific recommendations relative to the Allied Services Act.

2

**DEFINITION OF
AND RATIONALE FOR
SERVICES INTEGRATION**

BACKGROUND

Services integration is still an evolving art about which little is known. Furthermore, the very term "services integration" did not have a generally accepted meaning and the "the rationale for services integration is composed of partial arguments."[1] As a consequence, the first task of the study was to examine the rationale for, and develop a definition of, services integration.

There was a range of definitions and rationales advanced in various HEW materials and other existing literature. The following summary is designed to provide in brief terms the context within which a working definition and rationale were proposed for use in this study.

Several definitions of services integration were found in various HEW documents. It was defined both as an objective and as a process or activity. These aspects were usually not distinguished. Definitions of services integration as an objective included the following:

> A service delivery system which can provide all those services needed by a given client or community—constrained only by the state of the art and the availability of resources.[2]

According to a memorandum from Secretary Elliot Richardson, services integration aimed

> ... at developing an integrated framework within which ongoing programs can be rationalized and enriched to do a better job of making services available within the existing commitments and resources. Its objectives must include such things as: (a) the coordinated delivery of services

for the greatest benefit to people; (b) a holistic approach to the individual and the family unit; (c) the provision of a comprehensive range of services locally; and (d) the rational allocation of resources at the local level so as to be responsive to local needs.[3]

As a process or activity, services integration is defined by the ways in which particular services are combined or related across agency and program lines.[4] These are basically what have been identified as "integrative linkages" for the purposes of this study.

It is apparent from these statements and from the Gardner report[5] that services integration is intended to be a significant redirection of ongoing programs and of resources, even to a point of institutional change, rather than the overlay of new service activities on a fragmented base of continuing operations. Also, although services integration has attempted to overcome fragmentation "at the delivery level, at the state level, and at the Federal level,"[6] Secretary Richardson recognized that the "primary focus" is "the integration of services at the local level for the purpose of maximizing their actual benefits to people."[7]

The concept of services integration has developed in response to a fragmented pattern of service delivery in which separate programs, each individually developed over the years, meet separately defined needs. That categorical approach treats

the individual not as a whole being, but as a person with separate and separable problems which can be treated in isolation from one another.[8]

However, since needs are related, the consumer who has [several problems] must deal with a system which seems totally irrational. Rationalization of the service delivery system must occur from the bottom up.[9]

The problem was further stated in a presidential message, transmitting the proposed Allied Services Act of 1972 to the Congress: "For the uninformed citizen in need, the present fragmented system can become a nightmare of confusion, inconvenience and red tape."[10]

Thus, the primary recognized objective of services integration is to organize the delivery of services comprehensively around the needs of the person, family, or community. Because much of the existing organization of services is by function, however, this objective requires crossing existing program and agency lines. As ex-President Richard Nixon put it in his 1972 State of the Union message: "We need a new approach . . . which is built around people and not around programs. We need an approach which treats a person as a whole and which treats the family as a unit."

The ultimate goal or ideal of services integration was succinctly put in the presidential message transmitting the Allied Services legislation:

> Such plans could eventually make it possible to assess the total human service needs of an entire family at a single location with a single application.[11]

It is within this ideological frame of reference that the present study defines services integration.

A WORKING DEFINITION

At the onset of the study period, services integration was defined as the process by which two or more HEW categorical programs, with mutually compatible objectives, service elements, or client groups, are linked in order to allow treatment of an individual's or family's needs in a coordinated and comprehensive manner.

A slightly different definition, focusing more on the linking of services of two or more service providers rather than two or more grant programs, was subsequently proposed by the contractor and accepted by HEW. For purposes of this study, then, social services integration was defined as

> The linking together by various means of the services of two or more service providers to allow treatment of an individual's or family's needs in a more coordinated and comprehensive manner.

This definition embraces a wide range of HEW program activity. Virtually every HEW-assisted project that requires the services of more than one service agency for successful implementation is a potential services integration project.

However, by this definition, the instance of a single agency obtaining funds from two or more categorical grant sources is not considered services integration unless it involves the situation where two or more previously independent agencies have been consolidated into the single agency. Without that consolidation, the example involves solely considerations of the federal delivery system in joint funding, which are quite distinct from issues surrounding the integration of services of traditionally separate service providers at the point of service delivery. This study then focused on problems at the local delivery level, rather than dealing with problems of joint funding at the federal level.

The definition provides a further helpful restriction of focus by stressing the integration of services by previously separate providers. Thus, projects funded through "comprehensive" grants to a single entity through which two or more services are provided (for example, 314[e] funds to provide a range of health and health-related service through a single agency) would not be included in the study. This was considered appropriate because such situations do not present examples of linking together services of two or more providers. Services integration exists at the outset.

RATIONALE

Martin Rein has analyzed the need for integration of services, as well as attempted solutions, within an historical framework.[12] He identifies three types of problems in the organization and distribution of social services: (1) the dispersal of similar functions; (2) the discontinuity of related functions; and (3) incoherence when different functions are pursued without relationship to each other.[13]

This fragmentation has resulted in various felt problems, including: duplication of cash benefits, duplication of other services, multiplicity of independent and uncoordinated visiting, duplication of manpower, overuse of services by a small percentage of clients (multiproblem families), and poor access and underuse of services. Rein also points out that "the re-combination of fragmented specialized services can serve many goals" and that the federal government's statements include several competing and conflicting goals.[14]

HEW presents services integration in terms of several factors that are important concerns from a policy point of view but that are not intrinsic to integration by definition. These factors are (1) effectiveness (or quality) of service delivery; (2) efficiency (or economy) of service delivery; and (3) accountability of service delivery.

Although these factors are logically distinct from integration, a distinction is not made in many of the statements. Effectiveness and efficiency are seen by HEW as goals and/or assumed consequences of services integration. Effectiveness includes responsiveness to consumer needs and results that can be evaluated.[15] Efficiency includes economies of scale, and administrative efficiency, as well as the "multiplier effect" (also an aspect of effectiveness).[16] On this basis, efficiency should be considered an implicit part of the rationale for services integration.

HEW's use of the term "accountability of service delivery" refers primarily to local general purpose government and, through it, to the general public rather than to the service consumers.

When this background of "partial arguments" was reviewed within the context of this study's working definition of services integration, it appeared that the various rationales for integration can be incorporated in two general propositions. The first is that the availability of services to clients who need the services of more than one service provider is greater if delivery is integrated rather than fragmented. The second is that the efficiency in the delivery of services to clients who need the services of more than one service provider is greater if delivery is integrated rather than fragmented.* These two rationales became research hypotheses to be tested in this study.

Availability

In services integration terms, "effectiveness of service delivery" refers to the availability of service rather than its quality. Therefore, the issue of availability of service (health services, for example) rather than the quality of the service (whether the health service is competent, sensitive, and so on) is examined in the study. Two dimensions of availability are explored: (1) accessibility, which relates to initial client entry into the system; and (2) continuity, which relates to client movement within the system.

The questions examined are, (1) Are the services more accessible to the client than would be the case without the integrating linkages? and (2) Is the delivery of services to the client more continuous than would be the case without the integrating linkages?

Efficiency

"Efficiency" ostensibly results from integration of services in three major ways:
1. Reduction of duplication of service delivery.
2. Economies of scale:
    a. Some things can be done at less cost.
    b. Some things can be done that otherwise could not be done (for example, staff training).
3. Impact on problem solution. If the public investment in one service (such as job training) is to have lasting benefit only if another service (such as a job placement service) is also provided, the cost

---

*It should be noted that the proposition does not address itself to the question of whether a services strategy is more efficient than an income strategy. Examination of that question was not part of this study.

involved in assuring that the client gets the job placement services as well as job training may be justified in terms of protecting the investment in job training. This measure is referred to as impact on problem solution.

NOTES

1. Sidney Gardner et al., "Services Integration in HEW: An Initial Report," 2/26/71, p. 7.

2. Ibid.

3. Elliot Richardson, "Services Integration—Next Steps," Secretarial Memorandum, U.S. Department of Health, Education, and Welfare, 6/1/71, p. 1.

4. Contract no. SRS-71-37, p. 3.

5. Gardner, op. cit., pp. 18 and 48.

6. Contract no. SRS-71-37, p. 1.

7. Richardson, op. cit., p. 1.

8. Gardner, op. cit., p. 24.

9. Office of Field Support, Additional Materials for Services Integration Meeting, 9/3/71.

10. House Document No. 92-296, p. 2.

11. Ibid., p. 1.

12. Martin Rein, Social Policy, chap. 2, Coordination of Social Services (New York: Random House, 1970).

13. Ibid., p. 105.

14. Ibid., p. 119.

15. Office of Field Support, op. cit., p. 3.

16. Gardner, op. cit., pp. 8-9.

3

ANALYTICAL FRAMEWORK

In the study, services integration projects were viewed as consisting of the integrator (who may also be a provider of direct services) and autonomous service providers, which are organizationally independent of the integrator but which are tied to it by various integrating linkages. (In the case of consolidated human resource agencies, the term ''autonomous service providers'' refers to those departments that previously were organizationally separate and that have been made a part of the ''super-agency.'')

The term integrator refers to the organizational entity, and more particularly the board, staff, or person within the entity, responsible for coordinating the services of autonomous service providers (and its own services if the integrator should be a deliverer of services as well) through the development of integrating linkages.

Integrating linkages are the mechanisms that maintain the coordination of the service providers in a services integration project by tying together or consolidating the various administrative, fiscal, and service delivery functions each provider ordinarily performs separately.

In order to compare the integrators with respect to the development of linkages in the various projects and, in turn, the impact of the projects on service delivery to clients, three key factors were identified. These factors were authority over service providers, the intent or perceived role of the integrator (both in terms of project objectives and the objectives and/or philosophy of the integrator), and the resources or incentives under the control of the integrator. Functioning within the framework of certain authority relationships between integrator and provider, the integrator is guided by his intent to parlay the resources and incentives under his control into the development of integrating linkages.

CLASSIFICATION SCHEME

The projects studied were classified in two ways: (1) according to project characteristics, and (2) according to the kinds of integrating linkages the project illustrated.

This classification was based on several hypotheses:

1. That different configurations of project characteristics have different impacts on accessibility, continuity, and efficiency of service delivery.

2. That different configurations of project characteristics result in the development of different integrating linkages.

3. That different integrating linkages have different impacts on accessibility, continuity, and efficiency of service delivery.

4. The factors over which HEW has some control impede or facilitate the development of integrating linkages.

This classification was designed to enable the sample projects to be assessed according to (1) the impacts that different project characteristics have on accessibility, continuity, and efficiency of service delivery; (2) the impacts that different project characteristics have on the development of various integrating linkages; (3) the factors other than project characteristics that impede or facilitate the development of integrating linkages; and (4) the impacts that different integrating linkages have on the accessibility, continuity, and efficiency of service delivery.

Integrating Linkages

Administrative Linkages

1. Fiscal

Joint budgeting: A process in which the integrator sits with all service providers together or individually to develop a budget.

Joint funding: A process by which two or more service providers give funds to support service.

Fund transfer: Instances in which funds originally to be used for one service are shifted to be used for another service.

Purchase of service: Formal agreements that may or may not involve a written contract between the integrator and autonomous service providers to obtain service.

2. Personnel Practices

Consolidated personnel administration: The centralized

provision of some or all of the following: hiring, firing, promoting, placing, classifying, training, and so on.

Joint use of staff: The case in which two different agencies deliver service by using the same staff.

Staff transfer: The case in which an employee is on the payroll of one agency but is under the administrative control of another.

Staff outstationing: The placement of a service provider in the facility of another service provider.

Colocation: The stationing of staff by autonomous service providers in a common facility.

3. Planning and Programing

Joint planning: The joint determination of total service delivery system needs and priorities through a structured planning process.

Joint development of operating policies: A structured process in which the policies, procedures, regulations, and guidelines governing the administration of a project are jointly established.

Joint programing: The joint development of programmatic solutions to defined problems in relation to existing resources.

Information-sharing: An exchange of information regarding resources, procedures, and legal requirements (but not individual clients) between the project integrator and various service providers.

Joint evaluation: The joint determination of effectiveness of service in meeting client needs.

4. Administrative Support Services

Record-keeping: The gathering, storing, and disseminating of information about clients, including standardized and/or centralized case information; and procedures for flow of information.

Grants-management: The servicing of grants.

Central support services: The consolidated or centralized provision of services such as auditing, purchasing, exchange of material and equipment, and consultative services.

Direct Service Linkages

1. Core Services

Outreach: The systematic recruitment of clients.

Intake: The process (including determination of eligibility) resulting in the admission of a client to direct service.

Diagnosis: The assessment of a client's overall service needs.

Referral: The process by which a client is directed to another provider for services.

Follow-up: The process used to determine that clients receive the services to which they have been referred and, in general, help them negotiate the service delivery system.

2. Modes of Case Coordination

Case conference: A meeting between the integrator's staff and staff of agencies who provide service to a given family for the purpose of discussing that family in general or a specific problem, possibly determining a course of action and assigning responsibility among the agencies for implementing the solution.

Case coordinator: The designated staff member responsible for assuring provision of service by multiple autonomous providers to a given client.

Case team: The arrangement in which a number of staff members, either representing different disciplines or working with different members of a given family, work together to relate a range of services of autonomous providers to a given client. (The primary difference between case conferences and case teams is that the former may be ad hoc while the latter involves continuous and systematic interaction between the members of the team.)

Project Characteristics

There were four characteristics of projects that appeared a priori to be significant variables affecting services integration. One of the objectives of the study was to determine their importance to the success or failure of the integration effort. These characteristics and the range of possible variation within each characteristic are indicated as follows.

Organizing Principle for Service Clustering

Age group: Clustering of services needed to meet needs of an age group (for example, preschool, elderly).

Geographic group: Clustering of services, whether or not functionally related, required to meet needs of all residents in a service area.

Function: Clustering of services supportive of a primary functional mission (such as primary health care).

Problem group: Clustering of services needed to meet needs of problem group (for example, juvenile delinquents, drug addicts).

Mode of Client Entry

Entry through a central information and referral service directly connected to functional services (for example, core services in a neighborhood service center).

Entry through an independent information and referral service.

Entry through prime service linked to supporting services (for example, day care center).

Organizational Sponsorship

General purpose government (local, county, or state).
Private voluntary council.
Private nonprofit corporation.
Special purpose public agency.

Mode of Coordination

Voluntary coordination: In voluntary coordination, the integrator is responsible for the delivery of direct service itself as well as for developing linkages with autonomous service providers for other services that support or complement his own: for example, Head Start central staff are responsible for activities such as child development and nutrition, as well as for involving other service providers such as health practitioners and social services agencies in the implementation of a comprehensive Head Start program. (In this report, projects employing this mode of coordination are sometimes referred to as "voluntary projects.")

Directed coordination: In directed coordination, the integrator has the authority to mandate the development of linkages between legally subordinate service providers: for example, the office of the administrator of a human resource agency has the authority to compel the division heads to participate in joint planning, budgeting, evaluation, and so on. (In this report, projects employing this mode of coordination are sometimes referred to as "directed projects.")

Mediated coordination: In mediated coordination, the primary mission of the integrator is the development of linkages between autonomous service providers rather than the provision of direct service: for example, staff of a 4-C Committee, which, rather than providing day care services, relates the services of health providers, early childhood education specialists, and social agencies to the activities of day care centers in order to establish a network with the capability to plan, program, budget, implement, and evaluate comprehensive child development programs. (In this report, projects employing this mode of coordination are sometimes referred to as "mediated projects.")

SAMPLE SELECTION

Thirty projects meeting the definition of services integration were selected for study.[*] The projects in the sample are listed in

---

[*] In addition, an abbreviated study of four state-level efforts at services integration—in Georgia, Illinois, Maine, and Massachusetts—was undertaken. See Part II.

the Appendix. The sample could not be a random sample of all services integration projects because the universe of services integration projects being supported by HEW was unknown. In the first place, within HEW there was no consensus about what constituted a successful services integration project. Secondly, there was no centralized information system about the projects funded by HEW.

As a consequence, a classification scheme was developed that would provide examples of the linkages and project characteristics that were being studied. A sample of projects was selected that would fit this stratification.

Potential projects for the sample were drawn from a variety of sources: written information about projects (for example, 1,115 demonstrations), recommendations from regional offices, both written and oral, and recommendations of Central Office program staff (for example, Office of Child Development personnel concerning Head Start programs). Projects were sought that had been in operation long enough to have a "track record" and that had a reputation of having successfully tied together the services of a number of separate agencies.

The sample was designed to ensure that there was a reasonably uniform distribution of projects according to the four project characteristics and at least two examples of each integrating linkage. To ensure that these sampling requirements were fulfilled, all the projects were not selected at once. As field work on a set of projects was completed, the projects were classified according to their characteristics and linkages and another set was chosen to reflect those characteristics and linkages not yet examined.

Because of the large number of project characteristics and linkages to be studied in proportion to the size of the sample, it was not possible to look at a number of projects in which the only constant was a project characteristic or integrating linkage to be analyzed. The sample selected, however, did permit meaningful judgments about the significance of the various characteristics and linkages to be made.

CHAPTER

4

FINDINGS

THE INTEGRATION OF SERVICES IS NOT EXTENSIVE

The study reveals that integration of services is not extensive even in the projects recommended as being successful projects.[*] No project fully developed a majority of the linkages. In general, progress in developing linkages was slow, and internal difficulties complicated many of the projects. Many of the projects had not been in operation long enough to have developed many linkages and others were focusing primarily on service delivery and not integration. Other inhibiting factors are indicated in succeeding pages.

SERVICES INTEGRATION IS AN EVOLUTIONARY PROCESS

The study indicates that services integration is an evolutionary process. It takes time for services integration to occur—time for organization and implementation of a project, time for a project to attain legitimacy in the eyes of service providers, and time for participating agencies to develop a comfortable working relationship, often a necessary prerequisite to the coordination or consolidation of agencies' functions. It is difficult to implement a services

---

[*]Information within HEW about HEW-funded projects is frequently deficient. What was seen in the field was often much different from what HEW officials indicated was there. This was in part due to the fact that within HEW there was no consensus about what a successful services integration was and in part due to an inadequate information system in the department.

integration agenda. Once linkages have been made, they need continued attention and support in order that gains be protected and further progress made.

THERE IS A WIDE RANGE OF FACTORS THAT FACILITATE AND INHIBIT SERVICES INTEGRATION

Facilitators and inhibitors to services integration cover a wide range of factors. The study disclosed no single factor that was either beneficial to, or impeded, a majority of the projects. Rather, there were eight distinct categories of facilitators and inhibitors, and each category was comprised of many constituent elements.

In summary, services integration has a better chance of occurring when the sociopolitical leadership in the locality wants it to happen, when integration is a high-priority objective of the project, when the project director aggressively pursues coordination and has good contacts with important actors in the process, and when service providers have strong incentives to cooperate.

Conversely, services integration is less likely to occur even given the already unreceptive environment in which services integration must take place when the local leadership opposes change, when the integrator is so burdened by service delivery responsibilities and internal operations that he has no time to pursue coordination, when the project fails to define its mission as the development of integrative linkages, when service providers actively protect the status quo, jealously guarding their prerogatives, and when the project is poorly administered.

Superimposed on the local environment are the policies and procedures related to federal grant administration. These policies and procedures are beneficial when the integrator has control over service providers' funds and when guidelines suggest or require that the project coordinate its efforts with other service providers. However, these policies and procedures can be critical impediments when projects are buffeted by unclear and conflicting guidelines and funding uncertainties. These issues relate to project survival and must command priority at the sacrifice of coordination.

The more significant facilitators and inhibitors, each of which is susceptible to change by actions of HEW, are described below.

The Environment

The sociopolitical environment in which the projects function is an important factor, both positive and negative, in services integration. Support from government, community, and public and private funding sources—in terms of need for service delivery changes in general and by means of the project in particular—often enhances integrative efforts, while opposition exerts an important negative influence.

The local environment was found to be susceptible to change. If national leaders stress the need to overcome problems in the delivery system and if services integration truly becomes part of the national agenda, a local environment can be created that is more responsive to it. Those sectors of the community that are interested in, or have a stake in, improving the service delivery system are able to surface and unite for action. If adequate resources are available to local entities to encourage change, community consensus and support can be developed. If some emphasis is given to the desirability of a role in services integration for those bodies most able to affect the environment (such as local general purpose governments, influential citizens acting through health and welfare planning councils, consumer groups), those entities are more likely to undertake such roles and are better able to justify their initiatives.

Project Objectives and Priorities

A critical inhibitor to services integration is the lack of attention given to integrative efforts by the projects. This results from a variety of factors, most salient being an emphasis on service delivery responsibility and internal operations, and a definition of project objectives that does not recognize the establishment of integrative linkages as a central part of project mission.

Project objectives and priorities are susceptible to change. Clear emphasis in program guidelines and/or in technical assistance on the desirability of coordination can affect priorities and legitimize coordination efforts. In some projects it is clear that the integrator has developed linkages with other service providers only in response to federal requirements.

Project Director

The study provides support for the "great man" theory that the personality of the project director is one of the most important factors in services integration. In many of the projects, the director played the critical role in services integration. Leadership, persuasiveness, commitment, and personal contacts with political sources, staff of service providers, and the community appeared to be those attributes that had the greatest positive impact. On the other hand, the absence of administrative capability of some project directors had a negative effect on services integration.

Professional credentials were not essential. While there were some directors whose recognition and respect in their specialized profession made them more effective as integrators, there were other generalists who were equally effective.

Project Staff

A critical facilitator of service integration is the existence of a capable project staff whose mission is the coordination of providers and not service delivery. The expertise of such staff is important because the ability to help providers in programing, training, grants-manship, meeting federal requirements, and so on reinforces the providers' ties to the project.

Service Provider Objectives and Attitudes

The attitudes of service providers have great impact on services integration efforts. Where providers want to retain absolute control of funds, functions, and internal procedures and where they vie for control of the delivery system (which is probably normal organizational behavior), services integration is critically impeded. If, in addition, providers have their own power and influence with funding sources, attempts to overcome attitudinal obstacles are particularly hindered.

Provider attitudes can be changed or overridden if the authority and resources of the integrator are adequate. In addition, to the extent that the sociopolitical environment is changed, as previously outlined, the factions pressuring for change within these service providers can be assisted and reinforced. Service providers, most of which operate with public funds, can also be induced through guideline provisions and grant conditions to develop linkages with other providers.

Grant Administration Policies and Procedures

Grant administration policies and procedures can have a positive impact on services integration in the following ways:

Integrator Control of Service Provider Access to Funds

Services integration is facilitated to the extent the project integrator has control over service provider access to funding. This control enables the integrator to require provider participation in linkages as a prerequisite to receiving funds.

Single-point funding is a powerful tool for integration. The integrator, through whom funds flow to providers, can link services more closely if he is paying for them. In super-agencies, the director can obtain further cooperation from department heads if he is their funding source.

Open-Ended Funding and the Availability of Flexible Funds

The study indicated that the integrator's ability to integrate services is enhanced if the project is operating within the framework of an open-ended funding source such as Title IV-A. In such a project, the integrator could hold out the promise of nearly unlimited, constantly available funds for providers.

Conversely, projects functioning on grants of limited duration and fixed amounts encountered a variety of obstacles to linkage development as a result of their short-term expiration. Similarly, projects funded with demonstration grants (such as Section 1115) had difficulty in obtaining support from the community, developing linkages with providers, and making permanent changes in the delivery system.

Some linkages such as planning could not be accomplished with a short-term grant since they were continuous, long-range processes. Once linkages were developed, they had to be sustained—an effort a one-time grant cannot support.

In-Kind Contributions for Federal Funds

The opportunity to provide in-kind services instead of cash for local share can and in some cases has acted as an incentive to the integrator to seek out and involve provider agencies in services integration efforts. However, in many other cases, the making of the in-kind contribution has not resulted in a more closely-linked relationship between the donor and the integrator beyond the in-kind contribution itself.

On the other hand, grant administration policies and procedures can also act as an important impediment to services integration efforts. Unclear guidelines and funding delays and uncertainties can make the funding source part of the hostile environment in which the project must operate and can effectively cause projects to focus on internal operations to the detriment of coordination. These kinds of problems absorbed time of project staff, turned their attention to survival rather than coordination, and in some cases encouraged continued separation of potentially integrative processes.

SERVICES INTEGRATION RESULTS IN IMPROVED ACCESSIBILITY, CONTINUITY, AND EFFICIENCY

The divergent nature of the projects and the lack of baseline data coupled with the exploratory nature of the study made it infeasible to develop quantitative measures by which to assess impact on accessibility and continuity. The absence of data precluded the development of rigorous quantitative measures of the efficiency or cost effectiveness of services integration. Before and after cost figures are unavailable; the accounting systems employed prevent accurate isolation of costs attributable to integrative activities; several of the projects studied were too new to have developed reliable figures. Therefore, the findings that are offered here can be characterized as trends, evidence gained from partial success, and projections of probable longer-term impacts rather than rigid, quantifiable results.

With these qualifications, it can be said that services integration has a positive impact on accessibility, continuity, and efficiency of service delivery to clients. The direct economies achieved through integration did not appear to outweigh the costs of achieving integration, at least in the short run. However, if impact on problem solution is considered as a measure of efficiency, then a stronger efficiency argument can be made for services integration.

Accessibility

Integrative linkages among service providers in many of the projects have begun not only to make new services available to clients but also to expand the clientele receiving existing services. For example, integration has brought services to clients' neighborhoods and improved attitudes of traditional service provider staff, thus enhancing their ability and willingness to serve new client groups. It has also increased the number and effectiveness of outreach personnel to find and admit clients for service and led to systematic review of service requirements and resources resulting in development of needed services.

Continuity

Integrative linkages have affected continuity both by manipulating the fragmented service delivery system on a client-by-client basis and by administratively and programmatically rationalizing the system on behalf of all clients. Some projects have emphasized the core services of intake, diagnosis, referral, and follow-up supplemented by a variety of modes of case coordination (for example, case conference, case coordinator). These approaches have ensured that client acceptance into one service results in acceptance to other services, minimizing red tape and delay. Furthermore, they have facilitated initial assessment of overall service need and the delivery of specific services in a complementary, orderly and timely manner. These approaches have also prevented client loss within the service delivery system.

Projects have also affected continuity by concentrating on administrative linkages to identify service gaps and augment the resources of the delivery system to assure that the range of client needs can be met. These administrative linkages (such as joint planning or programing, purchase of service, and joint funding) enabled projects to commit agencies to provide a specific amount of service and to plan and deliver their service in a manner that complements the service of other providers. In addition, they have facilitated increased communication among service providers. Finally, a few projects have begun to utilize administrative linkages to weld providers into a tight-knit system that can plan, program, budget, and evaluate across a broad range of client needs.

Efficiency

Fieldwork indicates that it may not be possible to justify services integration strictly in terms of total dollar savings. Centralized/consolidated operation of core services, record-keeping, joint programing, joint funding, joint training, and/or central purchase of service arrangements on behalf of a number of service providers promote economies of scale, and coordinated staff utilization, funding, planning, and programing and evaluation help reduce duplication.

Although there are some cost savings resulting from economies of scale and reduction of duplication, they do not appear (at least in the short run) to equal the input costs of administrative and core service staff required to support integrative efforts. However, if one includes protection of public investment in services as a measure of efficiency, then a stronger case can be made for services integration on grounds of efficiency. If the public investment in one service (job training, for example) is to have lasting benefit only if another service (a job placement service, for example) is also provided, the cost involved in assuring that the client gets the job placement services as well as job training may be justified in terms of protecting the investment in job training. (This measure is referred to as impact on problem solution.)

THERE IS NO ONE BEST SERVICES INTEGRATION MODEL

Services integration can occur at various government levels with diverse sponsors, contexts, and activities. For example, the study included examples of services integration by state/local government/private agencies; with a variety of organizational modes; providing functional services ranging from child care to health care; focused on target groups, target areas, age groups; and occurring in hostile and favorable environments.

This study indicates that there is no one best services integration model. There were no indications of any significant difference in the impact that various project characteristics had on accessibility, continuity, and efficiency with the exception of "mode of coordination."

(On the basis of the information analyzed, it is not possible to assert that other project characteristics have no difference in impact. Because of the present state of the services integration art, isolating and measuring difference is exceedingly difficult, particularly in a small sample. It is particularly difficult to determine in precise, quantitative terms the impact any individual project had on accessibility and continuity and efficiency, and is virtually impossible to compare in precise quantitative terms the relative impact of different kinds of projects on those measures.)

Impact Varies According to Mode of Coordination

The projects studied fell into three general categories of coordination:

1. In voluntary coordination, the integrator is responsible for administering the provision of direct service as well as developing linkages between autonomous service providers: for example, Head Start central staff are responsible for activities such as child development, nutrition, and so on, as well as involving such other service providers as health practitioners, and social service agencies in the implementation of a comprehensive Head Start program.

2. In mediated coordination, the primary mission of the integrator is the development of linkages between autonomous service providers rather than the provision of direct service: for example, staff of a 4-C Committee, which, rather than providing day care

services, relates the services of health providers, early childhood education specialists and social agencies to the activities of day care centers in order to establish a network with the capability to plan, program, budget, implement, and evaluate comprehensive child development programs.

3. In directed coordination, the integrator has the authority to mandate the development of linkages between legally subordinate service providers: for example, the office of the administrator of a human resource agency has the authority to compel the division heads to participate in joint planning, budgeting, evaluation, and so on.

The impact of the project on accessibility, continuity, and efficiency appeared to vary according to the mode of coordination being employed.

Voluntary Coordination

In the projects studied that relied on voluntary coordination, the direct service provided was not previously available in the locality. Therefore, it is difficult to determine how much difference in accessibility is attributable to the fact that services are integrated as opposed to the mere fact that new services are available. It appears that when linkages have been developed, more clients receive the service because the linked service providers are more aware of and more readily make referrals to the service.

Positive impact on continuity occurs because the specific group of clients recruited for the project is guaranteed some services by external providers through such linkages as joint funding, purchase of service, joint programing, and staff outstationing. In addition, clients individually receive other services because of core services, which negotiate access to external services, coordinate service needs with the providers, and follow-up receipt of services. The provision of functional and supportive services by the project also increases client readiness to accept service from other providers.

With respect to efficiency, some economies of scale accrue from the assembly of a group of clients for service by a given provider. In addition, there is some reduction of duplication since the project provides core services, thus eliminating the need for service providers to engage in similar activities. However, the greatest impact on efficiency of these types of projects is their impact on problem solution by the provision of multiple services.

Mediated Coordination

Services integration implemented within the framework of mediated coordination utilizes administrative linkages (for example, joint programing, purchase of services, administrative support services) to impact accessibility and continuity. This occurs as a part of project efforts to rationalize the service delivery system by filling service gaps, increasing service relevancy, developing complementary service, and standardizing eligibility and intake procedures. These projects have significant impact on efficiency because arrangements are developed simultaneously for all clients rather than on a client-by-client basis.

Focus on the delivery system enables the integrator to disclose service duplication and overlap, and assess total needs. Moreover, the provision of staff expertise to providers has resulted in a redirection of existing service resources and a modification of delivery methods. In addition, the availability of staff to act on behalf of each provider to support cooperative efforts, act as grantsmen, negotiate with various funding sources, and so on can free the resources of the providers for service delivery.

Finally, this type of coordination has greater impact on problem solution than does voluntary coordination from the point of view of both numbers of clients affected by the project and efforts to make services more complementary in content and delivery procedures.

Directed Coordination

Review of services integration efforts within the framework of directed coordination was limited to general purpose government human resource agencies. Each agency studied was currently in the throes of a horizontal administrative reorganization and/or consolidation. Their efforts to develop integrative linkages (for example, consolidated planning, budgeting, evaluation) at the state level and to decentralize to the regional level through the development of single administrative structures in uniform regions are still in the formative stage. Presently, the state agencies are proceeding with limited tests of regional service delivery strategies through the use of demonstration projects. These efforts hold promise for future impact on accessibility, continuity, and efficiency of service delivery to clients.

The development of organizational structures to implement the formal authority of the human resource agency administrators should result in a planning capability to assess needs and resources, eliminate overlap and duplication, and fill service gaps, thereby promoting continuity in the delivery system and impacting efficiency. This planning capability is generally being aligned with budgeting, evaluation, and central record-keeping initiatives by these administrators.

Programing efforts and continued review of personnel utilization for the purposes of establishing joint use should produce cost savings and greater efficiency. Information-sharing and the availability of technical support services to agency divisions should promote both standardized and complementary service delivery, which will enhance continuity.

The development of integrated regional delivery systems should enhance service accessibility by using purchase of service arrangements to initiate information and referral, the establishment of multiservice centers, and so on.

However, these benefits for the most part have not yet been realized; in most cases, the payoffs for service delivery statewide will probably not be demonstrated for several years.

Impact Varies According to Project Objectives

The study revealed that project objectives affect the impact of a project on accessibility, continuity, and efficiency. The implicit and explicit objectives of services integration projects have affected the allocation of resources (time, personnel, money) devoted to and the approach taken in developing integrating linkages. Accordingly, these projects differ in the extent of their impact on the success measures of accessibility, continuity, and efficiency according to their objectives.

Where the objectives are limited to the manipulation of the service delivery system on a case-by-case basis, there is less impact on continuity and efficiency in terms of reduction of duplication since the delivery system itself remains the same.

Similarly, the single objective of bringing a variety of services into the clients' neighborhood (for example, most neighborhood service centers) limits impact on efficiency, largely because services are viewed by the integrator as discrete entities and not adapted to each other for maximum total effect. When these projects take a comprehensive approach to the identification and solution of client needs, continuity is enhanced. However, neighborhood service centers studied were typically limited in objective to providing core services and central record-keeping on a case-by-case basis with insufficient attention given to the coherence of the total delivery system.

Conversely, projects whose objectives emphasize the development of planning and coordinative arrangements between providers for the purpose of establishing a comprehensive and integrated service delivery system may have little initial effect, primarily because of the amount of time required to develop effective linkages. However, they indicate capacity to produce, over time, more extensive and lasting impact on accessibility, continuity, and efficiency. There were ample indications that the more mature projects of this type were beginning to have such impacts. For example, in one project the integrator has used such linkages as joint development of operating policies, programing, purchase of service, and so on, to develop a consortium of mental health providers in which intake by any one provider results in an immediate assignment for service by any other provider to which a client is referred.

Finally, approaches to integration that have begun with administrative consolidation (for example, conglomerate human resources agencies) were at too early a state of development to have had any discernible impact on the accessibility, continuity, or efficiency of service delivery to clients, although that was the objective of many of them.

DEVELOPMENT OF DIFFERENT LINKAGES REQUIRES DIFFERING RESOURCES AND INCENTIVES, VARYING PERIODS OF TIME, AND IMPACTS ON ACCESSIBILITY, CONTINUITY, AND EFFICIENCY IN DIFFERING WAYS

The integrator's ability to circumvent and overcome the resistance of service providers to coordinate their efforts largely relates to the resources and incentives available to induce cooperation. Power resources such as direct line authority over service providers or control over providers' access to funds allowed the integrator to make fundamental inroads in overcoming agency autonomy for the purpose of service integration, while the necessity to rely on persuasion generally resulted in more superficial gains.

Certain linkages can be made while still preserving organizational autonomy. Thus, direct service linkages and some administrative linkages (for example, information-sharing, joint programing, and so on) do not significantly encroach on agency independence and can be achieved when the integrator has few or no incentives beyond his persuasive ability. However, some administrative linkages lie close to the heart of agency governance—control over the organization's funds and personnel. These linkages can be achieved only when the integrator has substantial resources and incentives at its command.

Table 1.1, above, portrays an assessment of the kinds of resources and incentives needed to develop various linkages, the relative amount of time needed to develop them, and the importance of the linkage in terms of impact on accessibility, continuity, and efficiency. Because of the small size of the sample, the short operational life of many of the projects, and the difficulty of precisely measuring impact in general and in particular of isolating the impact of individual linkages, these relationships can be presented only as working hypotheses based on the experience gained over the past year in analyzing 30 projects. It is suggested that these hypotheses continue to be tested by HEW over time and in additional projects and that modifications be made as additional experience indicates.

No significant correlation between the project characteristics and the successful development of various kinds of linkages could be discerned, the one exception again being the mode of coordination employed. This, in turn, reflects the differing resources and incentives available to the integrator.

As might be expected, there was a general correlation between the use of direct service linkages and voluntary projects and between the use of administrative linkages and mediated and directed projects. In voluntary projects, the integrator was responsible for providing direct service to a specific client group as well as developing linkages with service providers. With little available time and no authority over service providers, emphasis was placed on establishing linkages that had immediate payoff in terms of getting services to clients. Integrators in voluntary projects related to providers only on a one-to-one basis as a general rule. Linkages were not consciously used to develop additional linkages.

On the other hand, the integrators in both mediated and directed projects were charged with the development of cooperative relationships between service providers rather than the provision of direct service and, in varying degrees, possessed the resources and incentives with which administrative linkages could be developed. Therefore, they placed their emphasis on the establishment of such linkages.

The integrators in mediated projects (except neighborhood service centers) also took an aggressive approach in developing linkages. Generally, they used one integrative linkage to involve service providers in others, parlaying the resources at their disposal into linkages to obtain wider participation by providers in project activities. Although the integrators did relate to providers on a one-to-one basis, this was generally a prelude to getting the providers to interact with each other.

However, in the mediated projects, there were two significant variables that affected the integrator's emphasis on, and ability to develop, particular linkages. These were cases where (1) the integrator controlled service providers' funds by virtue of single-point funding and (2) the organizing principle of serving all the needs of clients within a specific geographic area resulted in development of a neighborhood service center.

The integrators in mediated projects with single-point funding were guided not only by objectives related to rationalizing the total delivery system but also had considerable leverage to involve service providers in integrative linkages. Neighborhood service centers tended to focus their attention on assuring that service was provided to individual clients, and therefore initially used direct service linkages and only a few administrative linkages, such as colocation and central record-keeping. Therefore, in many respects, although neighborhood service centers generally conform to the definition of mediated coordination, the centers have more in common with voluntary coordination projects.

54

The types of resources and incentives under the control of the integrator under various project types are described below.

Voluntary Coordination Projects

In voluntary coordination projects, the major and almost sole resource available is the integrator's ability to persuade service providers to connect or to link their services with those of the prime service offered by the project. Only a few projects had as an additional resource the availability of funds to pay for some services if necessary. Given the lack of formal authority and the constant demands made on time and energy by direct service responsibilities, persuasion necessitated strong commitment and effort by the project director and staff.

Participation in the project was dependent on three related incentives acting on autonomous agencies; first was their perception that cooperation would assist or allow them to achieve their own organization's goals. A second incentive was the opportunity to expand clientele; projects gave service providers access to a concentrated target population, as well as making individual clients requiring specialized services easily available to them. A third incentive, in some projects, was the integrator's ability to be a bridge and buffer between the service provider (generally an established, traditional, and usually large service provider) and an unfamiliar client population. This was particularly important in instances where the client group involved was perceived as difficult or threatening by the service provider's administration or staff.

Mediated Coordination Projects

In mediated coordination projects, there was a staff whose primary mission was developing coordination among service providers. In a few other projects, the integrator also had control over service providers' access to funds.

Projects achieved their most significant leverage over service providers by virtue of their designation as the single conduit for certain federal funds. This single-point funding gave the integrator the capability both to deliver and control some or all of the service providers' financial resources. Service providers so urgently wanted funds to sustain or expand their direct service that they either actively solicited participation in the project or were willing to accept the integrator's coordination demands in return for new money.

55

In each project, the central staff could interrelate the activities of service providers partially because they were not competing to offer services to clients but instead assisted the agencies themselves. The integrative staff was a resource to service providers and, in the process of helping these agencies, affected their policies, procedures, and the ultimate delivery of services to clients.

Integrative staff was able to attain legitimacy in the view of service providers by demonstrating expertise useful to the agencies in accomplishing their own objectives and by relieving the agencies of administrative concerns, thus leaving them more time for service delivery.

The availability of expertise in a central coordinative staff was a major incentive to service providers to become involved in project activities and the integrative staffs implemented linkages to pave the way for agencies' participation in other linkages.

Neighborhood Service Centers

The critical resource available to the integrator was the neighborhood service center facility itself, which enhanced the connection of the autonomous service providers with the clients. Use of center facilities provided some incentives to the service providers for participation in the project. First, the location of the facility in the target area provided ready access to a concentrated population as well as making individual clients requiring specialized services easily available to the service providers. Second, the service providers were not bound by an organizational framework that altered their roles, objectives, or programmatic policies to any appreciable extent.

In each case, the center as a facility was not utilized as a bargaining device to develop a single coherent delivery system but rather just as a shelter for service providers. The various service providers were more than happy to respond to the "invitation" to relocate. This colocation of providers generally resulted in staff meetings, which in turn led to the development of other linkages— but usually in an unstructured way. Many of the existing linkages in neighborhood service centers were inherent in the project design rather than the conscious agenda of the integrator.

Directed Coordination Projects
(Human Resource Super-Agencies)

In the human resource super-agencies, there are diverse resources available to the integrator in the development of linkages among the previously separate service providers. First is the legislative mandate for reorganization. Typically, this reflects a legislative intent to reduce service fragmentation, achieve administrative economies, and establish unitary policy control over state human service agencies.

A second resource consists of the legal powers delegated to the integrator such as single-line authority over divisions of the agency, internal reorganization authority, budget and resource allocation authority, and comprehensive planning authority. (The extent to which the integrator has been given these powers varies from state to state.) Additionally, the integrator has access to a planning staff to review critically the existing systems of the service providers. He also has special project or demonstration funds to test new systems.

Controlling these resources, the agency administrators tended to follow a pattern in which planning and programing linkages were established first, with fiscal linkages and administrative support service linkages following in that order. In those cases, the clear intent of the integrator was to pursue linkages between division heads systematically and as quickly as they could be accepted, reserving the use of line authority only as a last resort.

GENERAL PURPOSE GOVERNMENT IS AN IMPORTANT FACILITATOR OF SERVICES INTEGRATION

Local general purpose government played some role in many of the projects. Involvement ranged from direct project sponsorship, funding conduit, and general support of the project to a barrier to project activities.

Analysis of the case studies to test the hypothesis that general purpose government is better able to sponsor effective services integration than are other organizational auspices (for example, special purpose public agencies, voluntary councils, private nonprofit corporations) yielded only a few tentative conclusions. Projects sponsored by general purpose government put somewhat more emphasis on the development of administrative linkages and less on direct service linkages and implemented linkages at a somewhat slower pace than do projects under other sponsorship.

However, the limited size of the sample and variations in the length of time projects under different sponsorship had been in operation make it impossible to ascribe the difference in type and timing of linkage development solely to the difference in organizational sponsorship. Other parts of the analysis indicated that projects vary not so much by type of organizational sponsorship as they do by mode of coordination.

Whether or not general purpose government is a more effective project sponsor, it is clear that support and aid to a project by general purpose government is an important facilitator of services integration.

THE CLIENT CAN BE AN IMPORTANT INTEGRATIVE FORCE

Although there was some degree of client participation in nearly two-thirds of the projects studied, dramatic variations in the role of clients appeared, ranging from pro forma membership on committees prompted by funding source requirements to client control of policy-making and project operations.

The extent of client involvement does not seem to vary by mode of coordination, except that the consolidated human resource agencies (examples of directed coordination) have not yet determined or developed organizational mechanisms to implement client involvement. The role of the client as integrator most nearly correlates with the extent to which clients initiated participation in the project, and this, in turn, primarily related to the level of organization and/or mobilization of client population at project inception. In some cases, this organization and/or mobilization was traceable to efforts by community action agencies; in others, to the experience derived from a shared problem (for example, parents of mentally retarded children); and, in a few cases, to the efforts of project staff.

Clients have caused the integration of services by identifying problems, soliciting local contributions to finance remedies to the problem, supporting responsive agencies within the delivery systems, lobbying for the availability of existing service to new clientele, changing service provider attitudes, acting as a countervailing force to the establishment of a conservative consensus by participating agencies in the development of project policy, and establishing service legitimacy in the view of potential clients by virtue of their involvement. In many cases, unfettered by traditional definitions of feasibility, clients have achieved positive, creative solutions to service delivery problems.

CONCLUSION

The services integration projects studied were operating in extremely diffuse social service environments made up of a variety of public and private agencies with competing claims to funds and authority. Developing that structure into a unitary system, even if it were desirable, could probably not be done, for several reasons:

1. There are various approaches to designing systems—according to problem or age groups, geographic areas, or functions—each of which has some defensible rationale.

2. There are various funding sources, and they are not likely to agree on a single system. Although the trend is toward more public involvement, private charity will not be totally supplanted.

3. Organized constituencies with congressional supporters lobby for services organized around a lead function, such as vocational rehabilitation or mental health, as the prime service with other services as auxiliary.

4. There is no consumer group pressuring for a unitary system.

5. There are a variety of other obstacles to unity, as suggested by the list of inhibitors uncovered by our fieldwork.

In summary, there is little support for a unified service delivery system either from service providers or from other sources.

While a unitary system may never be created, the study indicates that it would be feasible to create a more closely knit, although still pluralistic, system by getting providers to link services and enhancing the ability of certain agencies, such as general purpose government, to assume a leadership role in the pursuit of services integration. The study also indicates that such an effort has payoff to the client in terms of improved accessibility and continuity of service and to the taxpayer in terms of protecting his investment in services. This effort is the substance of services integration policy and necessitates certain actions by HEW.

5

RECOMMENDATIONS FOR A COMPREHENSIVE STRATEGY TO PROMOTE SERVICES INTEGRATION

There is the potential for services integration at all levels of HEW funding; however, to implement services integration, HEW must make a significantly greater effort.

There is no single approach to overcoming the obstacles to services integration. The effort must involve a variety of steps to facilitate the integration process and to shape the services integration product.

The study findings indicate that in order to achieve the greatest impact on accessibility, continuity, and efficiency, support should be focused on mediated and directed coordination projects since they pursue rationalization of the service delivery system on behalf of an entire class of clients rather than the manipulation of the delivery system for specific clients. Nevertheless, voluntary coordination projects should not be abandoned. While they currently rely on a coincidence of provider objectives to achieve services integration and concentrate on service delivery, a slightly greater investment of effort could produce effective services integration. Objectives and priorities of these projects can be expanded to include system change rather than being confined to system manipulation, and their capacity to implement these new directions can be enhanced by the availability of additional staff to focus on coordination among service providers rather than provision of direct services.

In sum, the study findings indicate a wide range of opportunities open to HEW to promote services integration. In order to take advantage of these opportunities, there must be a departmental commitment to services integration and the implementation of a comprehensive strategy to promote it. The major components of such a strategy are outlined below.

CREATION OF AN ENVIRONMENT RECEPTIVE TO SERVICES INTEGRATION

There are a number of steps that officials in HEW and other federal officials could take to create a local climate favorable to services integration. They include the whole range of activities that may be undertaken—speeches, national conferences, and so on—to establish in the minds of the public that the issue is a priority of the federal government.

This same climate must be established within the department in order for HEW to be able to undertake the rest of the program outlined below.

Study findings corroborate many of the recommendations of HEW's own task force on Administrative and Organizational Constraints to Services Integration. As emphasized in that report, many middle-level management staff are not in tune with the services integration policies of HEW. Likewise, services integration efforts have not reached many of the HEW program officials who make funding decisions and monitor grantee progress.

PROVISION OF SUPPORT SERVICES TO SERVICES INTEGRATION PROJECTS

The level and manner in which HEW provides advocacy, technical assistance, and monitoring support services to projects should be revised to facilitate implementation of a services integration policy.

The HEW Regional Offices should be deeply involved in the development and operation of local services integration projects. The Regional Offices, given a staff capability in services integration, could undertake provision of technical assistance and program monitoring to local projects, rather than central office staff.

Projects analyzed in this study that received guidance from the HEW regional staff included several of the services integration concepts in their objectives. Although their initial objectives did not focus on services integration, they were altered when assistance was provided by the HEW regional officers.

Advocacy

HEW has demonstrated a reluctance to intervene at the state or local level in support of a project it has funded. While this reluctance is often predicated on a desire to permit localities to manage their own affairs, it may be detrimental to services integration efforts.

HEW needs to be more supportive of the projects it funds and to assume an advocacy role in their behalf to overcome impediments to services integration. HEW may particularly have to assume an advocacy role with intermediate funding sources, such as state departments, which administer formula grant funds.

Also in an advocacy role, HEW should emphasize that all service providers receiving formula grant funds should coordinate their programs with local agencies that may be planning or operating an integrated delivery system in the providers' service area.

On-Site Technical Assistance and Training

In order to overcome the general lack of knowledge about services integration and its implementation and to alter the low priority given to coordination of delivery systems by service providers, HEW should provide sustained, on-site technical assistance and training as necessary during the development and operation of a services integration project.

Technical assistance should include the following:

1. Information about linkages—what they are, how they can be and have been developed. Linkages should be defined with examples of how projects with similar environments and clientele have effectively linked services of autonomous providers.

2. Information about the use of purchase of service agreements for the development of linkages.

3. Information about the qualities that should be sought in a project director over and above a certain level of management expertise as guidance to those who will be selecting project directors.

4. Forums for directors and staff concerning services integration and linkage development.

5. Techniques for involving service providers and local general purpose governments in project development and the decision-making process.

Technical assistance should stress the following:

1. Services integration is an objective of major interest to HEW and should be a project objective.

2. Linkage development is a tool to achieve services integration and not a goal in itself.

3. Involvement of service providers and representatives of the local general purpose governments (state, city, and/or county) in initial project development can be very important to project success.

Indirect Technical Assistance

HEW should develop a capability to provide indirect technical assistance through the development of a services integration information clearinghouse either within the department or an independent organization. (There are some precedents that suggest that an independent entity might more readily make qualitative assessments about services integration efforts and be able more quickly to disseminate informational materials.) Indirect technical assistance can include such items as the outcomes and processes used in Section 1115 Research and Demonstration Projects and Targets of Opportunity projects, model clauses for purchase of service agreements, alternative strategies for linkage development, and instruments by which to identify, monitor, and evaluate services integration progress.

Monitoring

The study found limited monitoring of services integration projects. Much of the monitoring that did occur was counterproductive and rarely focused on services integration. HEW should develop a system for monitoring services integration projects that (1) focuses on the achievement of services integration as well as the delivery of services; (2) applies flexible performance standards to focus on project objectives rather than preconceived objectives that do not relate to the project's functions; and (3) relies on HEW staff visits to project sites rather than on written reports by project staff.

Monitoring and technical assistance to services integration projects can be facilitated if it is based upon (1) reasonable expectations for linkage development; (2) determining which integrating linkages are important to develop; and (3) determining what can be done to enhance their development.

As part of this evaluation, a classification scheme and an applied analytical approach for analyzing services integration projects were developed and tested. Application to the project sample studied yielded some conclusions about relationships that, because of the size of the sample, can only be regarded as tentative. It is believed that the classification system, or something similar to it, would be a useful technique to be used by HEW in monitoring and evaluating other services integration projects as a way of determining what technical assistance needs might be and building up a broader base of experience and insight into the process and results of linkage development. It also would provide an organized system for interrelating the experience and insight gained from a variety of services integration projects.

ELIMINATION OF INTERNAL HEW CONSTRAINTS
TO SERVICES INTEGRATION

Many of the federal constraints to services integration disclosed by the study are not so much related to the inherent limitations of the categorical grant system per se as they are to the procedures, policies, and organization of HEW. There is a clear need for a staff within the department whose sole responsibility is coordinating HEW's services integration efforts and reorienting existing HEW staff to a services integration approach. (This recommendation supports that of the Task Force on Administrative and Organizational Constraints to Services Integration.)

This unit or staff should be organizationally placed in the office of the secretary. There should be counterpart units or staffs in each agency. This organization would be replicated in the regional offices with units in the regional director's office and in each regional commissioner's office.

The focus of the Washington staff would be in developing general policy and technical assistance materials; the focus of the regional staff would be the provision of direct technical assistance and development of indirect technical assistance materials. These staffs could also be the focus of the implementation of the Allied Services Act should it be enacted.[*]

There is also a need to experiment with alternative forms of organization that offer promise for a more integrated response by HEW to localities. For example, a single staff person might be authorized to represent all bureaus of SRS in a geographic area (for example, a large county of metropolitan area).

BUILDING SERVICES INTEGRATION INTO THE
HEW GRANT SYSTEM

A services integration policy should be built into a rationalized HEW grant system in which grant programs are coordinated, guidelines developed, and administrative procedures geared toward facilitating its implementation.

---

[*]See pages 301-3 below for more specific recommendations relative to the Allied Services Act.

Development of Program Guidelines Reflecting a
Services Integration Policy

HEW should write a services integration policy into program guidelines. Guidelines should make it clear that linkage development is a matter of significance to the funding source and that projects are expected to devote time and resources to it. This can occur if guidelines (1) indicate that linkage development is an eligible/required project expenditure; (2) encourage/require project reports to include the status of efforts to integrate service providers; (3) encourage/require provider participation on project policy-making boards and committees and in project development (a facilitator uncovered by this study); and (4) encourage/require a project to take specific steps that will result in the development of specific linkages.

For example:

1. Guidelines could require the integrator to develop formal, structured mechanisms for the participation of providers in the planning and programing processes.

2. Guidelines could stimulate joint evaluation by indicating how purchase of service agreements might be used to implement this process.

3. Guidelines could stimulate the development of centralized record-keeping by indicating a variety of methods for the sharing of case information rather than by specifying that one method be used. (Too often the differing requirements of provider agencies' funding sources and agencies' small clientele, make implementation of a single, mandated system untenable.)

Many of the discontinuities in regulations that make it difficult or impossible to use HEW programs jointly are administrative, not statutory, in origin. Administrative guidelines and regulations for formula grants and project grants should be thoroughly examined to determine what modifications will facilitate the joint use of HEW program funds.

HEW Funding Policy as a Means to Facilitate
Services Integration*

The case studies demonstrate that HEW policies and procedures concerning the allocation and use of grant funds can have either a

---

*Some of these proposals can be implemented through the planning and capacity-building grants and the administrative cost

positive or negative impact on services integration. They suggest ways in which HEW can use its funding authority to facilitate implementation of services integration projects.

Integrator Control of Provider Accessibility to Funds— Single-Point Funding

HEW should recognize that programs that might be set up through separate grants to individual service providers will result in greater integration if instead funds flow through a single local conduit. It should, therefore, consider single-point funding as a tool for services integration.

HEW might consider coupling this single-point funding procedure with a policy adopted by HUD in the Model Cities Program and stipulated in Title IV-A—a prohibition against the integrator itself providing the services if they can be obtained externally.

Open-Ended Funding and the Availability of Flexible Funds as Facilitators of Services Integration

HEW should explore further the services integration potential of Title IV-A and the impediments of grants of limited duration. It might consider means of compensating for the lack of open-ended funding programs and the particular problems inherent in limited-duration grants. One means of compensation might be the creation of a flexible pool of funds for services integration activities similar to those of the Target of Opportunity Program but that would be implemented as a continuing support program rather than a research and demonstration program.

These flexible funds, perhaps from R and D programs, would be used to finance linkage development and services integration activities rather than service delivery. They might also be used in a limited way for service delivery as an incentive for provider participation in a project.

The funds could be administered by a special HEW staff whose mission would be the coordination of HEW services integration

---

grants under the proposed Allied Services Act if it is enacted. However, there is a whole range of opportunities at the local level for assisting services integration outside the context of the Allied Services Act that should be considered as well: (1) in communities that will not be developing local allied services plans, (2) in individually HEW-funded projects that will not be part of a local allied services plan, and (3) in activities not related to eligible uses of those grant funds.

activities and whose organizational placement would permit it to cut across agency and program lines.

Funds for Support Services

HEW should consider the impact of support services on the service delivery system. Several projects relied on the provision of support services such as transportation to achieve continuity in service delivery. Funds for the provision of these services, however, were not readily available. HEW might (1) make it clear in guidelines that support services are eligible project expenditures, and (2) include in the funds awarded to a project sufficient amounts for the provision of support services.

Planning Grants to Facilitate Project Implementation

HEW should consider the institution of planning grants to projects for initial start-up and operating costs. The plan produced with these funds could focus not just on service delivery, but on the coordination process to be used in achieving services integration. The planning grants might come from the pool of flexible funds previously discussed. Technical assistance in linkage development should accompany these grants.

Provision of Funds for Project Staff to Concentrate on Services Integration

HEW should facilitate acquisition of staff to concentrate on services integration either by making staff an eligible project cost or by providing special staffing grants. HEW should realize that coordination is evolutionary and requires time to develop; therefore, staffing funds must be provided on a long-term and sustained basis and not within the framework of a one-shot, short-term grant.

In-Kind Contributions for Federal Funds as a Services Integration Tool

HEW should consider in-kind contributions as a tool to encourage integrators to establish connections with providers (1) by requiring integrators to develop linkages with donors, (2) by providing technical assistance regarding the services integration potential of in-kind contributions.

Purchase of Service Agreements as a Services Integration Tool

HEW can enhance the efficacy of purchase of service agreements

as a means to achieve services integration by (1) encouraging/
requiring integrators to make funding under purchase of service
agreements contingent on provider participation in linkage development; (2) providing, through technical assistance and guidelines,
information about the use of such agreements for linkage development, detailing what linkages can be developed at each stage of
project implementation; (3) indicating to state agencies administering formula grant funds (a) how purchase of service agreements
may be used and developed to promote services integration through
either program guidelines or technical assistance and (b) the types
of requirements that may be placed on project integrators who
obtain formula grant funds through purchase of service agreements
or enter into such agreements with other providers.

6

FACILITATORS
AND INHIBITORS OF
SERVICES INTEGRATION

Among the major objectives of this study was the identification and analysis of factors affecting the development and implementation of services integration projects. Some of the facilitators and inhibitors of services integration affected all facets of the project's development and implementation. They are discussed in this chapter. In addition, specific facilitators and inhibitors were identified that affected only particular integrating linkages attempted by the project. They are discussed in Chapter 7.

The factors at play in each project were identified and rated by the project field teams who performed the field interviews and analyses and thus had the closest perception of the subtleties of each project situation. The facilitators and inhibitors were then rated "critical," "major," or "minor" to indicate the intensity of their impact in the development of the project.

The listing of facilitators and inhibitors indicates the range of factors involved and the totals of the ratings indicate their general order of magnitude and frequency. There were a total of 52 facilitators and 36 inhibitors identified that affected overall project development.

The inhibitors and facilitators fall into 10 general categories of factors that either help or impede project development. These categories are (1) environmental influences, (2) service provider objectives and attitudes, (3) grant administration policies and procedures, (4) project structure and operations, (5) project staff, (6) technical and logistical factors, (7) role of director or board, (8) incentives for project participation, (9) integrator's objectives and priorities, and (10) service provider policies and procedures.

The first six categories apply to both facilitators and inhibitors while numbers 7 and 8 pertain exclusively to facilitators and numbers 9 and 10, to inhibitors. The individual facilitators and inhibitors that fall within and give definition to these categories appear in succeeding sections of this chapter.

FACILITATORS

Table 6.1 illustrates by category the facilitators that influenced project development and implementation. The summary data reflect the ranking of each category and the frequency with which the individual facilitator impacted the projects. None of the particular facilitators grouped under the categories listed occurred in every project studied. The most commonly occurring were found in less than half (approximately 49 percent) of the projects. Thus, while some facilitators clearly appeared more often than others, it is difficult to conclude that any one was the primary aid to services integration.

Within each category, there is a variety of related facilitators. In fact, the eight categories subsume a total of 52 identified facilitators acting upon overall project development alone. Thus, any effort at fostering the facilitators of service integration must embrace a wide spectrum of activity.

By far the most important factors facilitating services integration were (1) support from the external sociopolitical environment in which the project functioned; (2) the cooperative environment created when the direct actors in the project—the integrator and the other service providers—shared the project's objectives; and (3) the cooperative environment created when the service providers did not fear loss of control of their services or internal operations. Almost half of the facilitators fell into these categories.

TABLE 6.1

Summary of Facilitators

Rank Order	Category	Critical	Major	Minor	Total
1	Environmental influences	27	27	17	71
2	Role of director or board	26	15	8	49
3	Service provider objectives	15	18	8	41
4	Technical and logistical factors	15	15	7	37
5	Project structure and operations	12	9	14	35
6	Grant administration policies and procedures	13	9	14	35
7	Project staff	6	11	9	26
8	Incentives for project participation	11	10	3	26

The specific manner in which the project was carried out accounts for approximately 35 percent of the facilitators. These categories include the role of director or board, technical and logistical factors, project structure and operations, and project staff. The role of the director was rated as a critical facilitator in one-third of the projects.

Federal grant administrative policies and procedures (less than 10 percent of the facilitators) were not nearly so important as these local influences.

The following discussion examines the specific facilitators for each category. Conclusions are drawn on the effects of each facilitator as they impact entire projects.

Services integration was clearly facilitated if the environment of a project was supportive of (1) general change in the service delivery system with which the project was concerned and (2) the specific changes in the system that the project was designed to bring about (see Table 6.2). The environment was favorable for success if some, and preferably all, of the following recognized the need for change in the service delivery system and endorsed the project: (1) state and local (including county) government; (2) the community (community organizations, political factions, influential citizens, services users); and (3) service providers.

The most important facilitator in this category was active support from the public funding source (primarily local and state government). Government willingness to encourage or initiate change in the service delivery network and to support a demonstration project beyond merely funding the project appeared as a facilitator in over 45 percent of the projects. Only slightly less frequently appeared government support of the mix of project services and of the delivery and administrative procedures the project utilized.

Allocation to the director of formal authority over the total project was a prime facilitator in only five projects (Table 6.3). The personality of the director or assistant director was a more important facilitator than his formal authority. In fact (with a single exception) it was the "critical" factor in more projects than any other facilitator. In one-third of all projects examined, the director's leadership and commitment appeared as a critical major facilitator. His contacts with political sources assisted project development in one-quarter; his contacts with administrators and staff of service providers in almost one-sixth; and his contacts with community organizations and influential citizens in one-seventh. The central importance of the integrator's contacts was illustrated in the Boise Youth Service Bureau. In this project the program manager had no formal authority to coordinate autonomous services, but the esteem in which she was held by her contacts in provider agencies enabled her to legitimize the project in the community.

TABLE 6.2

Environmental Influences

Facilitators	Critical	Major	Minor	Total
1. Environment is supportive of general changes in the existing services delivery system:				
a. Service providers recognize the need for changes in the service delivery system.	5	6	5	16
b. Local and/or state government and/or public funding source is willing to support, encourage, or initiate changes in the service delivery system.	6	8	1	15
c. Community organizations, political factions, influential citizens, service users recognize the need for changes in the service delivery system.	1	2	6	9
2. Environmental influences are supportive of service delivery system change through the project:				
a. Active support of funding source beyond mere funding.	13	4	1	18
b. Support of community organizations, political factions, influential citizens, and/or service users	2	7	4	13
Total	27	27	17	71

72

TABLE 6.3

Role of Director or Board

Facilitators	Critical	Major	Minor	Total
1. Role of the director				
a. Director exerts his leadership and displays commitment to the project.	9	3	—	12
b. Director has contacts with				
(1) Political sources	5	2	2	9
(2) Administrators/staff in provider agencies	4	2	1	7
(3) Community	2	2	2	6
(4) Funding sources	2	—	2	4
(5) Professionals in areas related to the project	—	2	1	3
c. Director has formal authority over total project operation.	4	1	—	5
2. Community advisory board control over certain aspects of project operation	—	3	—	3
Total	26	15	8	49

73

TABLE 6.4

Service Provider Objectives and Attitudes

Facilitators	Critical	Major	Minor	Total
1. Service providers had congruent/complementary objectives with the project	9	6	2	17
2. Perception of project as a means to attain its own objectives	2	7	—	9
3. Willingness to submerge agency prerogatives in support of integration objectives	2	4	3	9
4. Willingness of service providers to consider themselves part of the service delivery problem	2	1	3	6
Total	15	18	8	41

74

Control by a community advisory board of certain aspects of project operation appeared as a facilitator in two voluntary and one mediated project.

Services integration was facilitated significantly when the integrator and provider agencies had shared or complementary goals (Table 6.4). This is particularly true when the integrator's only coordinating tool is persuasion—as in the voluntary projects and all but three of the mediated projects. In these cases, the integrator lacked such compelling leverage as control of funds so that mutually compatible goals became a paramount factor. Moreover, service providers in a mediated project usually had to meet new demands placed on them by virtue of their participation; clearly, a sharing of the integrator's goals would make them more willing to assume this onus.

The attitudes of service providers that could facilitate integration efforts primarily involve their desire to improve service delivery and their willingness to alter some of their traditional policies in order to serve in the project. The most frequently occurring facilitator of this type was provider willingness to expand clientele, often accepting not only more clients but a different type of client. For example, the hospitals affiliated with the Westside Mental Health Center began to treat members of the black and hippie population previously not served. This facilitator also appeared in neighborhood service centers where location enabled clients to secure services from providers such as health and welfare departments, previously so remote as to seem inaccessible to them.

The willingness of provider agencies to consider themselves part of the service delivery problem was another attitude affecting integration efforts. This was also prevalent in neighborhood service centers, which greatly depended upon the willingness of providers to colocate in a neighborhood facility to create a new service delivery network.

Services integration was also significantly advanced when service providers viewed their participation in the project as a means to achieve their own objectives.

Support services were particularly important in voluntary coordination projects and neighborhood service centers—both project types centrally focused on providing the client with his needed range of services (Table 6.5). Transportation especially helped fulfill that objective and so became a prime facilitator. Several neighborhood service centers, such as Crossroads Neighborhood Service Center, provided transportation because they were linked to service providers not located in the same facility or even in the project service area. For the same reasons, physical proximity of provider agencies facilitated project development with equal importance.

75

TABLE 6.5

Technical and Logistical Factors

Facilitators	Critical	Major	Minor	Total
1. Support services are provided:				
a. Transportation	1	5	1	7
b. Child care	1	1	—	2
c. Escort	—	1	—	1
d. Meals	—	1	—	1
2. Studies and task forces have identified needs	3	3	2	8
3. Standardized data collection/continuous feedback from providers	4	2	1	7
4. Physical proximity of service providers	2	2	3	7
5. Facility is well located in services area	4	—	—	4
Total	15	15	7	37

Each project had its own policies, procedures, and requirements governing its relationship with affiliated providers and clients. In general, projects whose development and implementation progressed most smoothly (1) involved providers in project development and the identification of needs and areas for consolidation and (2) were free from the bureaucratic, traditional, and/or political constraints that had characterized the autonomous service providers (Table 6.6).

In particular, the integrator's freedom from bureaucratic and political constraints facilitated mediated and voluntary projects by permitting them to be more innovative in their programs and procedures and to act quickly in implementing services.

Flexibility in use of funds, permitting support of a variety of purposes, was the most significant facilitator in this category (Table 6.7). It appeared primarily in neighborhood service centers that utilized either OEO, HEW Title IV-A, or HUD Model Cities supplemental funds.

Other major facilitators in this category were (1) project designation by its funding source as the sole conduit for channeling its funds; and (2) federal guidelines for fund use and administration. Project control over funds was a critical factor in three mediated projects as discussed in detail in Chapter 10 (p. 164-5). Federal guidelines set the parameters for integration in three voluntary projects—all programs for which the federal government specified the range of service to be provided and the provider agencies to involve.

Finally, the federal regulation separating welfare payments from provision of services to welfare recipients assisted the development of projects directly affected by the internal procedures of their state welfare departments. Since there was to be disruption in any case, the mandatory partial reorganization appears to have stimulated the state government to rethink and revamp its total organizational structure.

Staff availability and capability of the project as well as harmony in staff relationships with service providers were critical or major facilitators identified in most project types (Table 6.8). The most critical facilitator in this category (in five projects) was the existence of a coordinative and administrative staff concerned with interrelating the activities of service providers, serving as a resource for providers, and developing linkages. However, in the super-agencies, these facilitators were of lesser importance probably because of the state of development and prescribed lines of authority of the super-agencies.

The facilitators in the category of incentives for project participation were basically three kinds of incentives (Table 6.9):

TABLE 6.6

Project Structure and Operations

Facilitators	Critical	Major	Minor	Total
1. Service providers are involved in project development, identifying concerns and areas for consolidation	2	2	4	8
2. Integrator is free from the bureaucratic, traditional, and/or political constraints of the existing service providers	4	1	—	5
3. Service providers are members of project board/committees	—	1	4	5
4. Organizational consolidation	3	—	1	4
5. Project staff serve as liaison to each service provider	1	2	—	3
6. Ability of client to enter the service delivery system through any linked provider	1	—	2	3
7. Integrator has joint staff meetings with service providers	—	2	1	3
8. Membership of project director/staff on boards of service providers	1	—	1	2
9. Service area resident/clients are involved in project planning, development	—	1	1	2
Total	12	9	14	35

TABLE 6.7

Grant Administration Policies and Procedures

Facilitators	Critical	Major	Minor	Total
1. Flexibility of funds	4	2	1	7
2. Funding source designates integrator as the sole conduit through which funds are channeled	4	—	1	5
3. Requirements that income assistance be separated from services necessitating reorganization	3	—	2	5
4. Existence of guidelines for fund use/administration	2	1	—	5
5. Permissibility of in-kind matches for state or local share	—	1	2	3
6. Open-ended funding source	—	1	1	2
7. Federal, state, local requirements necessitating or encouraging the development of certain linkages such as joint budgeting, joint funding, and so on	—	1	—	1
Total	13	6	7	26

79

TABLE 6.8

Project Staff

Facilitators	Critical	Major	Minor	Total
1. Relationship between staff of integrator and providers				
a. Close working relationship of staffs	—	3	1	4
b. Confidence of provider staff in expertise of project staff	—	2	2	4
c. Staff committed to project and linkage development	—	3	—	3
2. Existence of an administrative/coordinative project staff	5	—	2	7
3. Trained staff with expertise	1	1	2	4
4. Staff developed rapport with clients	—	2	2	4
Total	6	11	9	26

TABLE 6.9

Incentives for Project Participation

Facilitators	Critical	Major	Minor	Total
1. Integrator has some control over service provider accessibility to funds	2	3	—	5
2. Integrator is a buffer between the service provider and the federal government and/or other funding sources	2	3	—	5
3. Integrator serves as a buffer or intermediary between clients and traditional service providers	2	3	—	5
4. Linkage is recommended by funding source	3	1	1	5
5. Space provided free or at a low cost	2	—	2	4
Total	11	10	3	24

1. Service providers participating in the project received some type of financial benefit.

2. The integrator functioned as a mediator or buffer in overcoming problems confronting provider agencies.

3. Linkages were developed at the suggestion of a prestigious external source.

All three kinds of incentives appeared most often in voluntary and mediated projects. In the first type, the project integrator possessed no authority to obtain cooperation of service providers, and incentives were essential to secure their affiliation. In the second, participation created new obligations for providers, and the incentives tended to offset those obligations. In the third, which primarily involved one neighborhood service center, service providers acceded to a government suggestion in the hope of securing additional funds. None of these incentives appeared as a facilitator among super-agencies where coordination is mandated.

Expectedly, access to funds appears as a common incentive, but it is worth noting that, typically, this facilitator was operative in mediated projects where the integrator controlled allocation of state-administered federal funds. In the United Family Services and the Phoenix Child Care Projects, the integrating staffs used their control of Title IV-A money to begin coordinating neighborhood service centers and day care centers, respectively, into a service delivery network. The Westside Mental Health Center core staff used its single-conduit control of federal and state mental health funds even more effectively. With this leverage, providers were induced to serve a new clientele, numerous integrative linkages were developed, and one provider that failed to comply with requirements was expelled from the project.

Another type of financial incentive to integration was availability of space in a project facility at low cost or no cost. This appeared as a facilitator only in neighborhood service centers, where colocation of providers was a factor in project success.

In five projects, the integrator's role as a buffer between providers and the funding source facilitated integration of services. This mediation was usually concerned with conflicts about fund use or the meeting of federal requirements. For example, in the Phoenix Child Care Project, central staff mediated a question of permissibility and cash value of an in-kind match that arose between one child care center and SRS. Notably, this buffer role of the integrator is the only facilitator in this category that affected the super-agencies examined by this study. In those cases, the super-agency director served as a buffer between service providers and the governor and state legislature in terms of annual appropriations.

The other buffer role of the integrator—as mediator between service providers and a new client group—figured as a facilitator in five projects, four of which were cases of voluntary coordination. As intermediary, the project would assemble population groups the member agencies wished to serve; additionally, it furnished a structured, unthreatening atmosphere in which traditional service providers could begin to interact with a new clientele they had regarded as hostile. In the Oakland Parent-Child Center, for example, the project provided such a setting in which the Red Cross could accommodate to a low-income minority group it desired to serve but traditionally had not served.

INHIBITORS

Table 6.10 summarizes the eight major categories of project inhibitors to services integration. Assessments of the impact of individual inhibitors are presented in the order of frequency.

None of the inhibitors included in these categories was a critical or major influence in more than approximately 20 percent of the projects in the sample. Thus, as with the facilitators, it is difficult to conclude that any one was a primary impediment to services integration for all or any one project type.

The number of times specific inhibitors were isolated for projects was less than for facilitators. In large measure this reflects an underlying assessment gained from the field work that conditions

TABLE 6.10

Summary of Inhibitors

Rank Order	Category	Critical	Major	Minor	Total
1	Integrator's objectives and attitudes	16	4	8	28
2	Service provider objectives and attitudes	9	11	5	25
3	Grant administration policies and procedures	6	8	11	25
4	Project structure and operations	8	5	5	18
5	Environmental influences	7	6	1	14
6	Project staff	2	4	6	12
7	Technical and logistical factors	4	5	2	11
8	Service providers policies and procedures	3	4	4	11

TABLE 6.11

Integrator's Objectives and Priorities

Inhibitors	Critical	Major	Minor	Total
1. Concentration on internal operations, programing, and service delivery precludes emphasis on linkage development	7	2	6	15
2. Integrator never intended to develop certain linkages	8	–	2	10
3. Integrator gave objectives other than services integration a higher priority	1	2	–	3
Total	16	4	8	28

TABLE 6.12

Environmental Influences

Inhibitors	Critical	Major	Minor	Total
1. Environmental influences opposing service delivery system change through the specific project	5	1	–	6
2. Negative attitudes or opposition of government to change in the service delivery system	1	3	–	4
3. Absence of service providers	–	2	1	3
4. Monopoly of service by one provider	1	–	–	1
Total	7	6	1	14

83

are generally hostile to services integration efforts. Thus, only those inhibitors that dramatically affected individual projects were identified.

The integrator's objectives and priorities have a high potential for detrimental impact (Table 6.11). The most important inhibitor was a project's focus on internal operations or direct service delivery rather than on the development of integrating linkages. It occurred, as would be expected, predominantly in voluntary projects in which the integrator was responsible for service delivery as well as coordination of other service providers. A related issue was the necessity for project staff to respond to a variety of immediate operational problems such as meeting government requirements, funding, project or contract renewal, and personnel administration, which limited staff focus on linkage development with and among service providers.

The next most important inhibitor in this category was the intention of the integrator not to develop certain integrating linkages that could contribute to overall project coherence and efficacy.

Another associated inhibitor was the integrator's placement of higher priority on other objectives. Although services integration may have been a formal objective of the integrator, in fact, the objective was not aggressively pursued because the integrator had more pressing service needs to meet or the funding source dictated that other objectives be given higher priority.

As in the case of the project facilitators, among the most significant inhibitors in a project's environment were the actions and attitudes of public funding sources, primarily state and local governments (Table 6.12). The negative posture of government toward change in the service delivery system inhibited the development and operation of three projects. Local and state government opposition or intervention in the service delivery and administration procedures inhibited the integration efforts of four projects. Government or funding source opposition to the latter was particularly detrimental to neighborhood service centers because they involve the colocation of many agencies funded largely through federal grants. The Crossroads Neighborhood Service Center in Dallas illustrates the degree to which this inhibitor can affect a project's attempts to create an integrated service delivery network.

The most detrimental attitude was the desire of service providers to retain agency prerogatives with respect to control of service delivery (Table 6.13). It appeared often in super-agencies in which the integrator was attempting to consolidate established, traditional state or local government departments with their own clientele, federal grants, and degree of influence.

In three projects, provider possession of independent influence with funding sources served as another impediment of integration by reinforcing agency autonomy and lessening the need for project

TABLE 6.13

Service Provider Objectives and Attitudes

Inhibitors	Critical	Major	Minor	Total
1. Desire to retain agency prerogatives	5	3	3	11
2. Divergence of objectives/service delivery aims from the integrator	2	4	1	7
3. Reticence of established service providers to consider themselves part of the service delivery problem	1	4	—	5
4. Linkage development was a low priority	1	—	1	2
Total	9	11	5	25

TABLE 6.14

Grant Administration Policies and Procedures

Inhibitors	Critical	Major	Minor	Total
1. Conflicting/unclear guidelines	2	2	3	7
2. Insufficient funds for project operation, implementation, expansion	—	1	5	6
3. Federal, state, local regulations inhibiting certain linkages such as joint funding, joint budgeting fund transfers	—	3	2	5
4. Demonstration nature of the project	1	2	1	4
5. Funding delays and uncertainties	3	—	—	3
Total	6	8	11	25

85

TABLE 6.15

Project Structure and Operations

Inhibitors	Critical	Major	Minor	Total
1. Service providers were not involved in project development	2	1	2	5
2. Failure to obtain precise service commitments/contracts delineating responsibilities with service providers	1	2	2	5
3. Insufficient authority of the director	2	—	1	3
4. Poor administration/management	1	1	—	2
5. Personnel turnover	1	1	—	2
6. Necessity for integrator to use its central office to enter into contracts with providers	1	—	—	1
Total	8	5	5	18

TABLE 6.16

Project Staff

Inhibitors	Critical	Major	Minor	Total
1. Conflicts/distrust between provider and integrator staffs result from:				
a. Changes in traditional procedures and the bureaucratic routine	2	1	1	4
b. Generalist or specialist approach to service delivery	—	1	1	2
c. Professional rivalries, snobbishness, elitist attitudes	—	—	2	2
2. Insufficient staff due to lack of funds to obtain staff	—	1	1	2
3. Staff lacking training, expertise, knowledge of providers	—	1	—	1
4. Laziness of staff	—	—	1	1
Total	2	4	6	12

affiliation. Finally, in five projects, representing each project type, the reticence of service providers to consider themselves part of the service delivery problem served as an inhibitor.

The categorical grant system served as an inhibitor of a few services integration projects by preventing project coherence (Table 6.14). Prohibitions against joint funding, fund transfers, and comingling of funds impeded the development of linkages necessary to integrate a project and its service providers. Demonstration grants were also sometimes an impediment to services integration. The demonstration nature of a project limited funding to a specific time period that was too short for success or discouraged participation of service providers and other funding sources. It also prevented the project from affecting permanent change in the service delivery system.

The most common inhibitor in this category was conflicting guidelines or information about grant administration from government sources. In one project, the integrating staff continually received conflicting information about the uses of Title IV-A funds from two agencies within HEW and from the regional and central offices. The operation of this same project was tenuous throughout its existence because of funding delays and uncertainties, another inhibitor in this category. These uncertainties threatened the entire project, hindered the development of a planning component, and nearly closed a child care center as a result of a dispute over an in-kind match.

The failure of the integrator to involve service providers in project development and to obtain precise service commitments from service providers were important impediments to integration. Factors of poor administration included inadequate role definition, unclear lines of authority, insufficient supervision, assignment of incompatible work tasks to staff, permitting contracts to lapse, and poor delineation of reciprocal responsibilities of the integrator and the service providers.

Finally, in some of the super-agencies insufficient authority of the director inhibited services integration.

The most commonly occurring inhibitor in the category ''Project Staff'' was conflict between the staff of the project integrator and service providers (Table 6.16). The conflict was most often a result of integrator-instituted or attempted changes in traditional service provider procedures and bureaucratic routine.

The most significant inhibitor in the category ''Technical and Logistical Factors,'' poor communication between the integrator and service providers, did not appear in mediated projects that had a separate staff geared to undertaking responsibility for project coordination of affiliated provider agencies (Table 6.17).

The second most important inhibitor appeared in three voluntary coordination projects with a small, circumscribed clientele. It again

TABLE 6.17

Technical and Logistical Factors

Inhibitors	Critical	Major	Minor	Total
1. Poor communication between integrator and service providers	2	2	—	4
2. Small size of project clientele compared to provider's clientele lessens integrator's bargaining position	—	3	—	3
3. Physical distance between:				
a. Service providers and integrator	1	—	1	2
b. Service providers and clients	—	—	1	1
4. Inadequate facilities for information collection and dissemination	1	—	—	1
Total	4	5	2	11

TABLE 6.18

Service Provider Policies and Procedures

Inhibitors	Critical	Major	Minor	Total
1. Service providers have different eligibility requirements	1	2	2	5
2. Service providers have different record-keeping procedures	1	1	2	4
3. Failure to return information to central recordkeeping unit	1	1	—	2
Total	3	4	4	11

reflects the difficulty encountered by project integrators lacking authority or incentives to achieve coordination of autonomous service providers.

The problem of divergent eligibility requirements plagued super-agencies and voluntary projects solely and in only one case resulted from statutory requirements (Table 6.18). In the others it was a willful reluctance to conform.

It is interesting to note that the effects of diverse provider recordkeeping procedures were not just linkage-specific as might be expected but rather impeded over-all project implementation and coherence.

7

**INTEGRATING
LINKAGES**

Integrating linkages are the mechanisms that maintain the coordination of service providers.* This chapter discusses each of the linkages. The analysis focuses on the types of projects in which each integrating linkage was likely to develop, on the factors that facilitate or inhibit its development, and on its impact in terms of improving the accessibility, continuity, and efficiency of service delivery to clients.

LINKAGES IN GENERAL

There are two distinct types of linkages—direct service linkages and administrative linkages. Direct service linkages tie together the provision of services to specific clients. Core services (outreach, intake, diagnosis, referral, follow-up) and modes of case coordination (case conference, case coordinator, case team) have immediate, direct results and focus on a client and his specific needs. Administrative linkages tie together or consolidate the management of service providers. These linkages (such as joint planning, joint budgeting, and joint use of staff) focus on developing an apparatus to serve a whole class of clients and their needs. Thus, the impact of these linkages on service delivery is more indirect. Further, they may have little initial effect on actual services to the client because of the time required to develop them effectively. However, though the benefits from these linkages may

---

*A complete list of linkages and their definitions appears on pp. 37-39.

not be realized until sometime in the future, their eventual impact will be generalized over the entire class of clients.

Correlation with Mode of Coordination

Generally, there is a correlation between the types of linkages used and the project's mode of coordination. Table 7.1 shows the relationship between linkage development and mode of coordination where there was so identifiable causal pattern.

Table 7.1 shows that there was a correlation (1) between the use of direct service linkages and voluntary projects and (2) between the use of administrative linkages and mediated and directed projects. In voluntary projects, the integrator was responsible for providing direct service to a specific client group as well as developing linkages with service providers. With little available time and no authority over service providers, emphasis was placed on establishing linkages that had immediate payoff in terms of getting services to clients. (See Chapter 11 and also section below on Core Service Linkages.)

On the other hand, the integrators in both mediated and directed projects were charged with the development of cooperative relationships between service providers rather than the provision of direct service. Therefore, emphasis was placed on the establishment of administrative linkages. However, within the mediated mode, there were two significant variables that affected the integrator's emphasis on, and ability to develop, particular linkages. These were cases where (1) the integrator controlled service providers' funds by virtue of single-point funding and (2) the organizing principle of serving all the needs of the population within a specific geographic area resulted in development of a neighborhood service center.

The integrators in mediated projects with single-point funding were guided not only by objectives related to rationalizing the total delivery system but also had considerable leverage to involve service providers in integrative linkages. (See Chapter 10.) Neighborhood service centers tended to focus their attention on assuring that service was provided to individual clients and, therefore, initially used direct service linkages and only a few administrative linkages, such as colocation and central recordkeeping. (See Chapter 12.) Therefore, in many respects, although Neighborhood Service Centers generally conform to the definition of mediated coordination, the centers have more in common with voluntary coordination projects.

Other aspects of linkage development also generally correlated with mode of coordination. In those directed projects that were consolidated human resource agencies, the initiatives of the agency

TABLE 7.1

Correlation with Mode of Coordination

	Voluntary	Mediated	Directed
Administrative Linkages			
Fiscal			
Joint budgeting	Negative	Positive[b]	Positive
Joint funding	None	None	None
Purchase of service	None	None	None
Personnel practices			
Consolidated personnel administration	Negative[a]	Positive[b]	Positive
Joint use of staff	None	None	Positive
Staff transfer	None	None	None
Staff outstationing	Positive	None	None
Colocation	None	Positive[c]	None
Planning and programing			
Joint development of operating policies	None	Positive[b,c]	Positive
Joint planning	Negative	Positive[d]	Positive
Information-sharing	None	None	None
Joint programing	None	Positive	None
Joint evaluation	Negative	Positive	Positive
Administrative support services			
Record-keeping	Negative	Positive[b,c]	None
Grants management	Positive	Positive[b,c]	None
Central support services	Negative	Positive	None
Direct Service Linkages			
Core services			
(Outreach, intake, diagnosis, referral, follow-up)	Positive	Positive[c]	None
Modes of case coordination			
(Case conference, case coordinator, case team)	Positive	Positive[c]	None

[a]Does not apply to joint training.
[b]Applies particularly to single-point funded projects.
[c]Applies particularly to Neighborhood Service Centers.
[d]Does not apply to Neighborhood Service Centers.

92

administrators tended to follow a pattern in which planning and programing linkages were established first, with fiscal linkages and
administrative support services following in that order. The clear
intent of the integrator was to pursue linkages between division heads
systematically and as quickly as they could be accepted, reserving
the use of line authority only as a last resort.

The integrators in mediated projects (except neighborhood service
centers) also took an aggressive approach in developing linkages.
Generally they used one integrative linkage to involve service providers in others, parlaying the resources at their disposal into linkages to obtain wider participation by providers in project activities.
Although the integrators did relate to providers on a one-to-one
basis, this was generally a prelude to relating the providers to each
other.

Conversely, integrators in voluntary projects related to providers
on a one-to-one basis as a general rule. Linkages were not consciously
used to develop additional linkages. In this analysis, neighborhood
service centers fell somewhere between other mediated projects and
voluntary projects. The colocation of providers generally resulted in
staff meetings, which in turn led to the development of other linkages—but usually not in a systematic manner. Also, many of the
existing linkages in neighborhood service centers were inherent in
the project design rather than the conscious agenda of the integrator.

Impact of Linkages on Other Linkages

Generally, no one linkage irrevocably leads to the development
of any other linkage; at the same time, however, any one linkage in
a given circumstance can facilitate the development of any other
linkage. Clearly, linkages are mutually reinforcing. A climate of
cooperation and coordination maintained through certain integrating
linkages engendered an environment in which other linkages could
occur. Figure 7.1 gives a visual indication of the impact of any one
linkage on the development of others.

However, the major variable in the extent to which one linkage
aided in the development of other linkages was the integrator—his
perceived role, his formal responsibility for service delivery, the
resources at his disposal, and the amount of time available to him
for linkage development. (See the comparison of project integrators
in Chapters 9 through 12.)

The impacts of purchase of service agreements and colocation
illustrate these complexities. Purchase-of-service agreements were
used either to secure specific services for given clients or to secure
participation by service providers in a range of integrating linkages
in addition to specific direct service commitments. (See section on

93

FIGURE 7.1

The Impact of Linkages on Development of Other Linkages

Linkage Aiding Development of Other linkages	Linkages Aided: Personnel — Consolidated Personnel Administration, Including	Personnel — Joint Training	Personnel — Joint Use of Staff	Planning and Programing — Joint Programing	Planning and Programing — Joint Development of Operating Policies	Planning and Programing — Joint Planning	Planning and Programing — Information-Sharing	Planning and Programing — Evaluation	Fiscal — Purchase of Services	Fiscal — Joint Funding	Fiscal — Joint Budgeting	Administrative Support — Record Keeping	Administrative Support — Grants Management	Core Services	Intake	Diagnosis	Referral	Follow-up	Modes of Case Coordination
Personnel																			
Joint Training			•				•							•					
Joint Use of Staff				•															
Colocation		•		•			•					•		•					
Outstationing		•		•		•	•					•		•					•
Staff Transfer		•																	•
Planning and Programing																			
Joint Programing	•		•				•				•								
Joint Development of Operating Policies	•			•		•	•	•	•	•	•								
Joint Planning																			
Information-Sharing				•															
Evaluation				•		•						•							
Fiscal																			
Purchase of Services				•	•	•	•	•				•	•		•			•	
Joint Funding	•			•				•			•								
Joint Budgeting								•		•									
Administrative Support																			
Central Support		•		•				•											
Record Keeping				•		•	•	•					•		•	•	•	•	•
Core Services				•		•		•				•							•

Purchase of Service, below.) While colocation had the potential to result in the development of other linkages primarily because of the sustained contact between service providers, the spontaneous generation of linkages based on physical proximity alone takes a long time to occur. In several cases, colocation became an end in itself rather than a means to develop wider coordinative arrangements. (See section on Colocation, below.)

Impact of Linkages on Success Measures

The development of linkages has been slow, and many projects studied have achieved only partial success in their implementation. Table 4.1 portrays an assessment of the kinds of resources and incentives needed to develop various linkages, the relative amount of time needed to develop them, and the importance of the linkage in terms of impact on accessibility, continuity, and efficiency.

ANALYSIS OF SPECIFIC LINKAGES

Fiscal Linkages

Fiscal linkages reached a stage of implementation in more than half of the projects in which these linkages were appropriate. Table 7.2 reflects the difficulty for the integrator (except in directed coordination) to involve service providers in analysis and redistribution of financial resources within the project's delivery system, because an agency's control of funding and resource allocation lies at the heart of an organization's autonomy.

Since purchase of service agreements did not implicitly threaten agency autonomy, it was used more often than any other fiscal linkage.

Purchase of Service

Purchase of service was the easiest linkage to implement, was implemented in nearly three-quarters of the projects attempting fiscal linkages, and did not depend on the degree of authority that the integrator had over service providers. Autonomous agencies were anxious to get additional money to maintain, improve, and extend the services they provided and therefore had a strong incentive to participate in this linkage.

TABLE 7.2

Development of Fiscal Linkages
(percent)

Linkages	Modes of Coordination							
	Voluntary		Mediated		Directed		Total of Three Modes	
	Linkages in planning or initial stages of development	Linkages partially or fully developed	Linkages in planning or initial stages of development	Linkages partially or fully developed	Linkages in planning or initial stages of development	Linkages partially or fully developed	Linkages in planning or initial stages of development	Linkages partially or fully developed
1. Joint budgeting	40	—	—	54	60	40	27	31
2. Joint funding	—	60	—	54	60	—	12	46
3. Fund transfer	—	—	—	—	20	—	4	—
4. Purchase of service	—	70	18	54	60	20	19	54
Percent of possible linkages:	11	35	5	43	59	18	17	35

Thus, integrators were primarily restricted in the development of purchase of service agreements by the amount of funds available to them for this purpose. Therefore, integrators operating with open-ended funding sources were most successful. In fact, integrators with flexible or open-ended funding sources were able to solicit cooperation of agencies not immediately receiving funds on the basis that funds could be available in the future.

Inhibitors to the use of purchase agreements in some of the projects associated with state government were either the state's inexperience with them or restrictive policies and procedures regarding them. An example of the latter appeared in the Delaware County Division of Social Services. State regulations mandated that negotiation of purchase of service agreements (and all third-party billings for services to the Division) be channeled through a centralized state purchasing authority. Many interested agencies were discouraged from negotiating purchase agreements by the prohibitive delays and administrative burdens entailed.

In the directed projects, the use of purchase of service agreements was at some stage of development in 80 percent of the projects, but implementation was under way in only 20 percent of the agencies. For instance, the Utah Human Resources Agency had not established a procedure for its divisions to enter into purchase agreements or even to identify the full range of services, eligible for reimbursement under state regulations (particularly with regard to Title IV-A), that could be purchased from other divisions.

Generally, purchase of service was used in a variety of ways, differing by project according to their mode of coordination. While voluntary projects reflected the highest percentage of implementation of purchase of service, its use was limited by the integrator to obtaining specific services for project clients from agencies already providing these services. Although these arrangements successfully obtained service for clients, purchase of service was never understood in a larger administrative context or seen as a bargaining tool. There were few demands placed on service providers in return for funds. Actually the amount of funds involved was normally so small a percentage of service providers' budgets that the integrators had no position of power from which to bargain.

The point, however, is that integrators in voluntary projects and neighborhood service centers made no effort to use purchase agreements to bind providers to the overall project. Although neighborhood service centers operated within the framework of mediated coordination, their primary focus on service to individual clients produced results similar to voluntary coordination projects. The linkages formed were based on existing congruence between the agencies' existing services and the projects' needs. The integrators frequently negotiated small procedural adjustments or modifications such as adapting the location or timing of service delivery to better serve the particular clients or conducting some special orientation or training. There was little attempt to make basic changes in the service content or delivery procedures, or to stimulate the agency to develop new services.

A contrast was provided by integrators in mediated projects that controlled service providers' funds by virtue of single-point funding. Purchase of service was one of the most critical integrating linkages in these projects.

In these cases, the integrator controlled either a sizable percentage of service providers' budgets or controlled the providers' access to all of those particular kinds of funds available for which the integrator was designated as sole conduit. Therefore, the integrator had leverage from which to use purchase of service effectively. These integrators were guided by their projects' objectives (to rationalize and develop a coherent service delivery system) to use purchase agreements as an instrument for binding service providers to coordinate within the context of other integrating linkages.

Thus, money was funneled to participating agencies primarily in return for various kinds of commitments. Westside Mental Health Center's purchase-of-service documents bound (with formal sanctions) the providers to such diverse commitments as participation in joint programing and immediate assignment of clients for service after intake by any other member provider.

Westside also used the participating agencies' endorsement of project objectives in the purchase document to resolve a variety of issues that arose later. For instance, service providers were unwilling to provide data necessary for evaluation because of their concern for patient confidentiality. The integrative staff used the language of the purchase-of-service agreements to demonstrate the project's right to invoke sanctions if the information was not forthcoming. In another case, Westside did invoke sanctions to suspend an agency that refused to participate in the joint programing of a comprehensive drug program.

However, because Westside had been operational longer than the other projects with single-point funding, it also demonstrated the evolutionary nature of an integrator's ability to use purchase agreements as a device to extend the integrative effort. Initially the integrator simply sought provider participation in such linkages as joint development of operating policies, joint programing, and so on, and attempted to demonstrate to the agencies the value of affiliation with Westside. Integrator staff served as an administrative buffer between the funding source and the service providers and furnished central support services in the form of program development and grantsmanship assistance. Then, as the agencies gained experience in working together, developed confidence in the central staff, and came to depend on the funds channeled through Westside, more expectations were placed on participating agencies in return for funds.

In the United Family Services Project, purchase-of-service agreements tied the neighborhood centers to the project, including participation in such other linkages as joint development of operating policies, evaluation, planning, and so on. Also, agreements were centrally executed on behalf of the neighborhood centers with county-wide service providers binding these providers to give preference to clients referred by the United Family Service Project's affiliated neighborhood centers while continuing to serve other clients.

Additionally, single-point funding gave these projects leverage to begin to secure service providers' participation in joint budgeting.

Joint Budgeting

The implementation of this linkage in the projects studied closely correlated with the formal and informal authority of the integrator over the service providers.

The integrators in all of the directed projects had begun initiatives in the area of budgeting, but implementation had started in only 40 percent, and even in these, budgets were merely reviewed centrally by integrators. Department heads did not join together to develop or review budgets nor was the budget process consolidated.

For projects in which the integrator lacked authority over service providers, the most powerful incentive for providers' participation in joint budgeting was the availability of additional money. The single-point-funded mediated projects had achieved a first step toward joint budgeting—review and approval of program proposals by each board, which uniformly included provider representatives. However, considerable reluctance remains. For example, while each day-care center in the Phoenix Child Care Project submitted a newly standardized budget form for such review and approval, few requests for revisions have been made; and each center continued to push for retention of the right to determine its own budget.

The HUB Neighborhood Service Center's failure to implement joint budgeting also demonstrates the need for incentives such as additional funds. On the expectation of receiving more federal funding, agency representatives comprising HUB's Board of Directors became enthusiastically committed to the development of joint budgeting linkages in the allocation of these funds. When no additional funds were forthcoming, individual agencies were reluctant to participate in joint decisions regarding existing programs. Eventually, agency representatives even lost interest in participating actively on the board.

Because of the factors cited above, no voluntary coordination project was implementing joint budgeting. However, voluntary projects did show the highest instance of joint funding of any of the modes of coordination.

Joint Funding

In the context of this analysis, joint funding refers to the process by which two or more service providers give funds to support a service. The prime motive for implementation of joint funding in 60 percent of the voluntary projects to which it was appropriate was the federal regulation allowing the use of in-kind contributions for projects' local share requirement. Some integrators consciously sought new service for clients, which, in turn, could be used as local share, while others were motivated by the need to develop local share, which, in turn, resulted in service to project clients. Whatever its focus, the ability to use in-kind contributions linked providers to the project and established some formal parameters of service (both proposed and delivered) to document local share for project records. In some cases, this initial contact eventually led to joint discussion about the content of the service to be provided. However, in the face of heavy administrative responsibilities and focus on direct service delivery, many voluntary projects went no further in the development of joint funding.

Similarly, integrators tended not to utilize the agency participation gained through in-kind contributions as a stepping-stone to involve providers in other integrative linkages. In many cases, agencies readily agreed to in-kind contribution since it involved no outlay of funds, but they were not pressed to join in other cooperative efforts simply because the integrator never considered this possibility.

An exception was Jackson County Head Start, where an arrangement was negotiated for payment by the welfare department for dental services to children in the Head Start and Health Start Programs. However, this additional joint funding linkage resulted from a federal condition on the Health Start grant and considerable technical assistance by HEW Regional Office staff. Another variation in joint funding appeared in the JFK Neighborhood Service Center, where all agencies located in the facility paid a pro rata portion (based on the number of square feet they occupied) of the center's operating expenses.

In mediated projects, joint funding was variously implemented in 54 percent of the projects. Its widest use was the combination of project funds with an allocation by service providers to realize shared objectives by making available new or extended service beyond either's sole financial capability. For instance, outreach services for both the Bacon County Neighborhood Service Center and the county community action agency were jointly funded; special education and vocational services were provided in the Atlanta Employment Evaluation and Service Center by virtue of joint funding between the Center and the Board of Education and the Area Technical School respectively; a Street Academy was operated in South Bend through joint funding between the Youth Advocacy Program and the local Urban League.

A different form of joint funding—fund pooling—was achieved by the United Family Services Project, which was the conduit for Title IV-A funds. Fund pooling was comprised of the following: (1) local match for Title IV-A funds was collected from a variety of sources (including some of the neighborhood centers); (2) IV-A funds were received by the project on the basis of $3 for every local dollar; (3) IV-A funds were then redistributed so that neighborhood centers able to generate large sums of local money received in return $2 for every $1 they collected with the remainder furnished to less fortunate centers on the basis of need as well as to support the project's integrative staff.

Finally, there were instances of joint funding in the sense that service providers were granted funds by independent funding sources contingent on the development of linkages with the project. For example, the comprehensive health center in Cincinnati's Over-the-Rhine neighborhood was funded by HEW because it served the same area as the HUB Neighborhood Service Center. Also, integrative staff of the Edison Drop-Out Project, in conjunction with a local employment and vocational service agency, obtained an agreement from the State Bureau of Vocational Rehabilitation to pay the local employment and vocational service to provide specific vocational assistance to Edison clients.

Only the Bacon County Neighborhood Service Center's use of joint funding to provide outreach service and the United Family Services Project's joint funding/fund pooling represented the utilization of joint funding to rationalize the service delivery system as opposed to its use for the purpose of providing additional direct service. In this connection, it is too early to assess joint funding in the directed projects studied, since implementation of this linkage was in the early planning stages of the 60 percent of the projects considering its use.

Fund Transfer

No project had implemented or even attempted a fund transfer. While in some instances projects petitioned and received waivers from federal agencies of other procedural obstacles to more effective integration of services, no attempts were made on behalf of fund transfers. It appears that federal restrictions on fund transfer have been sufficient to discourage any attempts to implement this linkage.

Impact on Accessibility, Continuity, and Efficiency

Accessibility

Joint budgeting and joint funding have increased client accessibility in complementary ways, primarily by allocating available resources to make available new services to clients with multiple service needs. In addition, client entry into integrated projects has been made easier through changes in rules and intake procedures resulting from joint funding agreements. Similarly, purchase-of-service agreements have also been used to standardize or centralize intake procedures among agencies. In Bacon County, where joint funding has been used to expand outreach services, more clients can enter the service delivery system.

Continuity

Joint funding and purchase of services have made it easier for clients to stay in the service delivery system through their use to connect a range of service providers to the project and by creating services that previously had not existed. In the case of single point funding, purchase agreements have given integrators the leverage to involve providers in other linkages.

Efficiency

Fiscal linkages have all directly or indirectly resulted in the elimination of duplicative service effort among agencies by combining similar services provided by two agencies to a common clientele. Further, joint funding and purchase of service have enabled existing service providers to increase the number of clients served.

PERSONNEL LINKAGES

The implementation of integrating linkages within the category of Personnel Practices was the least developed of any other category of linkages. It was at some stage of development in 42 percent of the instances in which these linkages were appropriate, and partially or fully implemented in only 31 percent of those. In general, coordination in the area of personnel practices was difficult to obtain because service providers jealously guarded their prerogatives. Implementation of these linkages shown in Table 7.3 reflected the degree of the integrator's authority over service providers and, to a lesser extent, the availability to him of incentives to encourage agencies to give up their authority.

TABLE 7.3

Development of Personnel Linkages
(percent)

Linkages	Modes of Coordination							
	Voluntary		Mediated		Directed		Total of Three Modes	
	Linkages in planning or initial stages of development	Linkages partially or fully developed	Linkages in planning or initial stages of development	Linkages partially or fully developed	Linkages in planning or initial stages of development	Linkages partially or fully developed	Linkages in planning or initial stages of development	Linkages partially or fully developed
1. Consolidated personnel administration	20	30	18	36	40	20	23	31
2. Joint use of staff	10	20	9	27	40	40	15	27
3. Staff transfer	—	—	—	27	20	—	4	12
4. Staff out-stationing	10	40	—	27	—	40	4	35
5. Colocation	—	10	—	45	—	40	—	31
Percent of possible linkages:	10	26	6	33	25	35	11	31

103

The primary facilitator of the development of personnel linkages was the desire of service providers to expand the range of services and improve the quality of their services with a minimum of cost. A related facilitator was shared or complementary objectives among service providers to develop new approaches to meet client needs.

The primary inhibitors to the development of personnel linkages were those factors that discouraged or prohibited service providers from relinquishing control over personnel policies and practices and from entering into cooperative staff arrangements with other service providers or the integrator. These general inhibitors included (1) fear of providers that they would lose control of staff; (2) integrator distrust of provider staff, and vice versa; (3) integrator and/or provider preoccupation with internal administration; (4) integrator disorganization due to poor administration, lack of state mandate, ambiguous guidelines, newness of project, and so on; and (5) lack of formal agreements.

Consolidated Personnel Administration

This linkage was at some stage of development in 60 percent of the directed projects in which it was appropriate, 54 percent of the mediated projects, and 50 percent of the voluntary projects. Partial or full implementation, however, was achieved in only 36 percent of the mediated projects, 30 percent of the voluntary projects, and 20 percent of the directed projects. These percentages are somewhat skewed because of the inclusion of joint training under this linkage; in many voluntary projects, joint training was the sole aspect of consolidated personnel services planned or implemented. Therefore, joint training will be discussed separately.

Most evident was the negative correlation between consolidated personnel administration and voluntary coordination, and the positive correlation between intent to consolidate personnel administration and directed coordination. Directed projects have both the authority to override agency recalcitrance, and are very interested in doing so, since they are primarily concerned with administrative reorganization and consolidation.

The only other projects uniformly making inroads in the area of consolidated personnel administration were those mediated projects that controlled service providers' funds because of single-point funding. These efforts centered around development of minimum personnel standards and centralization of staff recruitment. However, in one project, initial efforts by the integrator to centralize hiring and firing so effectively deadlocked all other cooperation that the attempt was abandoned, leaving considerable ill-will to be overcome among service providers.

Even in directed projects, however, stumbling blocks to consolidation of personnel administration developed. For example, rigid civil service requirements were major impediments in the San Diego Human Resource Agency.

Mediated projects, except neighborhood service centers, had made some progress implementing this linkage (see Chapter 10) based on their objectives of rationalizing the service delivery system and assisted either by single-point funding or joint funding agreements (Youth Advocacy Program). Implementation in the single-point funded projects was also facilitated by achievement of joint operating policies through full representation of service providers on policy boards and committees.

Implementation of joint training in isolation from other aspects of consolidated personnel administration did not appear in directed projects. In the other types of projects, instances of joint training range from staff meetings for purposes of orientation to regular in-service training programs. Some involve the project and one or several service providers individually; others bring the service providers together as a group.

Facilitating factors in several projects were a common need for staff training, joint or interrelated provision of service, and colocation. Common need for trained staff coupled with providers' lack of funds or expertise to carry out training individually, led to joint training efforts in the Phoenix Child Care Project, United Family Services Project, Jackson County Head Start, and the Edison Drop-Out Project. Colocation or staff outstationing in a common facility resulted in a perceived need for, and facilitated, joint training in the HUB and Hamilton Neighborhood Service Centers. In the Edison Drop-Out Project and Hamilton Neighborhood Service Center, commitment of provider staff to improving service delivery also facilitated joint training; while in the Galveston Child Development Project and Jackson County Head Start, complementary objectives also facilitated the linkage.

Joint Use of Staff

This linkage refers to cases where two or more agencies deliver service by using the same staff. Cases where there is a central administrative staff or consolidated provision of core services are not included here since these were considered instances of other linkages. (See sections on Administrative Support Services and Core Services, below.) Joint use of staff was at some stage of development in 80 percent of the directed projects in which it was appropriate, 36 percent of the mediated projects, and 30 percent of the voluntary projects. Similarly, this linkage had been partially or fully implemented in 40 percent of the directed projects, 27 percent of the mediated projects, and 20 percent of the voluntary projects.

In the directed coordination projects, this linkage appeared to be prompted by a desire to reduce duplication and grew out of a study of the functions of each of the divisions or departments. For example, the Utah Human Resource Agency is experimenting with the use of family service staff to provide probation services in sparsely populated areas.

Staff Transfer

Staff transfer involves shifting the administrative control of an employee from one agency to another. As such, this linkage strikes at the heart of agency authority and is very difficult to implement; it was achieved in only three projects. This linkage was attempted in the Portland Parent-Child Center but failed. It is in the planning stage in the San Diego Human Resource Agency.

Mutual interest in reaching more clients (improving access) combined with the availability of funds for additional staff through the project, facilitated staff transfer arrangements in the Portland Parent-Child Center and the Bacon County and HUB Neighborhood Service Centers. Many of the factors facilitating staff transfer in individual projects seem to reflect a recognition of common goals and a degree of trust (or at least absence of threat) between the project and the agency based either on the nature of their relationship or on mutual involvement in planning. Specific factors in the case of the Bacon County Neighborhood Service Center were that (1) the community action agency was facing a cutback in funds and hence in services; (2) the project had evolved from the community action agency; (3) there was a preexisting relationship between the project director and agency administrator; and (4) there was mutual recognition of duplicated efforts. Specific facilitators in Portland were the involvement of the service provider in the original planning for the project and the fact that the arrangement did not demand much from the service provider in the way of money or change in policies or procedures. In the San Diego Human Resource Agency, facilitators are the involvement of service providers in identifying concerns and areas of potential coordination, and a recently achieved organizational consolidation that gives the project director power over personnel and over departmental functions.

In addition to the unwillingness of service providers to relinquish administrative control, other inhibitors appeared in the Portland Parent-Child Center, where the linkage failed. These were internal chaos and poor project administration; the lapse of formal contracts and lack of defined expectations for the relationship between project and external service providers; and the lack of regular procedures for evaluating the staff transfer arrangement.

Colocation

This linkage was implemented in all of the neighborhood service centers, one regional office of a state super-agency and one super-agency. Since this integrating linkage is critical to neighborhood service centers, a detailed discussion of this linkage appears in Chapter 12. Only the major aspects of colocation are considered here.

Factors facilitating colocation fall into two broad categories, those contributing to the creation of the facility and those contributing to independent service providers' initial participation. The major facilitator for the existence of the facilities was availability of federal funds for construction. This was a key factor in JFK, Crossroads, and Bacon County Neighborhood Service Centers. A second important facilitator in each of the above were studies, surveys, or the work of task forces to identify needs in preparation for forthcoming or potential federal funds.

The availability of federal funds for services and staff fostered both development of the facilities and, once they were built, participation of external service providers.

The main factors inducing service providers to participate in the multiservice centers, beyond the lure of the facilities themselves, were their involvement in planning and implementing the project, various kinds of formal agreements, and commitment to shared goals. Contractual agreements, formal memoranda, or other formalized linkage agreements ensured sustained participation in the HUB, Kearns, and Bacon County Neighborhood Service Centers and may lead to development of other linkages in addition to physical colocation.

The only factors identified as inhibiting colocation were the spatial inadequacy of facilities, restriction on the number of participants, and the problem of obtaining facilities that met building code requirements.

Staff Outstationing

Staff outstationing included two situations: those where service providers outstation staff in the facility of a project that itself provides direct functional services and those where the integrator outstations staff in facilities of service providers. The latter occurred in few instances. Outstationing, not including colocation, appeared overall in only 38 percent of the instances in which it was appropriate.

Major factors facilitating outstationing of staff were the commitment to shared goals, the project's ability to act as a bridge or buffer between new clients and traditional agencies, the project's provision of particular services in order to meet its objectives, and the clout of the project or its backers. In the Oakland Parent-Child Center, Edison Drop-Out Project, and Youth Advocacy Program, the project was able to connect large, traditional agencies with poor, minority clients that the agencies regarded as rather threatening, and to facilitate and support continuing service relationships. In order to achieve specific objectives, three projects undertook to provide particular services that led naturally to outstationing of project staff in facilities of independent providers. In the Tri-County Project, diagnosis and referral staff of the project were stationed in high-volume public agencies; in the Youth Advocacy Program, project staff were stationed in various youth-serving agencies in order to provide consultation and improve service delivery; and in Delaware County it was planned that community organization staff of the Division of Social Services would be based in the community action agency.

Many other factors appeared to facilitate staff outstationing. The project director's efforts and skills were particularly significant in the Oakland Parent-Child Center and the Tri-County Project, while the persuasive talents of another staff member were equally helpful in the Edison Drop-Out Project. Requirements specified in federal program guidelines also facilitated staff outstationing; for example, the federal Parent-Child Center guidelines requiring a range of program elements, specific contacts, and working relationships with other agencies in the community, and a local match (which was dependent upon in-kind services).

Factors inhibiting staff outstationing in facilities of other providers fall into two groups—those related to the projects and those related to participating agencies. Inhibitors related to projects were poor administration, preoccupation with administrative matters brought on by internal crises or by situations in the community, internal chaos and conflict in the project resulting in failure to sustain linkages, and lack of clarity in project objectives. Inhibitors related to linked agencies were the defensiveness of old, traditional agencies and their bureaucratic resistance to innovation and limited or diminishing resources.

Impact on Accessibility, Continuity, and Efficiency

Accessibility

Personnel linkages have an uneven impact on accessibility. Within this category, colocation and outstationing have the greatest direct impact. Both increase accessibility of services by providing them in locations closer to the client group than formerly, and in facilities where clients go for other services. Staff outstationing brought new and additional services into the project's facilities and allowed service providers to reach and serve more clients or new client groups. Joint training also increases accessibility indirectly by changing attitudes of traditional service providers opening them to new client groups.

Continuity

The implementation of personnel linkages impacted on continuity in several ways. It allowed expansion of the range of services delivered to clients and also facilitated the movement of services to clients as opposed to moving clients to services. Also greater interagency contact resulting from the implementation of personnel linkages increased interagency communication, cooperation, and coordination. In addition, staffs of the various agencies could better map out the delivery of services to clients based on their increased understanding of other providers.

Efficiency

Personnel linkages had an important impact on efficiency, reducing duplicated effort by allowing various providers to combine their staffs or to use the staff of another provider in offering services. These linkages also permitted efficient allocation of scarce expertise and freed staff for other duties. Moreover, outstationing and colocation enabled clients to receive a range of services, increasing the potential impact on problem solution.

Joint training enhanced efficiency in four ways. First, it gave service providers training they could not otherwise afford. Second, economies of scale accrue from assembly of a group of staff requiring similar training. Third, trained staff are developed at less cost. Fourth, available expertise is utilized more fully.

Consolidation of other aspects of personnel services—that is, hiring, firing, promoting, placing, classifying—has not had any discernible effect on service delivery—perhaps because this linkage is generally not developed. It may be, however, that the impact of consolidated personnel services will never extend much beyond efficiency notably in terms of administrative economy.

PLANNING AND PROGRAMING LINKAGES

Planning and programing linkages were at some stage of development 70 percent of the times they were appropriate and actually

TABLE 7.4

Development of Planning and Programing Linkages
(percent)

| | Modes of Coordination | | | | | | | |
| | Voluntary | | Mediated | | Directed | | Total of Three Modes | |
Linkages	Linkages in planning or initial stages of development	Linkages partially or fully developed	Linkages in planning or initial stages of development	Linkages partially or fully developed	Linkages in planning or initial stages of development	Linkages partially or fully developed	Linkages in planning or initial stages of development	Linkages partially or fully developed
1. Joint planning	30	10	18	54	60	20	31	31
2. Joint development of operating policies	10	40	9	45	–	80	8	50
3. Information-sharing	–	60	9	81	40	40	12	65
4. Joint programing	20	50	18	81	40	40	23	62
5. Joint evaluation	30	20	27	63	60	20	35	38
Percent of possible linkages:	18	36	17	69	32	40	20	50

implemented nearly 50 percent of those times. Table 7.4 indicates that information-sharing and joint programing appeared most frequently, while joint development of operating policies appeared least often.

Successful development of these linkages appears to be related to the formal authority of the integrator over service providers and the availability of staff to pursue and support planning and programing activity.

Also, planning and programing linkages were most likely to develop when there were formal, structured mechanisms for the participation of service providers in decisions about project operations. Representation of service providers on project boards and committees in mediated and directed projects facilitated planning and programing linkages. For example, in the Westside Mental Health Center and the Phoenix Child Care Project, joint membership of service providers on functional committees facilitated the exchange of information on project procedures and federal guidelines governing project operation. In addition, these committees facilitated the joint development of program proposals.

Regular project staff meetings are another important administrative mechanism. Joint staff meetings between the super-agency administrator and department heads are of particular significance in the directed projects. By virtue of colation in neighborhood service centers, the convening of regular project staff meetings provided easy exchange of information, the identification of service delivery gaps, and the cooperative development of program strategies.

The major inhibitors of planning and programing linkages were factors that prevented or interfered with the existence of the facilitators identified above. For example, one inhibitor was the assignment of inappropriate staff representatives by service providers to serve on the governing board and functional committees of projects. In the HUB Neighborhood Service Center and the Oakland Parent-Child Center, the involvement of representatives on the policy and advisory boards who had little administrative authority in their respective agencies inhibited the capability of these bodies to make joint planning decisions or to implement joint programing efforts.

In the Westside Mental Health Center, on the other hand, some central staff members felt that appointment of administrative personnel as opposed to clinical staff from service agencies limited the capacity of a planning subcommittee of the Board of Directors to arrive at effective program solutions to internal problems of service delivery to clients.

Similarly, the lack of involvement of the total range of service providers on the advisory committees of the Boise Youth Service Bureau and Edison Drop-Out Project contributed to the lack of joint planning and programing attempts. Another major inhibitor to the development of planning and programing linkages in general was project objectives and/or federal regulations, which gave the integrators responsibility for direct service delivery. In these cases, staff had neither the time nor the perspective to devote to the development of these kinds of linkages with service providers.

Joint Planning

Four out of the five directed projects have instituted some kind of joint planning process. Also, over 70 percent of the mediated projects were attempting joint planning. The other mediated projects that have not attempted joint planning are sponsored by general purpose government and generally emphasize colocation. Three of these projects are neighborhood service centers.

Voluntary projects reflected the least incidence of joint planning. Nonetheless, joint planning was at some stage of development in 40 percent of the instances in which it was appropriate. However, it had been fully implemented in only 10 percent of these instances. In these projects, the integrators were primarily involved in day-to-day delivery problems. The problems and uncertainties associated with their yearly funding lessened their incentive to pursue longer range joint planning, rendering it possibly desirable at some future time but a low priority at present. Further, contacts with service providers were generally on a one-to-one basis, and developing a structured process for joint planning would have been a difficult task for many.

The absence of any authority over service providers and the fact that their clients generally constituted only a small fraction of the providers' total clients produced very little leverage for the integrators to use in obtaining participation from those other agencies.

The establishment of project objectives to create a single comprehensive service delivery system is a significant factor in the implementation of joint planning in directed projects. The centralization of the planning functions with sufficient and competent staff responsible for coordinating the planning activities of all service providers was another factor in facilitating the effort in these agencies.

Similarly, the objectives of mediated projects that were single conduits of service providers' funds (for example, Westside Mental Health Center, Phoenix Child Care, and United Family Service Projects) to rationalize the service delivery system gave them a clear incentive to pursue joint planning efforts. In addition, lacking the responsibility for direct service delivery, they were able to commit their time to the support of these efforts. But equally significant was the leverage that control of providers' funds gave them to begin to demand participation.

112

There were also general factors that inhibited joint planning. First, several of the projects were limited by the objectives that they set for themselves. For example, the JFK Neighborhood Service Center was intended to be a "supermarket" of services, and so joint planning was never acknowledged as an aim to be pursued.

Second, involving a wide range of service providers in a project caused integrators to be faced by historical and professional animosities between the agencies. In the Westside Mental Health Center, for example, professional jealousies among executive directors of the family service agencies over "discriminatory" practices that allocate major central staff administrative positions to medical doctors rather than to social science PhDs resulted in their separate incorporation as a subunit of family service agencies within the Westside consortium. This enabled these agency directors to enjoy additional autonomy from Westside in the planning and development of new programs while remaining eligible to receive funds through the project.

Other projects were trying to overcome agency reluctance to surrender their prerogatives by gaining participation in other less threatening short-range programing linkages before tackling joint planning.

Joint Development of Operating Policies

Joint development of operating policies is primarily concerned with establishment of a broad framework in which project operations can be carried out in a more coherent manner. To this extent, this linkage is exclusive of long-range planning and programing and has a much greater impact on project administration than information-sharing. For instance, joint development of operating policies was implemented by a governing board composed of service providers. These boards then established project policy including personnel policies, the selection of administrative staff, identification of additional funding sources, the approval of contracts and new programs, the establishment of by-laws governing project operation, and so on. Responsibility for the establishment of personnel policies and the hiring of project central staff were examples of the types of operating policies most frequently jointly developed among the projects studied.

This linkage was implemented in all the directed projects through an informal mechanism such as staff meetings rather than formal organizational arrangement. Moreover, these efforts are facilitated by the consolidation and centralization of authority in the office of an administrator in contrast to participatory authority, as exemplified by a board. Therefore, joint development of operating policies as it is discussed below does not include these related, but centralized, efforts.

Joint development of operating policies was being planned or attempted in 50 percent of the voluntary projects cases in which it was appropriate, and in 54 percent of the mediated projects.

The Westside Mental Health Center (mediated) represented the most developed example of this linkage both in terms of the formal existence of a board with various subcommittees involved in operating policies and the scope of activities in which these units were involved. Conversely, the JFK Neighborhood Service Center, while there is a governing board composed of the heads of the various agencies providing services, has not attempted to handle any operating policy issues. The HUB Neighborhood Service Center's governing Board of Managers was limited in that it included representation from only a small percentage of the total number of agencies providing services through the center.

Again, representation on the board by a majority of the project's member agencies and by personnel with administrative authority in their agency was very important in the development of this linkage. Other contributing factors included the willingness of the project director to encourage the sharing of authority and the existence of federal requirements mandating a specific structure for project operations.

Factors impeding the joint development of operating policies included negative attitudes on the part of service providers as well as organizational and functional problems. In some cases, agencies' representatives believed they would be ineffective in attempting to influence federal directives, which, in turn, impeded the initiative to jointly develop operating policies. The potential for meaningful participation by service providers was also limited when the integrator did not provide staff to support these activities or when meetings of the governing bodies (on which providers were represented) were so infrequently scheduled that service providers began to feel as though their participation was pro forma rather than genuinely related to project operations.

Some projects overdid the involvement of service providers on various overlapping boards and subcommittees. The structure was so elaborate and confusing that effective implementation of this linkage has been delayed. For instance, the Westside Mental Health Center includes eight subcommittees of the board of directors in addition to an administrative council. In the Phoenix Child Care Project, where the Project Committee (an overall steering committee) creates and delineates the function of standing committees as needed, the lack of clarification among the various committee members as to committee role and responsibilities delayed project programing and planning.

114

Information-Sharing

Information-sharing was implemented in more projects than any other integrating linkage except joint programing; it does not threaten service provider autonomy and is relatively easy to accomplish. This linkage was at some stage of development in 60 percent of the voluntary projects in which it was appropriate, in 90 percent of the mediated projects, and in 80 percent of the directed projects. These differences were due more to variation in project objectives than in authority of the integrator over service providers. Objectives such as administrative consolidation in most of the directed coordination projects and the establishment of a comprehensive and integrated service delivery system or the comprehensive approach to meeting all the needs of all the residents of a single neighborhood in mediated projects, stimulated the integrators to establish systematic information-sharing among service providers. In voluntary projects, integrators instead gave priority to provision of service to clients while contacting other providers to supplement service. Many had neither the time nor inclination to promote contacts between the service providers.

In many cases, information-sharing derived from, or was facilitated by, the implementation of other kinds of integrating linkages. For example, in the Seattle Senior Centers Project and Kearns Neighborhood Service Center, the development of a centralized information system evolving from central recordkeeping stimulated information-sharing. Also, any linkage that brought service providers together (for example, colocation) or brought providers into systematic contact with integrative staff (for example, outstationing) generally enhanced the probability that information-sharing would occur.

A related technique utilized most successfully in the Youth Advocacy Program was the assignment of a central staff representative to be a continuous liaison with specific service providers. This personalized channel for information-sharing was intended to assist the provider's administrative staff to revise their traditional mode of operation and to coordinate their service delivery through the project. This method was utilized to a lesser degree in the Westside Mental Health Center and on a broad basis in the Florida Human Resource Agency.

Otherwise, information-sharing is affected by the same facilitators and inhibitors that apply generally to planning and programing linkages.

Joint programing was at some stage of development in 70 percent of the voluntary projects in which it was appropriate, in 100 percent of the mediated projects, and in 80 percent of the directed projects.

Joint programing was a desirable way to bring providers together; and even when agencies did not fully subscribe to the broad objectives of the project, it was a useful linkage. Integrative staff focused on shared operational objectives of service providers around which to organize joint programing sessions to meet the needs of a particular client group or for specific programs.

Formal agreements (for example, membership agreements, purchase of service) provided the most frequent facilitator of joint programing. Formal contractual agreements in the mediated projects that were the conduit of funds to participating agencies were particularly useful in this regard.

The factors that were identified as facilitating information-sharing also contributed to the development of joint programing attempts. The mutual identification of a duplication of effort by service providers (sometimes within the context of information-sharing) and the availability of additional funding through the integrators to expand service delivery of an agency have contributed to various attempts at the development of joint programing to respond to an immediate problem or an identified service delivery gap.

Moreover, provision by the integrator staff of central support services to assist agencies in the development of program proposals was also an important factor in facilitating joint programing. Each of the mediated projects, except neighborhood service centers, used joint programing as a conscious strategy to integrate services.

Program development and grantsmanship assistance were offered by having such a specialist on the central staff to respond to requests by participating agencies on an as-needed basis. In the United Family Services Project, this resource person was able to use such requests to encourage joint programing activities between the neighborhood center asking for help and other centers operating such programs or between neighborhood center asking for help and other centers with similar problems in their neighborhoods.

This kind of assistance was also used in Westside to establish a coalition of specific agencies within the consortium for joint programing of a comprehensive drug project that later evolved into a professionally staffed component of the Westside Mental Health Center. The Youth Advocacy Program used this staff capability to encourage joint programing between three small agencies seeking Model Cities funding for related services and as a technique to establish ad hoc coalitions of service providers not previously involved in project activities.

The involvement of the integrator staff with service providers and their personal influence with representatives of service providers primarily facilitated joint programing among the voluntary projects.

As with the facilitators of joint programing, the inhibitors of this linkage largely duplicate those applicable to information-sharing, but additional obstacles were the lack of role definition among service providers and failure to establish clear lines of responsibility for program development in those projects under directed coordination. In voluntary projects, the lack of formal authority over service providers by the integrator was also an obstacle. Also, in the Neighborhood Service Centers and to a lesser degree in the Westside Mental Health Center, joint programing was discouraged by associated problems of reporting and data collection.

Evaluation

Evaluation was being implemented in only 38 percent of the cases to which it was appropriate. It was performed in two ways: (1) jointly, with participation of service providers, and (2) centrally, by the integrator or an external evaluator hired by the integrator.

Joint Evaluation

Joint evaluation appeared only in isolated cases and is response to requirements of the funding source. These were generally instances of single-point funding in which the integrator, in turn, imposed joint evaluation as a condition for continued funding of the service providers. The United Family Services Project represents an example of this situation. However, it is not well developed primarily because the integrator has not placed much emphasis on developing this linkage in the past. Joint evaluation of neighborhood center efforts occurred during meetings of the Board of Directors, composed of board members from those centers. This process has been structured and maintained by the central staff person assigned to evaluation efforts and by staff of the service providers (for example, the neighborhood centers). Staff of the centers recognized that failure to cooperate could lead to eventual withholding of funds by the board.

The Kearns Neighborhood Service Center demonstrated that a joint evaluation process must both circumvent the reluctance of service providers and then deal with the problems inherent in obtaining a data base—standardized case information. The integrator is faced by a multifaceted problem—including agency paranoia about being evaluated, confidentiality, acceptance of the need for evaluation, and logistics of record keeping—which only powerful incentives can resolve. Control of service providers' funds (that is, single-point funding) provides the integrator with such an incentive.

Ninety percent of mediated projects had some form of evaluation at some stage of development. The few examples of joint evaluation processes occurred in these projects, which comprised a network of formally committed providers and which had capable staff to structure and support such an evaluation process.

Other kinds of evaluation involving service providers had begun to occur in a few voluntary and mediated projects. However, in these ad hoc joint evaluation efforts, the integrator and one or two service providers undertook only limited assessments of the effectiveness of specific programs that they had jointly developed. These efforts focused on adjustments in specific programs rather than modifications of the projects' delivery system.

Central Evaluation

The only other systematic evaluation was conducted centrally by the integrator or an external evaluator under contract, did not involve service providers, and differed in the extent to which evaluation results were relayed back to the projects' central administrative staff. This kind of evaluation was conducted in eight projects, solely in response to requirements by the funding source. Performed in this way, evaluation neither encouraged cooperation among service providers nor was considered as a constructive tool by these agencies or, in some cases, by central staff. Generally, because of lack of involvement, an evaluation process connected to funding and performed by a third party was viewed by service providers as a critical, potentially destructive weapon. In the absence of any type of feedback, apprehension and suspicion among providers were reinforced. So, although some form of evaluation had positive implications for improving the service delivery system by virtue of examining interrelationships between providers, central evaluation (including evaluation by outsiders) did not appear to impact on the development of additional integrative linkages or weld providers together.

Central evaluation also confronted the problems inherent in obtaining a data base. In the Westside Mental Health Center, enforcement by the integrator of the broad language of its purchase of service agreements pertaining to acceptance of project objectives (for example, evaluation) forced resolution of the confidentiality issue, which had inhibited earlier evaluation attempts. The threat of withholding funds brought cooperation from recalcitrant hospitals and agencies, who had withheld information needed for evaluation on the ground that it violated client confidentiality.

While central evaluation was under development in 80 percent of the directed projects, it was primarily considered as a management tool to promote administrative efficiency and performed in isolation from the various department heads. On the other hand, 50 percent of voluntary projects undertook central evaluation, but primarily in response to funding requirements and, in many cases, only when a specific portion of the grant was earmarked for this purpose. Sometimes, third-party evaluation was also required. Although not required in other cases, integrators choose this method because (1) concentration on delivery of direct service gave evaluation a low priority, (2) central staff lacked the time and expertise to perform evaluation, and (3) integrators themselves lacked substantive incentives to involve service providers in joint evaluation.

Impact on Accessibility, Continuity, and Efficiency

Planning and programing has affected the accessibility, continuity, and efficiency of service delivery to clients by providing mechanisms to enable individual service providers to more effectively participate in a complementary service delivery system.

Accessibility

The study indicates that the joint development of operating policies may improve client accessibility obliquely, by stimulating staff initiative. Joint approval of project staff in United Family Services Project helped achieve a level of professional expertise in central staff to initiate and support planning and programing activities aimed at making services more accessible to clients.

Participation of service providers in the project design for some of the neighborhood service centers improved location of service in relation to clients, and in some instances, of services not previously available to area clients. Joint programing also increased accessibility. In the Westside Mental Health Center and Phoenix Child Care Project, service agency representatives cooperated with central staff to develop an annual programing and funding effort. This has resulted in the availability of more service and of services to fill identified gaps.

Furthermore, in Westside the coordinated effort of a drug council composed of representatives of halfway houses and existing drug rehabilitation agencies in the area resulted in development and funding of a comprehensive drug treatment program to combat an escalating area crisis. Joint programing in the United Family Services Project and the Youth Advocacy Program and unifying eligibility standards among day care centers in Phoenix Child Care Project have also eased clients' entry into existing and new services.

Evaluation impacted accessibility only indirectly, through monitoring the effectiveness of those service units, such as outreach and intake, that impact accessibility directly.

Continuity

Planning and programing has affected continuity of service provided to clients by identifying and eliminating service delivery gaps. For example, the HUB Neighborhood Service Center, through its bimonthly joint supervisory staff meetings, obtained expanded service from the Ohio Bureau of Employment Service to include job development. Joint memberships on a regularly scheduled policy board or committee enables service providers to appreciate their role as part of a single delivery system and to begin to identify the complementary aspects of each agency's objectives.

Planning and programing linkages enabled providers to plan and deliver their service in a manner that complemented the service of other providers. Joint development of operating policies impacts continuity in that joint selection of project staff who will be liaisons to the provider agencies increased the legitimacy of project staff, making it easier to develop arrangements with participating agencies to ensure client movement through the service delivery system.

Evaluation directly impacted continuity. For instance, joint evaluation enabled the central administrative staff of a federation of neighborhood service centers to identify gaps in the services provided to clients through their neighborhood units. Evaluation efforts enabled the central coordinative staff within the Florida Human Resource Agency to begin to spot bottlenecks to ease client flow between its line divisions.

Efficiency

Planning and programing linkages are beginning to have an effect, directly or indirectly, in reducing duplication, achieving economies of scale and impacting problem solution. However, particularly in these linkages, significant evidence of enhanced efficiencies should probably not be expected until after long-term operation of the projects.

Planning and programing linkages have already enabled individual providers to avoid or minimize duplication and overlap in their separate plans. For example, in Jackson County Head Start Project, joint programing for a summer migrant program was able to rationalize the services of many providers who had planned activities in this area; the resulting program saved almost three-quarters the cost of a previous summers' program planned and implemented by one provider alone.

Planning and programing linkages had also begun to achieve economies of scale at the project level. For example, in the Cleveland Mental Retardation Project, staff discovered that county school districts were having difficulty developing vocational education plans to meet amended requirements providing for a fixed level of expenditures for physically and mentally handicapped students. Staff convened and supported a group composed of representatives of the State Bureau of Vocational Rehabilitation, health and welfare planning council and county school districts whose joint programing efforts produced a prototype that school districts could adapt to meet state plan requirements.

There were no clear instances in which evaluation in the projects studied made any impact on efficiency apart from monitoring the performance of other activities that did directly impact efficiency.

ADMINISTRATIVE SUPPORT LINKAGES

Some type of administrative support services was being considered or implemented in 68 percent of the projects in which such linkages would have been appropriate. However, these linkages had been partially or fully implemented in only 45 percent of those projects. Table 7.5 shows the development of these linkages and their appearance most frequently in mediated coordination projects.

Record-Keeping

Partial or full implementation of a central or standardized client record-keeping system was partially or fully implemented in over 80 percent of the mediated projects in which the linkage would have been appropriate, 40 percent of the voluntary projects, and 20 percent of the directed projects.

Within the mediated projects, the most consistent success in implementing some form of this linkage appeared in neighborhood service centers and projects in which the integrator was the single conduit of funds to service providers. In the latter projects, the integrator's initiatives focused first on the standardization of the form in which client data was recorded by affiliated agencies. In the United Family Services and Phoenix Child Care Projects, linked providers serve different geographic areas. Therefore, the major need for exchange of client case data between providers was rare. However, the development of standardized data has been sought by the integrators for purposes of planning, evaluation, and grants-management.

TABLE 7.5

Development of Administrative Support Service Linkages
(percent)

Linkages	Voluntary		Modes of Coordination — Mediated		Directed		Total of Three Modes	
	Linkages in planning or initial stages of development	Linkages partially or fully developed	Linkages in planning or initial stages of development	Linkages partially or fully developed	Linkages in planning or initial stages of development	Linkages partially or fully developed	Linkages in planning or initial stages of development	Linkages partially or fully developed
1. Record-keeping	40	40	9	81	60	20	31	54
2. Grants management	10	50	9	36	20	20	12	38
3. Central support services	30	10	9	63	40	20	23	35
Percent of possible linkages:	28	34	10	65	46	23	23	45

Westside Mental Health Center has been faced by a number of different problems in its attempt to develop a standardized and centralized client data system for the use of service providers as well as central evaluation staff. First, the issue of confidentiality had to be overcome by eventually threatening to invoke sanctions in its purchase agreements with providers. (See section above on Purchase of Service.) Second, the integrator had to contend with the technical and logistical problems of developing a computerized capability to store and retrieve data.

Regardless of the type of coordination, the implementation of central, standardized record-keeping for projects serving a large number of clients was facilitated by the use of automatic data processing. Conversely, the problems of developing such a capability, as occurred in the Westside Mental Health Center, Bangor Office of the Maine Human Resource Agency, and the Delaware County Division of Social Services, have hampered the execution of planned record-keeping systems.

In the neighborhood service centers, central record-keeping was a feature offered generally as part of the initial agreements with providers who were to be located on-site. Colocation of service providers facilitated central record-keeping since the logistical problems inherent in data-gathering and retrieval were reduced. Off-site providers generally did not participate because of these constraints.

However, even in those cases such as the HUB Neighborhood Service Center in which service providers were involved in the development of the record-keeping forms, providers continued to use their own forms because of record-keeping requirements of their own agency, funding source, and so on, so development of this linkage actively created duplication.

In addition, because of the confidentiality issue, some neighborhood service centers have two record-keeping systems operating simultaneously. For example, Kearns Neighborhood Service Center staff and service providers jointly developed a client record system that provided standardized profile data, but each agency continues to do its own record-keeping.

Dallas's system of central record-keeping was rendered ineffective because of the confidentiality issue and because providers were not involved in developing forms with the result that the forms do not supply the data they needed. However, requirements of the center's funding source (State Department of Welfare) have resulted in a reevaluation of the system.

In the voluntary projects and some neighborhood service center projects, the integrator's clients constitute such a small percentage of the service providers' total clientele that the providers are unwilling to alter their record-keeping systems. Therefore, the integrators have partially implemented this linkage in a variety of ways. In some voluntary projects the staff take the individual forms of the service providers to the client for completion as part of the intake process. Other project staffs verbally convey to service providers what they consider to be significant information from their comprehensive records. In the Seattle Senior Centers Project, only information obtained at intake is standardized and centralized. Other projects have used standard forms already common among individual providers. For example, Jackson County Head Start provided participating doctors with a medical form widely used throughout the state, one that follows the child to elementary school.

Grants-Management

The grants-management linkage was at some stage of development in 60 percent of the voluntary projects where it was appropriate, in 45 percent of the mediated projects, and in 40 percent of the directed projects.

The major problem in implementing this linkage are the obstacles caused by funding source requirements that mandate almost unique reporting requirements for individual programs or services.

Many of the voluntary coordination projects maintained a posture of asking as little as possible of service providers by managing, on behalf of the providers, the few grants they received directly. This activity consumed a significant part of their attention, since many different reports were required of them. For example, although Jackson County Head Start received money from only one source, HEW (Office of Child Development), three separate sets of data had to be reported—health start, full-day/full-year head start, and part-day/part-year head start.

Also since little response was obtained by the integrator from the multiplicity of data that had to be submitted, the integrators' motivation for completing such reports was lessened.

Mediated projects that were the conduit of funds to service providers also performed the grants management function. Their single-point funding also placed the integrating staff in a position to help participating agencies by acting as an administrative buffer between the funding source and the service providers. The integrator negotiated solutions to concerns of the funding source on behalf of the agencies and interpreted regulations to the agencies. This assistance served to encourage involvement by small, newly established or conservative agencies that were reticent about confronting, by themselves, the myriad of regulations and paperwork required by various funding sources. It also served to tie those agencies more closely to the integrator.

124

Central Support Services

Central support services were at some stage of development in 72 percent of the mediated projects where it was appropriate, 60 percent of the directed projects, and 40 percent of the voluntary projects.

Implementation of this linkage varied directly according to the objectives of the various projects. The high percentage of implementation in mediated coordination projects is almost entirely due to its use in all the mediated coordination projects except the neighborhood service centers. In the latter, this linkage had been partially implemented only in the case of Kearns Neighborhood Service Center, where its use was restricted to the exchange of materials and equipment among on-site providers.

In the other mediated projects, the integrative staff viewed its role as assisting service providers. The ways in which this was accomplished varied from providing an outreach specialist to train and assist neighborhood center's staff in the United Family Services Project to furnishing fact-gathering, program development, and grantsmanship assistance in all the projects. Largely, integrative staff was able to attain legitimacy in the view of service providers by demonstrating expertise useful to the agencies in accomplishing their own objectives and by relieving the agencies of administrative concerns, thus leaving them more time for service delivery. (Because central support services is a critical feature of mediated projects, an expanded discussion of this linkage appears in Chapter 10.)

Central support services were a major incentive to service providers to become involved in project activities, and the integrative staffs implemented this linkage to pave the way for agencies participation in other linkages. An obvious reason these mediated projects were able to implement this linkage—especially as compared with voluntary projects—was the availability of a central, coordinative staff to provide these services.

Impact on Accessibility, Continuity, and Efficiency

Accessibility

Administrative support services linkages exhibited no direct impact on accessibility either separately or collectively. Centralized support services have indirect impact on accessibility by enhancing the effectiveness of other linkages (for example, outreach was made more effective through the training of outreach workers). However, such use of centralized support services was infrequent.

Continuity

Centralized/standardized record-keeping and centralized support services have a major, if indirect, impact on continuity by increasing the effectiveness of other linkages. Planning, programing, information-sharing, and evaluation all benefit when information can be retrieved from a centralized and standardized case information system. Furthermore, the centralization of records encourages service providers to come together when some function involving all of them requires the use of these records.

Diagnosis, referral, and case coordination, all of which are major elements of continuity, are positively affected by a centralized/standardized record-keeping system, for the staff handling these functions to have immediate access to a client's records greatly enhances continuity. Similarly, access of providers to full client information enables them to deliver their service in a manner that accommodates the need for, and provision of, other services. As a natural consequence, it follows that standardized forms and procedures enabled clients themselves to move more freely between agencies embraced by the system.

Centralized support services in the form of consultation can impact continuity in many ways, depending on the nature of the actual services provided. For example, program development and grantsmanship assistance enabled providers to fill gaps in the delivery system, augmenting total service and financial resources of the system. Technical assistance—like centralized fact-gathering—helps ensure that existing services are responsive to the needs of the client population. In general, the provision of central support services helped agencies to provide complementary services since consistent staff assistance from the perspective of the total delivery system is rendered to all providers.

Efficiency

Administrative support services probably have a more immediate and direct impact on efficiency than any other linkage category. The centralization of record-keeping, reporting, and support services reduces duplication of effort among service providers. Integrator or provider requiring client records need not contact each service provider to acquire information. The onus of meeting reporting requirements is removed from provider agencies by centralized grants management.

In addition, the concentration of scarce expertise in the form of central support services allows a more efficient allocation of that resource among the service providers. The availability of this expertise was especially important to the service providers linked to the United Family Services Project. Furthermore, central support staffs have an overview of the service delivery system that enhances their impact on problem solution.

CORE SERVICE LINKAGES

Core service linkages were found in some form in 70 percent of the projects in which they were appropriate and were fully or partially implemented in over 50 percent. They were more fully developed and utilized in the voluntary projects and the neighborhood service centers. The core services being provided seemed to vary somewhat in intent, role within the project, and significance according to modes of coordination being employed.

In voluntary projects, core services linkages were fully or partially implemented in nearly 70 percent of the projects in which they were appropriate and were planned or beginning in an additional 14 percent. Because these projects focused on a finite client group and, in most cases, the integrator was responsible for providing some direct services, core services were often carried out by integrator staff through their ongoing contact with the clients. Although the degree of systematization varied, core services (except for outreach) were generally performed on a case-by-case basis. They were somewhat limited by the lack of standardized procedures or even general commitments agreed upon by the integrator and independent providers. The small size of many of these projects limited bargaining power of the integrator and made major reorganization of the system unlikely. Participation neither involved any commitment from autonomous providers nor required them to change anything else they did. In some cases, providers were not even aware that core services were being provided.

The following factors contributed to the emphasis on core services in voluntary projects. First, project objectives committed them to augmenting their services to clients with a range of services obtainable only from other agencies. Second, core services can, to a great extent, be completely carried out by the integrator's staff, without involved negotiations or arrangements with other providers. Third, core services are the traditional casework response to a fragmented system. Fourth, they meet at least some immediate client needs and thus have manifest short-term results, whereas administrative-level integrative efforts generally take longer to accomplish anything.

Core services were fully or partially implemented in only 53 percent of the mediated projects in which they were appropriate. Several mediated projects (the Westside Mental Health Center and Phoenix Child Care, United Family Services, and Cleveland Mental Retardation Projects) have either deemphasized or totally neglected the development of core services, instead concentrating on the development and provision of administrative support services to external providers.

In all but one of the neighborhood service centers, core services as a group and individually were more developed than other integrating linkages. For the two centers that originated under the Neighborhood Center Pilot Program, a plan for consolidated core services was a requirement for funding. In the centers, core services are provided by the integrator for all clients of the colocated units of participating agencies, and for clients of some off-site providers as well. They are generally provided by one or two units, with the five core services combined in various ways. The goals of core services parallel those of the centers themselves: to expand services at the lowest possible cost; make the services more accessible and effective; meet total needs of the clients; and avoid duplication of services. In contrast to other integrating linkages in the neighborhood service centers, planning, and development of core services involved the participating providers only minimally. However, there is much more acknowledgment that the integrator is providing the core services than with the voluntary projects, but lack of participation by service providers in planning core services has led to some difficulties.

General Facilitators and Inhibitors of Core Services

In general, development of core services, particularly intake, diagnosis, referral, and follow-up was facilitated or inhibited by the willingness or unwillingness of external providers to relinquish control over these procedures, and to support their operation. Various types of factors affected this in the different projects studied. Centralized or joint provision of each core service requires participating agencies to relinquish authority in different degrees. Outreach and referral requires almost no relinquishing of authority while intake infringed on agency prerogatives to the greatest extent in that clients are placed in a direct service by another agency.

This consideration affected which core service linkages were attempted or successfully implemented in various situations. The integrator's ability to require or persuade autonomous agencies to relinquish some control was an important facilitator. Factors contributing to this were formal agreements and sanctions; the commitment and skill of the project director and, to a lesser degree, of staff; the incentive constituted by the core services themselves; and other incentives such as funding resources possessed by the integrator. Conversely, the absence of these factors impeded the development of core service linkages.

The presence or absence of formal agreements and sanctions significantly affected the development of core service linkages. In the voluntary projects the integrator had no authority over participating agencies, and formal agreements were generally lacking. The reliance on informal working arrangements frequently resulted in dependence on the ongoing efforts of individual staff and on the continuing passive good will of autonomous agencies. Although the integrators in neighborhood service centers likewise had no authority over participating agencies, some formal agreements were developed. In at least one case, these were helpful in defining expectations and commiting service providers to a certain degree of participation. The mere presence of formal agreements was not necessarily sufficient. For example, in another neighborhood service center, written agreements stated that the city agreed to furnish space to provider agencies in exchange for a commitment to provide specific services to clients and to cooperate with the goals and total functioning of the center. The lack of authority over participating agencies and of agreed-upon sanctions when an agency failed in its commitment rendered the "agreements" meaningless. In this case, the time span between development of the center (1967) and the negotiation of linkage agreement (1969-71) apparently weakened the bargaining power of the integrator.

In contrast, in one directed project the contract that binds participating agencies to certain service arrangements is a major factor contributing to centralization of core services. The contract obligates agencies to accept referrals of multiproblem clients and to supply feedback to the information system. The project was able to develop such effective contracts due to the state government's strong support, and to the backing of the local United Fund.

The commitment, efforts, and skill of the project director also affected development and successful implementation of core service linkages. Although crucial in many of the voluntary projects due to their total dependence on persuasion, this factor made a significant difference wherever it appeared. In some projects, the director's effectiveness in developing and maintaining linkages was limited by the way his role was defined in terms of degree of authority or responsibility for administration and provision of direct service. In cases where the project director actually functioned in a coordinative capacity actively seeking cooperation and resolving disputes, core services as well as other linkages were enhanced.

The involvement of service providers in planning and developing the provision of core services, both before and during implementation, is another significant factor. Opportunity for participating agencies to influence the way core services were provided increased their commitment to the system and willingness to utilize and cooperate with it. The methods for involving providers included planning meetings and participation on project boards or committees.

Participation of the providers also resulted in systems that were in fact workable and helpful to the providers. Absence of such input resulted in agency resistance, or in the development of awkward mechanisms—as with the Crossroads Neighborhood Service Centers, where an extremely elaborate system of information flow in either disregarded or implemented in a way that is not helpful.

Service providers' confidence in the ability of integrator staff to perform core services was crucial. In one neighborhood center, lack of training of core service staff detracted from utilization of centralized core services and gave providers an excuse not to fulfill their commitments, thus resulting in a continuous deterioration of core services. In another, most agencies were not willing to delegate responsibility for core services to a central staff, citing doubts about the qualifications of the integrator's core service staff as justification. In many voluntary projects, the integrator's ability to connect autonomous service providers with clients, in large part a function of the core services provided, constituted the major incentive for participation. This could be more fully recognized and deliberately used. Core services resulting in bringing clients into the system were also an incentive in one neighborhood center.

Other incentives facilitating development of core services in various projects included well-located facilities at little or no cost, and the integrator staff's ability to be a buffer between "difficult" or new clients and traditional service providers. Frequently, these incentives were not used as bargaining points by the integrator.

Two other types of factors importantly facilitated or inhibited core service linkages: project objectives, and federal guidelines and technical assistance. In many projects, objectives both called for and limited the provision of core services. For example, most voluntary projects sought to provide a group of clients with a range of services oriented around a primary service provided by the integrator. Although core services were the key to obtaining needed services from outside agencies, staff's responsibility for service delivery and focus on the needs of a finite group of clients resulted in manipulation of the service delivery system on behalf of the client group or on a client-by-client basis rather than an attempt at rationalization of the system.

In somewhat different ways, the objective of some neighborhood centers also resulted in a perspective that limited core services. This occurred in projects where the service delivery problem was originally viewed as physical, so that the goal was primarily to bring service providers into the clients' territory and closer to each other. Where the problem was viewed more as one of coordinating and relating services—that is, where the objective was broader—core service linkages tended to be seen differently.

Projects operating according to some type of client-demand model tended not to develop core services as extensively—especially outreach, follow-up, and diagnosis of overall needs. These projects included two divisions of social services operating according to the TAP model* and two neighborhood centers. Significantly, all four projects were sponsored by state government, and the integrator was a branch of the Department of Social Services. Their objective was basically, as stated by one project, "the development of new service delivery mechanisms for welfare recipients that will increase their self-sufficiency and decrease their dependence on the system, while providing them with specific assistance designed to meet specific requirements." (Self-sufficiency was defined as "not requesting service.") These projects did not probe for related problems or needs and left it up to the client to come back if service was not obtained or was insufficient. This approach not only inhibited development of core services but also served to keep clients out of the system rather than help them.

Federal guidelines and technical assistance also affected core service linkages, by both their content and implementation. As noted earlier, neighborhood service centers developed within the Neighborhood Center Pilot Program were required to develop centralized core services. But the federal requirements calling for participation by service providers in project development were not always carried out in a way that required them to make a meaningful commitment or allowed them significant input related to the scope and content of core services. Guidelines relating to Office of Child Development programs, such as parent-child centers and Head Start projects, also require core services as a way of obtaining a range of services, but do not allow funds for staff to develop arrangements at the system level.

Individual Core Service Linkages

The following discussion describes the state of development of individual core service linkages as illustrated in Table 7.6 including examples of the ways each was implemented in various projects, and the facilitators and inhibitors that were specific to that linkage.

Outreach was fully or partially implemented in one half of the projects studied. Of the five core service linkages, outreach affects agency prerogatives least. Outreach was conducted in various ways, usually by the staff of the integrator. In a few cases the combined staff of the integrator and the local community action agency

*This refers to a separation of services reorganization plan developed under the auspices of the American Public Welfare Association.

131

TABLE 7.6
Development of Core Service Linkages
(percent)

	Voluntary		Mediated		Directed		Total of Three Modes	
Linkages	Linkages in planning or initial stages of development	Linkages partially or fully developed	Linkages in planning or initial stages of development	Linkages partially or fully developed	Linkages in planning or initial stages of development	Linkages partially or fully developed	Linkages in planning or initial stages of development	Linkages partially or fully developed
1. Outreach	—	70	9	36	60	20	15	54
2. Intake	20	60	—	54	40	20	15	50
3. Diagnosis	10	80	9	45	40	20	15	54
4. Referral	20	80	—	63	80	20	23	62
5. Follow-up	20	50	—	63	40	40	15	54
Percent of possible linkages:	14	68	4	53	52	24	17	53

provided core services to take advantage of existing skills and resources, expand services, and reduce unit cost. In many projects, outreach depended upon establishing relationships with other agencies in the community and keeping them informed of project services so that field staff could identify and refer potential clients. In some projects, the integrator's staff conducted intensive door-to-door recruitment. In one small project, outreach teams composed of a member of the social work staff and clients participating in the program were highly successful both in recruiting door to door and in setting up information tables at locations such as the local welfare department and a crowded clinic.

In those voluntary projects where the integrator provided direct service, participating agencies relied on the integrator's staff to perform outreach with respect to the project's specific clients but outreach was conducted only when the demands on the time of the staff for direct services permitted. In two neighborhood service centers, all on-site and many off-site agencies relied fully on centralized outreach to inform residents of their services. One directed project also conducted active outreach that supplemented and improved upon, rather than supplanted, the outreach efforts of the participating agencies.

Several projects were not committed to reaching more clients, and provided no outreach beyond disseminating general information (for example, flyers), which did not prove effective. Apathy toward outreach was typical of state welfare departments and neighborhood service centers utilizing the TAP or other versions of client demand model, as well as one neighborhood service center whose municipal sponsor had no real interest in improving service accessibility.

There was a tendency among some integrators—especially those involved in some form of community organization—to combine the outreach and community organization functions. This practice held promise of impacting both accessibility (by putting the outreach function in the hands of people who know the community and its residents) and efficiency (by minimizing the potential for duplication of services). In general, the most effective outreach efforts were those that involved face-to-face contacts—with clients, with service providers, and with individuals likely to encounter potential clients.

The primary facilitator of outreach was the willingness and ability of the integrator and/or external providers to serve a growing number of clients. This included the desire of service providers to tap new client populations previously inaccessible due to factors such as distance, poor rapport, or insufficient staff. For example, the Oakland Parent-Child Center provided outreach for the Red Cross through its ability to relate to a minority clientele that the Red Cross had difficulty approaching. The integrator, in many cases, was able to compensate for the service providers' outreach deficiencies and reach a previously unserved client population.

Accomplishing this required integrator staff knowledgeable in the ways of the target community, good rapport between outreach staff and clients, integrator location conveniently near the target clientele, and responsiveness of the outreach staff to the needs of the service providers.

Other than inability or unwillingness to accept additional clients—both to some extent institutionalized in the TAP model—the primary inhibitors of outreach were project newness (and concomitant disorganization) and the integrator's direction of outreach staff more toward community organization and service provision than toward client identification. The latter inhibitor was often a corollary to the unwillingness or inability of the integrator to expand its clientele.

Although intake was at least partially implemented in half the projects (including six voluntary and six mediated), it was rarely fully implemented. This is due to the fact that accepting clients for service is a basic prerogative of social service agencies, one they are usually most reluctant to give up.

Intake took different forms according to the organization and size of the projects. In the voluntary projects, intake to the direct services provided by the integrator admitted clients to many, but not all, of the services provided through the project. For example, intake admitted the family to all services provided by staff of one integrator and to services provided at the project's facilities by outstationed staff or participating agencies, while other agencies carried out their own intake when clients were referred to them. In another case, the forms required by all major service providers were completed at intake, and admission to the program automatically qualified each child for specialized services from all providers except one.

Four of the six neighborhood service centers had a central intake unit through which clients entered the system and were relayed to specialized services. The unit responsible for intake often provided other core services, most frequently diagnosis and/or referral, as well as counseling, and was either responsible for or closely involved with centralized record-keeping. In most cases the intake unit utilized a standardized form that eliminated repetitive interviews and filling out forms, but did not ensure that clients would in fact receive particular services.

In the Westside Mental Health Center, admission to the service system at one point qualified the client for all services. In other cases (for example, the Phoenix Child Care Project), projects were beginning to develop standardized eligibility requirements and intake procedures to be employed by participating providers.

Facilitators and inhibitors were those generally applying to core services. A particularly important facilitator was the existence of integrator personnel knowledgeable in the functions and procedures of service providers; while primary inhibitors were the unwillingness of service providers to standardize diverse, often incompatible intake procedures, and objections of service providers to actual or perceived lack of expertise of intake workers. (This also relates to diagnosis.) Integrators that used paraprofessionals for intake functions were particularly vulnerable to this criticism, especially from external providers that relied on professionals for these jobs.

Diagnosis (the assessment of total client needs) was fully or partially implemented in over half the projects including all but two voluntary projects. Diagnosis or screening appeared in a variety of forms with varying degrees of systemization. In voluntary projects, integrator staff carried out diagnosis of each client's total needs to determine what services would be provided in what sequence. When the integrator was itself a functional service provider, diagnosis was at first focused on that particular service, while other needs were assessed as they related it. Some of these projects carried out an assessment of total needs when the client entered the system; in others this was done in the course of participation in the program.

In several other projects, including some neighborhood service centers and welfare departments, diagnosis was performed by intake workers at the time of intake. In some cases this was an in-depth process of screening and counseling that explored the client's present problems and identified others; in others, the assessment of needs is partial and limited to those professed by the client himself. In all projects, diagnosis within specific functional areas, such as health, was done by the individual provider.

When diagnosis resulted in the development of a comprehensive plan for service, it had great potential impact on continuity and problem-solution, by affecting the provision of referral and follow-up, as well as planning and evaluation. For example, projects such as Jackson County Head Start and HUB Neighborhood Service Center, through screening for a variety of possible programs developed a specific program tailored to each client's needs. This made it possible to provide a number of services concurrently, adapting them so as to enhance each other. Projects that did not provide diagnosis, or failed to develop an overall plan of service, tended to refer clients to different services sequentially, and failed to utilize services in relation to each other.

The primary facilitator of central diagnosis was the integrator's holistic approach to client needs. Autonomous service providers' confidence in the ability of the staff performing a centralized function was also especially important in the case of diagnosis. Also client confidence in the diagnostician and in his ready access to services was necessary to ensure full disclosure of information.

Self-declaration of need appeared in the Delaware County Division of Social Services, the Bangor Office of the Maine Human Resource Agency, and the Kearns and Hamilton Neighborhood Service Centers.

From one point of view, self-declaration facilitates diagnosis in that the client is able to express his needs as he views them, and thus to map out his own services plan. On the other hand self-declaration may lead to incomplete or incorrect diagnosis, resulting in inadequate delivery of services, and reduced impact on problem solution.

The requirement of confidentiality appeared as an inhibitor of diagnosis in some projects, since it restricted information that could be made available to the integrator or other service providers.

Referral was the most developed of the five core service linkages. Referral generally entailed less sacrifice of sovereignty than any other linkage with the exception of outreach. It was a major task of the integrator in many projects but had a wide range of application. In some instances the integrator simply informed a client where and how to go about getting a service; in others he contacted service providers to facilitate entry by relaying information, setting up appointments, or modifying service delivery. In some cases standardized forms served to introduce the client and relay information regarding his needs to service providers. Agreements negotiated with providers were most effective in prohibiting rejection of clients.

In most voluntary projects, referral was hampered by lack of standardized procedures agreed upon by the integrator staff and autonomous service providers. Where referral was conducted on a case-by-case basis totally by the integrator staff, it was nonetheless effective due to staff's commitment and interest in the clients. However, this procedure is time-consuming and inefficient.

In the Tri-County Project, contracts defining agency participation required them to honor referrals made by project staff. Referral was enhanced (that is more clients actually got to and obtained services to which they were referred) by (1) such ancillary services as transportation, escort, advocacy, and baby-sitting and (2) a continuing relationship between client and the staff member making the referral. These several factors all made clients more able and willing to seek and continue other services.

Factors specifically facilitating referral were thorough staff knowledge of which service providers were available and how they function, personal ties of members of the integrator staff with staff of providers, and the "clout" of the integrator, project sponsor, or those associated with the project. The primary inhibitor was the unwillingness of providers to accept clients due to lack of funds, lack of facilities, or hostility toward client population and/or integrator. Other negative factors were failure to articulate services by functional specialty (producing an ambiguous service delivery matrix) and long waiting times or extensive red tape at the referred service provider.

Follow-up was fully or partially implemented in over half the samples, including five voluntary, seven mediated, and two directed projects. Although extremely time-consuming, follow-up seems to be crucial to assure that clients get services. In many projects, follow-up consisted of informal contacts made by the integrator's staff, with varying degrees of regularity and systemization. Often it depended on the initiative and persuasive ability of integrator staff. Three neighborhood service centers and several other mediated projects carried out regular follow-up of all referrals made by using a system of records and written information flow and/or by worker contact, usually on the telephone.

In one project the case coordinator maintained a ''suspense file'' on each client to keep track of what services had been provided. The Tri-County Project required each service provider to report to the integrator the status of the service provided. This same project was utilizing a computerized information system for follow-up, and several others were planning to do so. Projects using a client demand model left it up to the client to judge whether adequate service was received, and thus there was no follow-up.

Specific factors that facilitated the development and effectiveness of the follow-up linkage include standardized procedures and forms among the service providers and the integrator, and an automatic feedback system from service providers (preferably by computer, for large systems).

Major specific inhibitors are lack of time and effort by staff, the issue of confidentiality, and the informality of integrator-provider relations. Confidentiality has been a major stumbling block to effective follow-up. Many service providers, especially physical and mental health providers, are constrained from relaying case information, and this inhibits development of a follow-up process providing the necessary detailed information.

Impact on Accessibility, Continuity, and Efficiency

Accessibility

Outreach and intake were the core services linkages directly affecting accessibility. Where outreach was fully implemented, it functioned to bring potential clients into the service delivery system through such techniques as door-to-door canvassing, leaflet distribution, word of mouth, the media, and working through other agencies in the community likely to come into contact with potential clients and so refer them to project services. The implementation of a common intake function enhanced accessibility to the service delivery system in a number of ways. The primary impact was due to opening the total range of services to the client, with a reduction in the waiting time and red tape. The ability of a client to enter the system at many points including in some instances the clients' home, enhances accessibility.

Continuity

Continuity benefited because individual clients received additional services as a result of core services that assessed needs, negotiated access to external services, coordinated needs with providers, and followed up receipt of services. Many of the projects got clients to services that were previously unavailable to or not utilized by them. Core services played the major role in increasing continuity of service delivery in the voluntary projects where more systematic approaches were infrequent. Although this case-by-case process is time consuming and inefficient, it was very often the major source of continuity in what was—and will be for some time—a largely fragmented and irrational service delivery system. Also, the neighborhood service centers that had the greatest impact on continuity were those that implemented the linkages of intake, diagnosis, referral, and follow-up.

Although the primary impact of outreach was on accessibility, continuity was also enhanced by the outreach process. By making potential clients aware of a variety of services available, outreach encouraged them to seek a total set of services.

The specification and clarification of eligibility requirements inherent in centralized intake, and the limiting of the intake function itself to a single experience, removed barriers to client movement between services.

Diagnosis, as defined, impacted continuity by identifying the client's total set of needs, allowing construction of a comprehensive plan. A centralized, comprehensive diagnostic process eliminates sequential service delivery (where the client must return to the caseworker after receiving each particular service). The opportunity for the worker to get a total view of a client's problem, including sets of underlying or interconnected needs, enables provision of services in a coordinated and mutually enhancing manner.

Since no single provider can meet the total range of a client's needs, the referral process in some form is vital to achieve continuity. Referral impacted continuity through getting clients to a number of services and by increasing their knowledge of the service delivery system and allowing them to form direct relationships with other providers, which makes future service provision easier. The primary impact of follow-up is on continuity. Some form of follow-up is necessary in order to maximize the ease with which clients move through the delivery systems, and ensure that individual clients actually obtain needed services.

Efficiency

Central core services eliminated the need for each service provider to carry out these functions, thus reducing duplication and freeing provider staff for functional services. This led, of course, to economies of scale. In several cases, outreach staff became a vehicle for combining various activities, such as community organization, health screening, advocacy, and, in one case, intake.

Referral specifically impacted efficiency by fully utilizing existing resources and programs and avoiding duplication of effort. Follow-up, coupled with evaluation and planning, provided a check on the present allocation of time and money in the system to ensure optimization of effort.

The greatest impact on efficiency at this point is that on problem solution that results from improved continuity of service delivery. Intake, diagnosis, referral, and follow-up positively impacted problem solution by identifying mutually aggravating needs of clients, providing services in combination so that they were more effective, and ensuring that clients receive needed services.

Consolidated Provision of Core Services

In many projects the same unit or staff provided several or all core services. In other projects clients had to see a succession of workers. Each core service enhances the effect of the others; so it is important that all are realized within a project and when they are interrelated or consolidated, their effectiveness and continuity are increased. Close coordination of these services allows each to be better provided and saves both staff and client time.

In general, it seems useful to combine intake, diagnosis, referral, and follow-up, while outreach is best combined with functions requiring rapport with the community, such as community organization. (However, in some cases it was helpful to perform intake of clients in their homes.)

Handling intake, diagnosis, referral, and follow-up together reduces the time involved in the total process, ensures maximum knowledge of client data, and allows rapport to develop between worker and client. The provision of service is improved because, for example, the person who makes the original referral is more likely to have an easier time in follow-up because contact has already been established with the service provider regarding that particular client.

Service is also more effective because the support the clients gets from the project staff enables him to make better use of other services. This occurred particularly in voluntary projects where there was ongoing contact, counseling, or other supportive services. Client trust in project staff increased their ability and willingness to utilize the services of other providers. Some projects attempted to provide core services through one staff person (case coordinator) who was responsible for the client as long as he was within the system. More importantly, attempts to provide unified core services in several projects resulted in identification of weaknesses and gaps between the provision of various individual core services, thus leading to further consolidation.

Another aspect of the way core services are delivered is significant. Many Neighborhood Service Centers and other larger projects placed heavy reliance on use of forms to transmit information on clients and service delivery. Although a system of paperwork and forms is to some extent necessary, particularly where large numbers of clients and several providers are involved, it does not in itself either get clients to services or enhance continuity and sometimes merely increases an administrative burden on staff. In one project, an elaborate system of communication and built-in feedback between the component units and the service providing agencies did not (for a variety of reasons) function in a way satisfactory either to staff of the center or to that of participating agencies. Such ends/means displacement is a constant danger.

CASE COORDINATION LINKAGES

Three modes of case coordination—case conference, case coordinator, case team—were utilized in the projects studied. The primary difference between case conferences and case teams is that the former includes external providers and may be ad hoc while the latter may only involve the integrator's staff and includes continuous and systematic interaction between the members of the team.

Table 7.7 illustrates that over half of the projects studied had some mode of case coordination in planning or in some stage of execution. The fact that case teams were the least used is related to the fact that they require the most organized and continuous effort. Case teams and case conferences were viewed as different approaches to the same purpose and, therefore, rarely appeared together. In contrast, the use of case conferences was tied to the use of case coordinators, especially when the case coordinator was responsible for one or more of the core service functions (except outreach). The individual responsible for the provision of intake, diagnosis, referral, or follow-up was in a position to perceive the need for case conferences and convene representatives of the various service providers. Furthermore, a group meeting as a case conference usually had one individual responsible for coordinating its decisions and directing the client accordingly.

The heavy use of case coordinators and conferences by voluntary coordinated projects can be traced to their dual role of

TABLE 7.7

Development of Case Coordination Linkages
(percent)

| | Modes of Coordination | | | | | | | |
| | Voluntary | | Mediated | | Directed | | Total of Three Modes | |
Linkages	Linkages in planning or initial stages of development	Linkages partially or fully developed	Linkages in planning or initial stages of development	Linkages partially or fully developed	Linkages in planning or initial stages of development	Linkages partially or fully developed	Linkages in planning or initial stages of development	Linkages partially or fully developed
1. Case conference	10	70	9	54	—	—	8	50
2. Case coordinator	—	70	9	36	—	—	4	42
3. Case team	—	40	9	9	—	—	4	19
Percent of possible linkages:	3	60	9	33	—	—	6	44

141

functional service provider and integrator, with the latter role performed primarily to augment the range of service. This direct involvement of the integrator's staff in securing functional services requires systematic contact with external providers in order to coordinate the delivery of services to clients.

Case conferences are a traditional part of social work and are generally held irregularly on an ad hoc basis in response to a crisis or accumulation or problems. In practically all projects they were used unsystematically. When there was no recognized case coordinator, case conferences were generally arranged by social service staff in the voluntary coordination projects or by intake workers in the neighborhood service centers.

Case coordinators were used in a deliberate attempt to provide a comprehensive approach to service delivery. For example, in one neighborhood service center, particular intake workers were responsible for clients until either the service plan was completed or another agency assumed primary responsibility for case management. In one voluntary coordination project, community workers performed this role by providing referral and follow-up, as well as counseling and advocacy. In another, the health and social service coordinators each had responsibility for ensuring that needed services were obtained within their respective functional areas.

A few projects utilized case teams to ensure provision of a range of services in a coordinated and mutually enhancing manner. The greater the range of services provided internally by the integrators, the more they tended to use case teams rather than case conferences. (This is evident in the Yeatman Neighborhood Service Center, Galveston Child Development Project, Jackson County Head Start, and Oakland Parent-Child Center.) For instance, one voluntary project utilized teams composed of a case worker, paraprofessional, and community organizer in its approach to improving family living patterns of Aid to Families with Dependent Children (AFDC) recipients. In another, a team composed of a vocational rehabilitation counselor and a caseworker was responsible for each client from intake through an extended diagnostic process to job placement. It helped the client obtain services provided by the integrator as well as by autonomous agencies and was responsible for referral and follow-up and maintaining records of service. In all cases where teams were used, team members related to each other regularly, developing a service plan, exchanging information on clients, and evaluating progress.

Facilitators and Inhibitors of Case Coordination

Modes of case coordination tended to be regularly used where the desire to provide a comprehensive approach to service delivery was the underlying rationale for the project. A major factor facilitating the development and use of case conferences and case coordinators was a close working relationship among service providers, leading to mutual understanding of each other's operations and objectives. (In some cases this was furthered by physical proximity or colocation.) Case teams were facilitated by the integrator's provision of multiple services, which resulted in awareness of the need for ongoing coordination and made regular contact easier to achieve.

The major inhibitors of the development of case conferences and case coordinators were (1) project staff concentration on internal matters rather than on the development of linkages (in some projects this was related to the short term of operation or the demonstration nature of the project, both of which led to a "wait-and-see" attitude on the part of service providers; (2) the lack of adequate service provider staff to commit to the case conferences due to their immediate service responsibilities; and (3) the informal nature of the ties between the integrator and service providers.

Impact on Accessibility, Continuity, and Efficiency

Accessibility

The impact of case coordination on accessibility was negligible.

Continuity

The various forms of case coordination had a strong impact on continuity. By involving external providers in solving individual case problems, the integrator ensured smooth movement of the client from one service to another and ensured that the service delivery package was tailor-made to the client's full needs. In addition, the case coordinator, especially when supported by an adequate follow-up system, aided the client in negotiating the system and ensured that service providers met their obligations. Case teams, although infrequently implemented, seem highly effective in achieving continuity, both because they operate more continuously and because they tend to foster a staff with various specialized skills.

Efficiency

Case coordination also impacted efficiency. By mapping in advance parameters of service delivery, service providers were able to avoid duplication of effort and were better able to impact problem solution by ensuring the comprehensiveness of the service delivery package. The cost effectiveness of the services delivery is not likely to improve in the short run, but over the long run costs may be lowered through experience gained in problem solution.

8

THE CLIENT
AS INTEGRATOR

There was some degree of client participation in slightly more than 60 percent of the projects studied. In a few other projects, community residents participated on project advisory committees, but these residents were neither current nor potential project clients. Dramatic variations in the role of clients appeared, ranging from pro forma membership on committees prompted by funding source requirements to client control of policy-making and project operations.

The extent of client involvement did not seem to vary based on mode of coordination except that the consolidated human resource agencies as examples of directed coordination have not yet deter- nor developed organizational mechanisms to implement client involvement.

Projects reflected ranges that included variables of the nature and extent of client involvement and also the role of the client as client-initiated or staff-initiated. The role of the client as integrator most nearly correlated with the extent to which clients initiated participation in the project. This, in turn, primarily related to the level of organization and/or mobilization of client population at project inception.

In many projects, the extent of client mobilization was traceable to the work of local community action agencies. For example, in the United Family Services Project, residents, organized by the community action agency (CAA), mobilized when the CAA terminated its funding of local neighborhood service centers. While the local United Fund agency that had funded some of the neighborhood service centers was negotiating with the State Welfare Department for funds under Title IV-A to finance those centers that the CAA terminated, a committee consisting of two residents from each serviced neighborhood was created from a large ad hoc meeting of consumers. This body, now the Board of Directors of the United Family Services

Project, negotiated with the United Fund agency for the 25 percent local match for Title IV-A funds and pressured the United Fund to approve community control instead of United Fund control.

Client policy-making boards were established for each neighborhood. Through their power to approve proposals by prospective neighborhood center sponsors, some former sponsors were replaced by agencies judged more responsive to community needs. On the neighborhood level, clients participated in social action that has led to the provision of service by recalcitrant providers, while the federation of these neighborhood centers has consolidated and legitimized pressures on providers serving more than one neighborhood.

Consumer pressures also indirectly produced the Cleveland Mental Retardation Project and contributed to many of the successes that project achieved. In this instance, consumers rallied around a common concern—services for the mentally retarded. Pressures generated by these politically active, middle-class, concerned parents to do something about inadequate services stimulated a subcommittee of the health and welfare planning council to study the problem. This study recommended the creation of a special unit of the council and the acquisition of staff. From this beginning, the project developed, and consumer representation was included in its policy-making committee.

An integral part of the project was the support of an advocacy role for these consumers consisting of community education concerning mental retardation and the need for new, expanded, or improved services. These consumers lobbied for effective legislation and obtained support for bond issues to finance services. Undaunted by preconceived definitions of "impossible" situations, these consumers obtained funds, service, and changes in provider agencies' policies critical to the achievement of project objectives.

There were instances in which staff initiatives directed toward the involvement of clients provided the opportunity for consumers to play an important role in services integration. In the Westside Mental Health Center, staff partially conceived of consumers as a countervailing force on their Board of Directors otherwise comprised of affiliated service providers. Since the board was to provide a forum within which many administrative linkages were to be implemented, staff viewed consumer participation as a means to prevent development by agencies of a conservative consensus relative to operating policies, joint planning, and so on. Early planners also viewed client action as a means by which to get local matching funds from local general purpose government. They were correct.

Staff and consumers in Westside Mental Health Center also could and did unite in order to establish a posture of quick programmatic response to the needs of the community. Further, participation by consumers had begun to promote the kinds of attitude changes necessary for providers who were beginning to serve a new kind of clientele.

Sometimes, clients exerted an indirect influence on services integration. In a few cases, agencies saw the existence of a mobilized client constituency as a potential threat to their existing operations and established integrative linkages with the project to preclude militant action against their agency by these organized client groups. On the other hand, it is possible that in some cases a mobilized client constituency acted as an inhibitor to integration by causing some agencies to avoid developing linkages with the project because they were threatened by the project's constituency. However, the field research was not designed to determine whether or not such agencies existed.

9

**COMPARATIVE ANALYSIS
OF DIRECTED
COORDINATION PROJECTS**

DEFINITION OF DIRECTED COORDINATION

Directed coordination is that relationship between an integrator and a number of services providers where the service providers are legally subordinate to the integrator. The integrator has direct line authority over the providers to require that they coordinate service delivery either with respect to a geographic area, a function, or an age group.

In directed coordination, the integrator has the authority to mandate the development of integrating linkages among the service providers. In particular, such powers include authority to compel participation by service providers in a single system of planning, programing, budgeting, evaluation, and implementation of social service delivery.

SUMMARY DESCRIPTION OF THE DIRECTED COORDINATION PROJECTS

Common Factors and Project Characteristics

This chapter analyzes five projects employing directed coordination. In these projects, previously separate service providers were placed under the direct line authority of the integrator.

The five projects can be described generally as human resources super-agencies. Four super-agencies at the state level are examined. These are the Department of Health and Rehabilitative Services, Florida; the Department of Social Services, Utah; the Department of

Health and Welfare, Maine; and the Executive Office of Human Services, Massachusetts. One super-agency at the county level, San Diego, is also examined.

There are several characteristics that are shared by all five projects. Each is organized to provide services within the boundaries of a political entity. Four states and one county are the jurisdictions for service delivery.

Each project is organized under the auspices of general purpose government and has legal status in that it was created through state legislation, local charter, or local ordinance. The power, duties, and organizational structure are described in legislation.

Typically, the creation of state and county human resources super-agencies has resulted from a major reorganization of general purpose government.

Each project provides services to more than one client group of the population within its jurisdiction. Therefore, each project, through its responsibility for services to a diverse population in a selected geographic area, is concerned with a broader system of service than the voluntary of mediated coordination projects included in the study.

Services provided by the directed coordination projects have mixed organizational structures focusing on functions, age groups, and problem groups.

Location of services is characterized by decentralization. Services are typically provided by the states through county or district offices. At the county level, services may be provided through neighborhood locations.

The mode of entry to the service system available through each project is through a prime service and then to the other services of the project supportive of the prime service. In this instance, the prime services for entry into the system are composed of the major services of the organizational divisions of each project. The client enters through the services of any one of the divisions and is then referred to other services of the agency as needs are identified.

The effects of these characteristics on service delivery are discussed further in this study.

Summary Description of Projects

Department of Health and Rehabilitative Services, Florida

The Florida Department of Health and Rehabilitative Services was created as part of a major state reorganization in 1968. Twenty-two agencies, boards, commissions, and program offices were combined to create the department. It is now the single state agency for public health, welfare-social services, mental health, retardation, vocational rehabilitation, youth services, aging services, drugs and alcoholism services, and correctional institutions.

The department is organized into seven line and two staff divisions. Line divisions are corrections, youth services, mental health, retardation, vocational rehabilitation, family services, and health. Staff divisions are administrative services and planning and evaluation. A separate office for drug abuse programs is located in the office of the department director.

Service providers as reflected by the organizational structure are under the direct line authority of the department director. Administrative support functions of accounting, fiscal control, personnel, and purchasing are assigned to the division of administrative services. Comprehensive health planning, community medical facilities planning, comprehensive rehabilitation planning, and research and evaluation functions are assigned to the division of planning and evaluation.

Services are currently provided through decentralized substate district operations for each line division. While each division has its own separate service delivery system, services are coordinated through departmental level planning, programing, and budgeting.

Department of Social Services, Utah

The Utah Department of Social Services was created as part of a major reorganization of Utah state government in 1967. Subsequent amendments and additions to state legislation have resulted in a single state department responsible for public health, welfare-social services, aging services, drugs and alcohol services, mental health, corrections, and Indian affairs.

The organizational structure of the department consist of seven line divisions under the administrative direction of the department director. Line divisions of the department are health, family services, corrections, mental health, aging, alcoholism and drugs, and Indian affairs. Lay boards have been retained in the state organizational structure. A separate board for policy making is attached to each division. The division director (service provider) reports to both the division board and the department director.

Each service provider maintains separate administrative support systems including accounting, fiscal control, personnel, and purchasing. Planning, programing, and budgeting functions, which are also decentralized to the divisions, are coordinated among service providers by a small staff in the department director's office.

Each line division has a separate and distinct system of service delivery. Services are decentralized to the substate districts and county levels depending upon population density. Services are

150

coordinated for the client through referrals from one division as a prime provider to another for support services.

Coordination of the overall service delivery system is achieved through regular departmental level staff meetings.

Department of Health and Welfare, Maine

The Maine Department of Health and Welfare was created as part of a major reorganization of Maine state government in 1936. The department is the single state agency responsible for public assistance, social service, public health, and vocational rehabilitation.

Five bureaus are under the direct line authority of the department director. These divisions are health, medical care, rehabilitation, social welfare, and administration. Administrative support services for the service providers are completely centralized in this bureau of administration. Planning, programing, and budgeting for each of the bureaus (service providers) are decentralized to each; however, they are under the direct supervision of the department director.

Coordination of separate service delivery systems takes place through departmental level staff meetings chaired by the director. Services for the departments are decentralized throughout the state.

Executive Office of Human Services, Massachusetts

The Massachusetts legislature established the Massachusetts Executive Office of Human Services as part of a major reorganization of state government in 1969. The Executive Office presently supervises the existing state departments and commissions responsible for drug addiction, rehabilitation, mental health, public assistance, social services, programs for the blind, youth services, veterans services, and corrections.

Though the creation of the Executive Office did not include substantial revision to existing state departments, it is responsible for the planning, programing, budgeting, and administrative direction of the departments placed under its control.

Services are decentralized and provided through separate district systems for each department under this umbrella of the Executive Office.

Human Resources Agency, San Diego, California

The San Diego Human Resources Agency was created as part of a general reorganization of San Diego County government in late 1971. Six of the county social service oriented departments were placed within the agency. These are Department of Public Welfare,

151

Probation Department, Honor Camps (correctional facilities), Department of Veterans Services, Senior Citizen Department, and Office of Mexican-American Affairs.

For administrative purposes, two county commissions were placed within the agency though the lay boards were retained. These are the Human Relations Commission and the Economic Opportunity Commission (the local community action agency).

Service providers included in the agency operate under the direct line authority of the agency administrator, who, in turn, reports to the county's chief administrative officer and Board of Supervisors.

In addition, the agency has a community advisory board with nine members. The functions of the board are to advise the agency administrator on policy, program implementation, and evaluation of services.

COMPARISON OF THE PROJECT INTEGRATORS

The five directed coordination projects can be compared in terms of three characteristics. These are the authority of the director over the previously independent service providers, the goals and objectives for development of a cohesive service delivery system, and the resources and incentives for the development of coordinated services among the service providers.

Authority over Service Providers

There are four essential powers granted to agency directors in the creation of the state or county human services super-agencies studied. These are as follows:

1. The power of single line authority over the line divisions of the agency. This includes the power to appoint and dismiss division heads and to direct the internal affairs of the various divisions.

2. The power to conduct internal reorganization of the department. This includes the power to create and/or abolish divisions, to reassign functions to other divisions, and to create consolidated offices for departments' administrative services and planning.

3. The power of budgeting and allocation of resources to the line divisions. This may be expressed in terms of a power to review and approval over all division budgets or power to establish a central departmental budget function.

4. The power to conduct comprehensive planning for the functional services provided by the department.

The extent to which these powers have been granted and the methods in which they have been used to achieve services integration varies in each of the cases. The following discussion describes the goals and objectives with which those powers have been utilized and the resources and incentives available to the agency director.

Goals and Objectives of the Integrator

Four basic goals are being pursued in varying degrees by the directed coordination projects as the powers and direct line authority are being exercised by super-agency directors. These are (1) improvement in the quality of service delivery of the previously separate providers, (2) strengthening of the planning capacity of the new agency to plan comprehensively for a broad range of services, (3) unification of the service delivery system to reduce duplication, particularly in the provision of core services, and (4) decentralization of service delivery along geographic lines rather than functions and services of the previously separate service providers.

In Florida, the goal of the super-agency was to develop a unified organizational structure from the previously separate departments, a departmental program budgeting system, and a strong planning and evaluation capacity as a means to weld together a cohesive state service delivery system. Direct line authority of the secretary has been used to emphasize among division directors a mandate to integrate departmental programing and services within the state. That mandate is expressed in a departmental policy to provide comprehensive community-based services "which promote maximum self-sufficiency for individuals and their families and which enable persons to remain in or return to their own homes and communities."

In Utah, an organization and management study is being used by the super-agency to address the questions of how the department could develop a consistent approach to social services and how to weld the department into a cohesive service group. Clearly, the intent of the study was to determine methods for strengthening the organizational structure and moving toward services integration. Recommendations included abolishing division boards in order to obtain direct line authority over divisions and restructuring the department with consolidated staffs for administrative services, budgeting, planning, and evaluation. The reorganization proposal also called for consolidation of field staffs into a division of technical assistance. In effect, the organizational proposals would strengthen and utilize the powers of the executive director.

153

In Massachusetts, an HEW demonstration grant has been used to provide planning staff in one substate region to begin development of a common core services system for state services. Interdepartmental committees have been used for planning comprehensive child care services, services for handicapped children, community-based correctional activities, and drugs and alcohol services. The intent in these instances was improvement in the quality of services and improved accessibility and continuity of services.

In Maine, the powers of the super-agency director have been used to create a centralized administrative services staff and a regional organizational structure for welfare-social services. A major reorganization proposal is before the next session of the legislature, which will include assigning the functions of mental health, mental retardation, corrections, and aging services to the department. Following reorganization of the department, regional directors will have line authority over all departmental field staff in a substate district. The reorganization proposal provides for a consolidated planning staff at the central office and substate district levels.

In San Diego, the agency administrator has been using joint staff meetings and an interagency planning committee to develop agency objectives and identify potential areas of cooperation among service providers. To this extent, the county super-agency reflects the pattern of preliminary steps taken by the state super-agencies in the first six months of existence. In each of the states, these discussions were undertaken before identification of goals of an integrated service delivery system.

Resources and Incentives Available to the Integrator

There are five major types of resources available to the integrator in the development of linkages among the previously separate service providers. First is a legislative mandate to develop a cohesive service group. Second is the resource of legal powers delegated by law. Third is the availability of special project or demonstration funds to test new systems. Fourth is development of planning staff capacity to examine critically the existing systems of the service providers. Fifth is the incentive of increasing federal funding participation in services.

The mandate for services integration in Florida is being carried out in pilot projects for services consolidation and coordination, long-range planning in each functional service to reduce institutionalization, and analysis of existing departmental programs to develop linkages in core services and continuity for the same client groups between areas of specialization.

Resources available to the department have included special demonstration project funding, which has helped fund planning and evaluation staff, as well as a legislative mandate to develop a strong service system. The principal incentives to the extensive review and continuing redesign of the state service system has been the funding flexibility of Titles IV-A and XVI.

In Maine, the department has been pursuing development of planning and computer-based records and financial management systems as a means to improving delivery of state services. To that end, demonstration funds have been placed on development of a computer-based system of administration of assistance payments and organization at a regional level for separation of social services from income maintenance. The department, however, has not developed a central staff for planning and evaluation of all departmental services.

Field staff for all bureau are being colocated in regional service facilities. A model central core services system of outreach, intake, information, referral, and follow-up is being developed through a test in one bureau along substate regional lines.

Not all human service functions are assigned by law to the department in Utah. In that state's substate district experiment to improve service delivery, the governor's support, as an additional resource, has been instrumental in obtaining the cooperation and participation of other state agencies responsible for service functions such as vocational rehabilitation, education, and employment.

In Massachusetts, an HEW staffing grant is being used to fund a staff to work with the regional staffs to attempt to improve the delivery of services of the providers in the Executive Office of Human Services.

It is expected that this staff will undertake such activities as design of a standard intake system for all categories of services. Consumer interest will be strongly represented in the actions of this team, which will work with community groups to determine gaps in the service system and with agencies to correct them. Primary emphasis will be given to welfare programs.

COMPARISON OF INTEGRATIVE LINKAGES AND TECHNIQUES USED BY INTEGRATORS

The directed coordination projects used a number of integrative linkages to affect the service delivery system. In particular, planning and programing and fiscal linkages may be used more extensively in directed coordination projects than in voluntary or mediated coordination. These directly affect the organizational setting and funding arrangements for provision of core and direct services. Table 9.1 reflects linkage development in these projects.

TABLE 9.1

Linkage Development in Five Directed Coordination Projects

Linkages	Linkages in Planning or Initial Stages of Development (percent)	Linkages Partially or Fully Developed (percent)
I. Fiscal		
1. Joint budgeting	20	80
2. Joint funding	60	—
3. Fund transfer	—	—
4. Purchase of service	60	40
II. Personnel practices		
1. Consolidated personnel administration	40	20
2. Joint use of staff	60	40
3. Staff transfer	20	—
4. Staff outstationing	20	60
5. Colocation	40	20
III. Planning and programing		
1. Joint planning	80	20
2. Information-sharing	40	60
3. Joint programing	60	40
4. Joint development of operating policies	—	100
5. Joint evaluation	60	20
IV. Adminstrative support services		
1. Record-keeping	40	20
2. Grants-management	20	40
3. Central support services	20	40
V. Core services		
1. Outreach	80	—
2. Intake	80	—
3. Diagnosis	80	—
4. Referral	100	—
5. Follow-up	80	—
VI. Case coordination[*]	—	—
Percent of total possible linkages	42	24

*Linkages in this category deemed inappropriate.

156

Planning and Programing

The planning and programing linkages include joint planning, joint development of operating policies, joint programing, information-sharing, and joint evaluation. In each case, the planning and programing linkages occurred to some degree. The typical pattern was first information-sharing through joint staff meetings under the integrator. In this setting, the previously separate service providers began to develop jointly with the integrator the operating policies of the agency. Staff support for joint planning and programing then developed on the basis of perceived need by the integrator and service providers for a structured planning process.

In Florida, initial staff meetings of the service providers served to begin an exchange of information regarding each provider's programs, services, resources, procedures, and legal requirements. Joint development of operating policies evolved from the staff meetings through the concern of the integrator to reduce conflicts in separate policies of the service providers.

Approximately one year following creation of the Florida super-agency, a division of planning and evaluation was established with responsibility for departmental planning, programing, and evaluation. However, these tasks are not performed solely by the division. Rather, the division staff works with counterparts in each service provider to examine its total service delivery system, assess needs, and jointly develop programs. The division then serves as a focal point for drawing together the separate systems of service providers.

In Utah, there are only two staff members in the Office of the Executive Director charged with responsibility for departmental planning and programing. As in Florida, information-sharing and joint development of operating policies are performed in the context of staff meetings of the service providers under the integrator. Planning, programing, and evaluation remain separate staff functions within each service provider, while staff in the director's office serve as coordinators of departmental planning activities.

Maine exhibits many of the same characteristics. Information-sharing and joint development of operating policies are performed through staff meetings under the direction of the department commissioner. Planning, programing, and evaluation functions remain separate in each service provider. Most of the planning issues dealt with at the departmental level have centered around management of the social services system. For this purpose, the commissioner has a small staff supporting the individual service providers. Preliminary plans have been developed, subject to approval of the Maine legislature, to implement a single service system for the department.

Massachusetts is using committees composed of representatives of each service provider supported by staff in the Office of the Secretary to perform planning and programing activities related to specific client areas. In so doing, planning activities cross organizational lines of the service providers. Examples include planning and programing services related to handicapped children, alcoholism services, community-based correctional services, health care in institutions, and comprehensive child care services. As in the other cases, information-sharing and joint development of operating policies occurs through staff meetings of the service providers under the direction of the integrator.

In San Diego, staff meetings with the integrator are beginning with information-sharing. The county super-agency has not yet progressed to development of other planning linkages. The super-agency has, however, established an interagency planning committee. In programing, service providers have been jointly developing a youth service bureau.

Fiscal

The most important fiscal linkage in directed coordination projects is joint budgeting. This linkage, in fact, reflects an exercise of a specific power over the service providers delegated by law to the integrator.

Budget powers over service providers were delegated to the integrator in Florida, Utah, Maine, Massachusetts, and San Diego County. Florida has a program budgeting system that facilitates development of a joint budget for the department reflecting programs and priorities.

In Utah, the budget of the service providers must have approval of the board governing each service provider as well as the integrator. It is the integrator, however, who makes the budget request presentation for his department as part of the governor's recommended budget message to the state legislature.

In San Diego, service providers prepare preliminary budgets for review by the agency administrator (integrator). The agency's budget is then consolidated and presented to the chief administrative officer and county board of supervisors.

While joint funding and fund transfers had not been implemented in any of the cases, plans are being developed for joint funding of services in Florida and Massachusetts. Plans for and beginning implementation of purchase of services among service providers is occurring in each of the cases. In particular, Florida is using purchase of services provisions in Titles IV-A and XVI as a focal point for an extensive review and analysis of all departmental programs and services.

158

Personnel Practices

Consolidated personnel administration is often viewed as a typical characteristic of directed coordination projects. However, the four cases do not bear this out.

In Maine, the super-agency has consolidated traditional personnel functions organizationally through a division of administrative services. Florida, on the other hand, is establishing general policies and procedures to guide personnel practices in the department though staff to support the personnel system remain in each service provider. Service providers in Utah deal directly and individually with the state personnel office in the context of approved and budgeted positions. However, a plan has been developed for a consolidated office for administrative services including traditional personnel functions. In Massachusetts, while there is a staff member in the Office of the Secretary charged with coordinating administrative services, staff to support the personnel system remains with each service provider.

In San Diego, the individual service providers deal directly with the county civil service commission in matters of personnel administration.

Joint use of staff is beginning in both Florida and Utah through demonstration projects. Both states have projects where core service staffs are jointly used by all departmental service providers (Kearns, Utah and Palm Beach County, Florida). Outstationing of staff of one provider in the facilities of another provider is routinely occurring in each case as a means of providing services to eligible clientele. Examples include stationing of social services staff in correctional reception centers or vocational rehabilitation counselors in correctional facilities or facilities of social service providers.

Colocation of service providers' staff in a common facility is occurring in Florida, Utah, and Maine. Particular examples include special projects in Florida and Utah (Palm Beach County and Kearns, respectively). Maine is assembling a series of regional facilities as a common facility for staff of all service providers in the department.

Administrative Support Services

Of the three linkages, central support services, grants-management, and record-keeping, the central support services of consolidated accounting, auditing, purchasing, and materials management predominate. Both Florida and Maine have centralized staffs for these functions with equal organizational status to the service

159

providers. Grants-management functions in each of the cases remain decentralized to the service providers with responsibility for implementation of work associated with each grant. However, service providers in each case meet with the integrator for purposes of reviewing activities and resolving problems associated with grants management.

Utah, Florida, and Maine have been developing, through demonstration projects, unified record-keeping systems regarding services to clients. Each has not yet applied the system to statewide use, though portions of the system such as assistance payments and Medicare benefits have been implemented on a statewide basis. Massachusetts is using staff from the Office of the Secretary to begin work on standardization of client data.

Core Services

The direct services linkages of core services include outreach, intake, diagnosis, referral, and follow-up. For the most part, the service delivery systems of the service providers in each case are separate and distinct. However, demonstration projects are being used in Florida, Utah, Maine, and Massachusetts to begin to develop a unified core services system for all service providers in the department.

In Florida, the Palm Beach County project includes a single core services staff of state employees. Another variation is a contract between the State and Metropolitan Dade County to provide core services for the state service providers.

In Utah, the Kearns demonstration project includes a core services staff for service providers of the super-agency and other service providers in state government. (Employment services and vocational rehabilitation are examples.)

Similarly, a core service staffing and management system plan is being tested in regional offices in Maine.

In Massachusetts, a portion of the work associated in developing standardized case data includes an examination of the possibility of a central core services staff.

IMPACT ON ACCESSIBILITY, CONTINUITY,
AND EFFICIENCY

The success measures used in this section to describe the impact of the directed coordination projects are increased accessibility to the client to enter the service system, the continuity with which the client moves through the system of services, and efficiency resulting from elimination of duplication of service delivery and economies of scale.

Impact of the directed coordination projects is primarily limited to instances where, following creation of the super-agency, internal reorganizations are considered to develop improved points of entry into the system of services. Though in different stages of development, demonstration projects in Florida, Utah, Maine, and Massachusetts will eventually create a common system of core services as the point of access to the direct services of the providers in the super-agency. Similarly, Florida, Utah, Maine, and Massachusetts are pursuing the development of improved community-based services and deemphasizing institutional services.

While improvement in community-based services among the separate providers increases accessibility, it is the provision of core services across the range of providers as in the Florida and Utah demonstration projects that substantially affects the continuity of services to the client.

The legislative intent in each case and expressed in the creation of the super-agencies has been to achieve administrative efficiencies over the previous pattern of separate service providers. Reduction of duplication can occur through use of a common core services system and supporting records system.

Issues of economies of scale, however, present another situation. Development of a comprehensive planning staff in Florida represents development of a function within the super-agency that could not have otherwise been done. Similarly, preliminary plans in Florida to develop joint facilities for extensive diagnostic and evaluation services for both clients of vocational rehabilitation and retardation services represents reduction in costs to perform similar and associated services.

FACILITATORS OF DIRECTED COORDINATION

There are a number of factors that facilitate development of the characteristics of services integration through directed coordination projects. These are the organization of the project (in this case a super-agency) by means of legislation; the delegation of specific powers to the integrator over the service providers; the extent to which the integrator is able to promote internal reorganization of the super-agency after its creation; and the use of demonstration grants to develop new systems.

The definition of a directed coordination project indicates a degree of authority over the service providers. The most extensive powers of direct line authority, powers of appointment and dismissal of directors of service providers, control over service provider budgets, and power to undertake internal reorganizations, were granted in the creation of the Florida, Maine, and San Diego super-agencies. In Utah, the integrator must work with lay boards attached to each division (service provider). He shares power of appointment and budget review with the division boards. In Massachusetts, the secretary has direct line authority and budgeting control over service providers but does not have the power of appointment or internal reorganization. Therefore, he is dealing with an organizational status quo.

Within the limitations of powers delegated to the integrator, demonstration grant funds have been used in the four state super-agencies to develop new systems of service delivery. Greater organizational change is anticipated in Florida and Maine where the integrators have the power of appointment of directors of service providers and the power to affect internal reorganizations of the department. Both Utah and Massachusetts super-agencies are limited in these powers; however, they have the strong support of the governors to obtain cooperation of service providers in revamping the states' service delivery system.

In San Diego, because of the short history of the agencies, these powers have not yet been tested in obtaining changes in internal organization and modification of service delivery.

INHIBITORS OF DIRECTED COORDINATION

There are two major inhibitors to the development of character-istics of services integration among directed coordination projects. First is the lack of flexibility in state and local appropriations. Second is a history of recalcitrance among service providers to relinquish control of their separate service delivery systems.

In the first instance, which particularly applies to the states, legislative bodies are reluctant to grant a great deal of discretion in appropriations for services. For the most part, the legislatures tend to look for traditional services in budget requests and appro-priate funds for those specific services. Florida is one exception, where the secretary has discretionary authority to transfer up to 5 percent of the departmental budget.

Therefore, the departmental planning process must be closely tied to the budget cycle and a strong case built for major changes. This is one of the contributing reasons that major system changes are being undertaken as demonstration projects with other funding sources.

Secondly, the possession of specific powers by the integrator does not automatically change attitudes of the previously separate service providers. Rather than strongly asserting the formal powers, the integrator tends to attempt to create a cooperative atmosphere for coordination of services among the various providers. Again, a strategy of demonstration projects provides a setting to illustrate payoffs to the providers. The history of each project indicates a slow process initiated by the integrator to break down the reluctance of the individual service providers to relinquish control of separate service systems and participate in the creation of a unified departmental service system.

10

**COMPARATIVE ANALYSIS
OF MEDIATED
COORDINATION PROJECTS**

DEFINITION OF MEDIATED COORDINATION

In mediated coordination, the primary mission of the integrator is the development of linkages between autonomous service providers rather than the provision of direct service. Therefore, the integrator focuses on improving the functioning of the service delivery system rather than obtaining or changing specific services on behalf of an individual client.

SUMMARY DESCRIPTION OF THE MEDIATED COORDINATION PROJECTS

Common Factors and Project Characteristics

This chapter analyzes five projects employing the mode of mediated coordination. It does not include projects classified as neighborhood service centers. They are considered separately in Chapter 12.

The five mediated coordination projects included in this chapter are a mental health center in San Francisco, a mental retardation project in Cleveland, a child care project in Phoenix, a juvenile delinquency prevention project in South Bend, and a federation of neighborhood service centers in Pittsburgh.

These five projects share a number of common characteristics. The integrators do not serve clients directly, although the agencies affiliated with the projects relate to large numbers of clients. For example, neighborhood service centers federated through the United

Family Services Project served an average of 4,150 clients per month between January and September 1971 while the centers participating in the Phoenix Child Care Project provide day care to more than 1,000 children.

The focus of these projects is the creation of an integrated service delivery system organized around a specific problem group in three cases (Youth Advocacy Program, Cleveland Mental Retardation Project, United Family Services Project), function (Westside Mental Health Center), or age (Phoenix Child Care Project).

Three of these projects are sponsored by private, nonprofit corporations while the remaining two projects are performed under the aegis of a private voluntary council—in each case the local health and welfare planning council.

The effect of these characteristics on service delivery is discussed further in this study.

Description of Projects

Community Council Child Care Project: Phoenix, Arizona

The Community Council Child Care Project, a component project of the Maricopa County health and welfare planning council, was designated by the Arizona State Department of Public Welfare in mid-1970 as the single conduit of Title IV-A day care funds for 19 private and public agencies providing day care services in this 9,000 square mile county. The United Fund provides the local share for Title IV-A funds. A Project Committee composed of an equal number of representatives from three categories—the health and welfare planning council, professional and public agencies responsible for the provision of child care, and clients—is responsible for carrying out the objectives of the project. A child-care task force consisting of all public and voluntary day care and Head Start directors provides additional coordination, plans cooperative programs, and servies in an advisory capacity. The Project Committee is also seeking recognition as the local 4-C Committee.

A small administrative staff hired by the health and welfare planning council is regarded as the integrator. The staff supports the activities of the various committees of the project, coordinates the activities of its funded centers, and develops a network for integrating agencies and resources related to child care.

Greater Cleveland Mental Retardation Development Project: Cleveland, Ohio

The Greater Cleveland Mental Retardation Development Project, a component project of Cleveland's health and welfare planning council from 1966 through 1970, was an HEW research and demonstration project to develop an effective system welding autonomous public and private agencies to serve the mentally retarded in the metropolitan area. A small central staff, functioning as the integrator, worked under the direction of a subcommittee of the council.

United Family Services: Pittsburgh, Pennsylvania

United Family Services is a nonprofit corporation designated by the Pennsylvania State Department of Public Welfare as the single conduit of Title IV-A funds to a federation of 11 neighborhood service centers in and around Pittsburgh and funded in mid-1970. (The United Fund provides the majority of local match for the Title IV-A funds.) These neighborhood centers provide clients who qualify for public assistance or Title XIX medical assistance with the basic services of information and referral, follow-up and crisis intervention, supplemented by supportive service in such areas as employment, housing, health, law, home and money management, child care and development, and education and training.

The board of United Family Services, composed of two representatives from each neighborhood center's client-dominated policymaking Family Service Committee and five representatives of the health and welfare planning council, provides policy direction to a central administrative staff. This staff functions as the integrator.

Westside Community Mental Health Center: San Francisco, California

Beginning implementation in 1969, Westside Community Mental Health Center is a nonprofit corporation designated by the County Health Department as the single conduit of state and federal mental health funds to a consortium of 16 agencies (for example, hospitals, medical clinic, social service agencies, half-way houses) providing mental health services to residents of one five-square catchment area of the city.

Emergency, outpatient, inpatient, partial hospitalization, and aftercare services provided by the consortium members are coordinated by a central administrative staff funded by an NIMH staffing grant. Policy for the project is developed by a Board of Directors composed of representatives of the 16 consortium agencies and elected neighborhood residents. The center director and staff are the integrators.

Youth Advocacy Program: South Bend, Indiana

The Youth Advocacy Program develops opportunities and alternatives to meet the needs of delinquent and potentially delinquent youth between the ages of 15 and 25 in and around South Bend. The project was funded in mid-1970 through the local Urban Coalition with a three-year research and demonstration grant from HEW's Youth Development and Delinquency Prevention Administration. Receiving policy direction from a committee of youth, the central administrative staff is supplemented by field representatives stationed at established community agencies (for example, School District, city government, recreation commission, Model Cities agency). The central staff and field representatives function as the integrator.

COMPARISON OF THE PROJECT INTEGRATORS

Three factors—authority over autonomous service providers, the intent of the integrator, and resources under control of the integrator—affected the development of integrative linkages and the impact of mediated projects on service delivery.

Authority over Service Providers

By definition, the integrative staff of mediated projects do not have formal authority over the service providers participating in project activity. Most of the projects attempted to compensate for agency autonomy by developing membership agreements, letters of commitment, and so on, to bind agencies to the objectives and authority of the project. These agreements were executed with all participating agencies and preceded purchase-of-service agreements with those agencies that were to provide direct service under the aegis of the project.

The projects differed only in degree of formality and range of conditions and sanctions imposed by these agreements. For example, in one project, the membership agreement signed by participating agencies not only outlined the types of cooperative arrangements in which the agencies must participate but also affirmed the authority of the project's central administrative staff to coordinate those activities of the service providers that were part of the project.

Intent of the Integrator

The perceived role of the integrator, both in terms of project objectives and the objectives and/or philosophy of the integrative staff, has affected the allocation of resources (time, personnel, money) devoted to, and the approach taken in, developing integrating linkages. The objectives of these projects stressed rationalization of the service delivery system rather than manipulation of the system on a client-by-client basis. They uniformly specified activities such as planning, coordination, resource mobilization, and program development. Some also included increasing the availability of service, while the Youth Advocacy Program and the Cleveland Mental Retardation Project also emphasized increasing the relevancy of existing services.

Moreover, the integrative staffs all placed priority on the development and support of types of interaction between service providers that had not occurred prior to their intervention. The very model structure enabled them to do so without responsibility for direct service delivery; these staffs had both the perspective of the total delivery system and the time available to initiate and pursue coordination among service providers. Finally, the integrators in these five projects recognized that project success primarily depended on the changes that only service providers were empowered to make; and therefore, the integrators used a range of techniques to parlay the resources and incentives at their command to achieve integrating linkages and to gain legitimacy for them in the eyes of service providers, clients, and community powers.

Resources under the Control of the Integrator

In mediated coordination projects, there was a staff whose primary mission was developing coordination among service providers. In a few projects, the integrator also had control over service providers' access to funds. (The ways in which integrative staff used these resources are described in the next section.) Each project had and used staff expertise to develop linkages. Three of the projects (Phoenix Child Care Project, United Family Services Project, and Westside Mental Health Center) were the sole conduit of federal funds to service providers. This fact significantly affected their success in initiating coordinative arrangements between agencies and the techniques they used to develop them. On the other hand, the limited funds available to both the Youth Advocacy Program and the Cleveland Mental Retardation Project prompted different approaches to modification of the service delivery system.

Other resources that were common to some, though not all, of the projects were (1) the professional stature and/or "clout" of integrator personnel and (2) the integrator's access to a client group seen by the service providers as hostile or fearsome. Both of these factors affected the initial (or continued) willingness of agencies to consider cooperating with proposals of the integrative staff. For example, the influence or control over resources of a project's sponsor carried over to the integrative staff. One project was sponsored by the health and welfare planning council, which allocated United Fund money that financed or provided seed money for new programs to many agencies the integrator wanted to involve in the project. Therefore, when approached by the integrative staff, these agencies were predisposed to try to cooperate.

In the case of the Youth Advocacy Program, sponsorship by the Urban Coalition (composed of influential people in the community) gave the project enough initial legitimacy in the view of service providers to allow its integrative staff to begin discussions about participation by these agencies in the project. Likewise, professional stature can produce a similar effect, as illustrated in another project in which the professional standing of the project director enhanced the readiness of fellow professionals heading service agencies to cooperate with project staffs' overtures.

Moreover, resources took the form of personal relationships existing between integrative staff and agency executives, legislators, private funding sources, and so on. These relationships predated project development and helped the integrators to achieve their objectives. For instance, the integrator's personal association with state legislators and high state officials enabled one project to circumvent much of the red tape connected with funding. This success encouraged participating agencies to cement their association with the project.

In three projects the integrator's easy relationship with a client group regarded as militant or hostile also produced a certain initial willingness of service providers to discuss cooperation. Fear of prospective clients by service providers seemed related both to a recognition of past negligence in meeting these clients' needs and to concern that pressure generated by the client group would threaten agency survival. Association with an organized militant client group achieved local share funding for two projects and cooperation from previously unresponsive agencies for another.

COMPARISON OF INTEGRATIVE LINKAGES AND TECHNIQUES USED BY THE INTEGRATORS

While there was broad similarity in the types of integrative linkages used by mediated coordination projects to affect service delivery to clients, those projects that controlled the funds flowing to service providers developed more linkages than did the other projects. Linkage development in the five projects is illustrated in Table 10.1.

TABLE 10.1

Linkage Development in Five Mediated Coordination Projects

Linkages	Linkages in Planning or Initial Stages of Development (percent)	Linkages Partially or Fully Developed (percent)
I. Fiscal		
1. Joint budgeting	—	60
2. Joint funding	—	60
3. Fund transfer	—	—
4. Purchase of service	—	60
II. Personnel practices		
1. Consolidated personnel administration	40	40
2. Joint use of staff	—	20
3. Staff transfer	—	—
4. Staff outstationing	—	40
5. Colocation	—	—
III. Planning and programing		
1. Joint planning	—	100
2. Information-sharing	—	100
3. Joint programing	20	80
4. Joint development of operating policies	—	60
5. Joint evaluation	40	60
IV. Administrative support services		
1. Record-keeping	20	60
2. Grants management	—	80
3. Central support services	—	100
V. Core services		
1. Outreach	—	—
2. Intake	—	—
3. Diagnosis	—	20
4. Referral	—	20
5. Follow-up	—	20
VI. Case coordination		
1. Case conference	—	20
2. Case coordinator	—	20
3. Case team	—	—
Percent of total possible linkages	5	41

170

The Linkage Potential of Single-Point Funding

The Phoenix Child Care Project, United Family Services Project, and Westside Mental Health Center achieved their most significant leverage over service providers by virtue of their designation as the single conduit for certain federal funds. This single-point funding gave the integrator the capability both to deliver and to control some or all the service providers' financial resources. Service providers so urgently wanted funds to sustain or expand their direct service that they either actively solicited participation in the project or were willing to accept the integrator's coordination demands in return for new money.

Therefore, early in the projects' evolution, a reciprocity developed in which the promise and delivery of funds made the service providers willing to do what the integrative staff wanted—namely, join together to develop and set policy for the projects. As a result, some or all of the service providers were involved in the development of the project and subsequently participated in determination of operating policies. Half of the Westside Mental Health Center's board of directors was composed of staff of the service providers, while the United Family Services Project's board was composed primarily of representatives of the policy boards of the neighborhood centers and the Phoenix Child Care Project's board and task force came in part from both day-care center directors and related service providers. Participation by service providers on the projects' board of directors in Westside and United Family Services enabled their representatives to share in the selection of the integrative staff, which, in turn, strengthened that staff's effectiveness in working with providers.

In mediated coordination, it is possible to see a cumulative process of linkage development, beginning with this initial involvement of service providers in project development. Their association with the integrator is next loosely formalized through membership agreements, primarily signifying acceptance of project objectives. It is then cemented by a purchase-of-service agreement, which specifies reciprocal rights and responsibilities. The Phoenix Child Care Project's agreements were limited to rudimentary stipulations pursuant to the flow of funds for direct service. On the other hand, Westside Mental Health Center's purchase-of-service documents bound the providers with formal sanctions to such diverse commitments as participation in joint programing and immediate assignment of clients for service after intake by any other member provider. In the United Family Services Project, purchase-of-service agreements tied the neighborhood centers to the project. Also agreements were executed on behalf of the neighborhood centers with countywide service providers to give preference to clients referred by affiliated neighborhood centers, while serving other clients constrained only by the project's client eligibility standards.

Moreover, building on shared decision-making at the board level and central fund administration, each of the projects had begun incrementally to establish procedures for joint budgeting through requirements for review and approval of program proposals by the board. These same conditions have produced in the United Family Services Project a joint funding arrangement—fund pooling. Fund pooling, as described in an earlier chapter, resulted in the redistribution of Title IV-A funds so that neighborhood centers able to generate larger scale contributions received in return $2 for every $1, with the excess furnished to less fortunate centers on the basis of need in addition to supporting the project's integrative staff.

Single-point funding also placed the integrative staff in a position to help its participating agencies by acting as an administrative buffer between the funding source and the service providers. The integrator negotiated solutions to concerns of the funding source on behalf of the agencies and interpreted regulations and data requirements to the agencies. This assistance served to encourage involvement by small, newly established, or conservative agencies that would otherwise be deterred by the bewildering requirements of the various funding sources.

Other integrating linkages that correlated with these "single conduit" projects were systematic information-sharing between providers and consolidated personnel administration. In each case, information-sharing was operative at both the board level and through at least one additional organizational mechanism—for example, Westside Mental Health Center's clinical advisory councils, the United Family Services Project's neighborhood center directors' meeting, and the Phoenix Child Care Project's Title IV-A center directors' meeting and child care task force. Consolidated personnel administration was advanced by such means as developing minimum personnel standards and centralizing staff recruitment. However, the sensitivity of this linkage is seen in the experience of one project, where initial efforts by the integrator to centralize hiring and firing so effectively deadlocked all other cooperation that the attempt was abandoned, leaving considerable ill-will to be overcome.

The linkages above were most fully developed in projects in which there was single-point funding, but apart from this resource, all five projects had a central staff. The following discusses what the presence of a coordinating staff adds to a service delivery system.

The Linkage Potential of Coordinating Staff and Expertise

In each project, the central staff could interrelate the activities of service providers partially because they were not competing in delivery of services but were engaged in assisting the delivery agencies. The integrative staff was a resource to service providers and, in the process of helping these agencies, affected their policies, procedures, and the ultimate delivery of services to clients.

These central support services ranged from the integrator's employment of one auditor to work with all participating agencies to the provision of programing and grantsmanship assistance. Although offered in a variety of ways, program development and grantsmanship always stimulated development of new services in the total delivery system, exploring new concepts and sources of sponsorship. In some cases, central staff prepared standardized checklists to guide the development of specific types of programs by a variety of agencies and obtained commitments from the funding source(s) to withhold money from programs not submitted in the prescribed format.

In the Cleveland Mental Retardation Project, the integrative staff persuaded a funding source to approve only those applications submitted in accordance with a ''Self-Evaluation Checklist'' prepared by that staff for agencies and organizations applying for funds to establish or support residential care facilities for the mentally retarded. All parties involved benefited from this device. It gave the applicants a structured process for developing a residential care program, while at the same time it gave the funding source a technical standard against which to assess applications. Finally, the ''Self-Evaluation Checklist'' was a way for the integrative staff to influence the range and content of programs and ensure that they would be developed to meet community needs and force providers into a process of program assessment.

Some projects had a program development and grantsmanship specialist on the central staff to respond to requests by participating agencies on an as-needed basis. In the United Family Services Project, this resource person was able to use requests for such assistance to encourage joint programing between the neighborhood center asking for help and other centers operating such programs or other centers with similar problems in their neighborhoods.

In addition, the use of program development expertise to encourage collaboration between agencies was also used within the highly structured Westside Mental Health Center to initiate a coalition of specific agencies within the consortium to jointly program a comprehensive drug project—it later evolved into a professionally staffed component of the Center.

This combination was also used by integrative staff to involve nonparticipating agencies in project activities. For example, the Youth Advocacy Program used this expertise both to encourage joint programing between three small agencies seeking Model Cities funding and as a technique to establish ad hoc coalitions of service providers. In this instance, because the Youth Advocacy Program's objectives related to institutional change (which service providers could not fully endorse since they were the institutions), integrative staff focused on shared operational objectives around which to organize joint programing and information-sharing sessions to meet the needs of a particular client group or for specific programs.

In addition, the Youth Advocacy Program included a special variation in the use of program development capability to integrate services. In order to realize its objectives of advocacy, the project outstationed staff (field representatives) in major community institutions. Once on site, these field representatives were able to secure partial agency acceptance by helping to develop new programs within the agency and also seek funds outside the agency.

Another central support service provided by integrative staff in the five projects was general fact-gathering activity. Staff was able to assert themselves in the view of service providers and influence their activities by becoming the source of information not only about funding information but also about the needs of the client population. Possession of this kind of data had two kinds of effects. First, service providers came to the integrative staff for documentation of need to complete requirements of funding requests in which the staff would not otherwise have been involved. As a result, integrative staff was able to suggest program or plan modifications so that service delivery gaps could be filled and overlap eliminated. In the Cleveland Mental Retardation Project, staff was requested by the county to prepare the initial plans for new state-mandated county boards to plan and deliver services to the mentally retarded, enabling the integrative staff to chart the objectives and program of these important additions to the service delivery system.

Second, fact-gathering was used as a rationale to prepare directories of agencies serving the client population. Development of these directories enabled (1) integrative staff to work with individual agencies to define their role within the service delivery system, (2) agencies to view themselves and each other as part of a total delivery system, (3) agencies to satisfy their concerns about having an avalanche of new clients by seeing the variety of services presently available from other providers, and (4) smaller agencies to obtain public awareness of their services.

Further, as an outgrowth of, and corollary to, these kinds of program development and fact-gathering activities, integrative staff developed joint training opportunities for service providers. Joint training sessions not only focused on the improvement of service quality but also attempted to expand the agencies' awareness of their relationship with other services necessary to meet the range of client needs and increase the contacts between agencies in the service delivery system. Associated with the issue of training (and in response to requirements of state legislation that controlled some of its funds), the Westside Mental Health Center established a consultative unit composed of the integrative staff and various employees of the participating agencies to provide technical assistance to consortium members, community groups, and so on.

Finally, the availability of staff whose only task was to facilitate cooperation and coordination between agencies and to assist agencies permitted a score of miscellaneous activities to be undertaken that would not otherwise have occurred. The following are some of these endeavors: coordination and evaluation of short-term projects arranged by service providers; development of standard administrative forms and procedures, intake and eligibility policies, and record-keeping formats; representation of agencies on related committees and planning groups (for example, both the Phoenix Child Care Project and the Youth Advocacy Program served on local manpower planning committees); and preparation of community information materials.

In general, the integrators in these five projects operated within the framework of their authority relationships with other agencies, their perceived role and whatever resources they controlled, to coordinate the activities of various service providers by developing linkages between them.

IMPACT ON ACCESSIBILITY, CONTINUITY, AND EFFICIENCY

These projects, whose objectives emphasized the development of planning and coordinative arrangements between agencies, have little initial effect, primarily because of the amount of time required to develop effective linkages. (For example, the Cleveland Mental Retardation Project's attempt to involve the school district in one program took three years.) However, the projects indicate capacity to produce, over time, extensive and lasting impact on accessibility, continuity, and efficiency. There were sufficient indicators that the more mature projects were beginning to have such impacts.

Accessibility

The clearest examples of efforts that impact accessibility are provided by the most mature projects—Westside and Cleveland. In the Westside Mental Health Center, joint determination of operating policies, information-sharing, and joint programing produced standardized intake and eligibility procedures, which allowed a client to enter at any consortium agency and be referred to any other—including the 24-hour crisis clinic, itself an example of enhanced accessibility. Accessibility was also enhanced in Cleveland when administrative linkages, combined with short-term funding, produced an information and referral unit that was taken over by the county's Mental Health and Mental Retardation Board after the project ended.

In addition, the Cleveland Mental Retardation Project used such linkages as joint programing, information-sharing, and central support services to change the service delivery system for the mentally retarded. The following indicate some of these changes after integration: nine times as many retarded adolescents and adults were reportedly receiving services through the Bureau of Vocational Rehabilitation; four times as many retarded youngsters with an IQ under 50 obtained special schooling; and there was a 30 percent increase in enrollment of educable retarded youngsters in public school programs.

Continuity

The projects used administrative linkages (for example, joint programing, budgeting, information-sharing, purchase of service, administrative support services) to impact continuity. These linkages are employed as part of project efforts to rationalize the service delivery system by identifying and filling service gaps, increasing service relevancy, developing complementary service, and standardizing eligibility and intake procedures. These administrative linkages enabled projects to commit agencies to provide a specific amount of service and to plan and deliver their service in a manner which complemented the service of other providers. In addition, they facilitated increased communication among service providers. Finally, a few projects have begun to utilize administrative linkages to weld providers into a tight-knit system that can plan, program, budget, and evaluate across a broad range of client needs.

Efficiency

Services integration within the framework of mediated coordination had significant impact on efficiency because arrangements are developed simultaneously for all clients rather than on a client-by-client basis. Focus on the delivery system enables the integrator to disclose service duplication and overlap and assess total needs. Moreover, the provision of staff expertise to providers has resulted in a redirection of existing service resources and a modification of delivery methods. Therefore, the projects contribute to solution of delivery problems both quantitatively (the number of clients affected) and qualitatively (the effort to make services more complementary in content and delivery more expeditious). In addition, the availability of staff to act on behalf of each provider to support cooperative efforts, act as grantsmen, negotiate with various funding sources, and so on, could free the resources of the providers for service delivery.

In this connection, the United Family Services Project provided an interesting variation on impact in terms of economies of scale. Because of the linkages between the neighborhood centers, the efforts of individual centers to make services available to its clients made those services available to clients of other centers. For instance, when one center negotiated with a hospital with a countywide service area to treat its clients, that hospital became a resource to the other neighborhood centers.

FACILITATORS OF MEDIATED COORDINATION

Analysis of these projects disclosed many external factors (that is, outside the control of the integrator) that enhanced the integrator's ability to develop linkages between service providers.

First, in several cases, the environment was conducive to innovation. In the Cleveland Mental Retardation Project, there was a coincidence of several factors including increased militancy of parent group soliciting funds for programs for mentally retarded children, the interest of the Kennedy Administration in the field of mental retardation and the recommendation of subcommittee of the health and welfare planning council for increased emphasis on mental retardation. In the Westside Mental Health Center, the county health department was looking for ways to experiment in organizing the delivery of mental health services and had prior experience delegating the administration of its programs through purchase of service agreements. In other projects, one-time funding for services to low-income clients had terminated, prompting community pressure for something to be done.

Second, factors relating to the project's funding source promoted integrative efforts. For instance, in the Westside Mental Health Center and the Phoenix Child Care and United Family Services Projects, the funding source preferred to channel funds through a single entity. In addition, activities of the United Family Services and Phoenix Child Care Projects were appreciably enhanced because of the open-ended funding source in that funds were always available and the integrator did not have to make choices between providers but could involve them all in project activities. In one of the single-conduit projects, several agencies participated in all of the cooperative activities, not because they were presently receiving funds through the project but rather because there were funds to be had in the future. Lastly, certain requirements of the funding sources, especially in the Westside Mental Health Center, have stimulated the development of standardized client data for the purpose of evaluation, joint planning, and so on.

177

Third, being part of a new organization or an agency that had not yet developed bureaucratic, traditional, and/or political constraints allowed the integrative staff considerable latitude and flexibility in testing methods to achieve cooperation.

Fourth, in several cases, mostly clearly in the Youth Advocacy Program and the Westside Mental Health Center, certain service providers participated in project activities because they viewed their involvement as a way to influence other more traditional participating agencies. Finally, services integration efforts were enhanced when the objectives of the project coincided with the objectives of service providers with respect to maximizing services with existing funds, expanding service, and making services more effective and accessible.

INHIBITORS OF MEDIATED COORDINATION

The primary obstacle to services integration efforts was the length of time involved in developing the project itself and in perfecting linkages between service providers. For instance, in the Cleveland Mental Retardation Project, the initial recommendation that gave impetus to the project came in late 1962; a one-year planning project was approved in late 1964; the project was approved in early 1966 and ended in 1970, with the final implementation report completed in the fall of 1971. Also, in the Westside Mental Health Center, a psychiatrist in the community sent letters to five service providers in 1966 soliciting their cooperation; Westside did not begin until 1969. Therefore, in the Cleveland Mental Retardation Project and Youth Advocacy Program—both short-term demonstration projects—the limited funding period was, and is, in and of itself, an obstacle to the project.

In addition, there were other factors relating to funding source that inhibited integrative efforts. Funding delays and uncertainties consumed such a large part of the integrator's attention that developing linkages between service providers necessarily assumed a lower priority. Further, these delays and uncertainties also resulted from unresolved guidelines and conflicts between federal and state officials in formula grant programs—for example, Title IV-A. In addition, the negative attitudes of the funding source caused difficulties for the integrators. For example, in the Phoenix Child Care Project, the state welfare department's conservatism and reluctance to become involved in Title IV-A created stumbling blocks for the project at every turn. And in the case of the Cleveland Mental Retardation Project, the funding source pressed the integrator to provide direct service, thereby hampering efforts to focus available energy on developing linkages between providers.

178

A second inhibitor is best illustrated in the Westside Mental Health Center and the Phoenix Child Care Project. In an effort to involve service providers in a variety of cooperative efforts, an elaborate committee structure with overlapping memberships was developed. However, it appeared that the proliferation of committees was instead making the project structure increasingly incomprehensible to participating agencies.

Third, a variety of problems were generated because of reluctance of service providers to participate in the project. These included a reluctance to be involved in federal programs with their concomitant regulations and paperwork, to consider giving up their own prerogatives, to entertain the notion that they were part of the service delivery problem, and to participate with integrative staff who did not share their professional credentials.

A final inhibitor to the development of integrating linkages was the initial priority given by some of the integrators to program development expanding the service delivery system. This emphasis absorbed attention that would otherwise have been directed to establishing systematic, structured cooperation between service providers.

11

COMPARATIVE ANALYSIS
OF VOLUNTARY
COORDINATION PROJECTS

DEFINITION OF VOLUNTARY COORDINATION

In voluntary coordination, the integrator is responsible for the delivery of direct service itself as well as developing linkages with autonomous service providers for other services that support or complement his own, for example, Head Start central staff are responsible for activities such as child development and nutrition, as well as for involving other service providers such as health practitioners and social service agencies in the implementation of a comprehensive Head Start program.

SUMMARY DESCRIPTION OF THE
VOLUNTARY COORDINATION PROJECTS

Common Factors and Project Characteristics

This chapter analyzes five projects employing voluntary coordination. The five projects are a Drop-Out Prevention Project in Philadelphia; and Early Child Development Program in Galveston, Texas; Parent-Child Center projects in Portland, Oregon and Oakland, California; and a Head Start project in Jackson County, Oregon.

These five projects share a number of common characteristics. Each serves a relatively small client group: the smallest serves 55 families with preschool children (Portland Parent-Child Center) and the largest 250 high school students (Edison Drop-Out Project). In each, the integrator delivers a specific service to the client group and seeks to augment that service with others provided by autonomous organizations.

Because its client group is characterized by age or problem, each of the projects is involved in a much smaller system of services than would be one serving the diversified population of a selected geographic area.

The mode of entry to the service system in each project is through the prime or initial service and thence to the services supportive of and linked to the prime service. In each project, the prime service may be characterized as the education of children or adolescents. The supportive or linked services are an array that include nutrition, health, social services, vocational training, parent education and training, and family counseling.

The sponsor in three of the projects (Oakland and Portland Parent-Child Centers and Jackson County Head Start) is a private, nonprofit corporation. The other two projects (Edison Drop-Out Project and Galveston Child Development Project) are sponsored by a special-purpose public agency.

The effect of these characteristics on service delivery is discussed later in this book.

Summary Description of Projects

Edison Drop-Out Prevention Project: Philadelphia, Pennsylvania

The project serves 250 tenth-graders in an attempt to reduce the dropout rate. It directly provides an alternative education program oriented to individual needs and interests. Limited supportive services include medical and dental care, vocational education and administration, and legal aid.

The project sponsor is the Philadelphia Board of Education, which is also responsible for policy. Administrative responsibility is delegated by the board to the principal of Edison High School, who serves as the project director. There is a community advisory board composed of community workers, businesses, and representatives of community service organizations.

Administrative staff under the project director directly responsible for obtaining voluntary supporting services to the project are the assistant project director and the client service coordinator.

The project is financed through a Title VIII grant from the Office of Education, HEW. The project began operations in July 1971.

Galveston Early Child Development Program: Galveston, Texas

The project serves approximately 200 children through three components—day care, special education for the physically and mentally handicapped, and a bilingual program. Four other providers

181

deliver supportive services, including primary and secondary health care and social services.

The project sponsor is the Galveston Board of Education, which is also responsible for policy. There is an advisory board composed of 50 percent parents of the children served by the project and the other 50 percent public officials and community leaders.

Contact with supportive service providers is the responsibility of central school district staff. The project director plays a second role in obtaining voluntary coordination from the linked service providers. The assistant director is responsible for consumer participation and works directly with the parents and the community.

The project is financed through Section 1115, Title IV-A of the Social Security Act, and state special education funds. The project began operations in September 1971.

Parent-Child Center Project: Oakland, California

The project, currently operating out of two centers, serves children up to age three and mothers of 70 families on both a full- and part-time basis. The focus of the project is the enhancement of child development. Direct services provided by the project are education, nutrition, and social work counseling. Ten other providers deliver linked services, which include vocational training, health care for the mothers, and parent education related to child development and health.

Project sponsor is the Frederick Burke Foundation. Overall policy decisions are the responsibility of the project's board (Policy Advisory Committee) composed equally of parents in the program, community residents, and professionals representing supportive child care and social service agencies.

The project director and the staff social worker are primarily responsible for initiating and/or maintaining contact with the supportive service providers. In addition, the project staff function as a unit to unite the specialized elements of the delivery system.

The project is financed through the Parent-Child Center Program of the Office of Child Development, HEW. The project began operations in September 1969.

Parent-Child Services Project: Portland, Oregon

The project, currently serving 55 families (project capacity is 75 families), directly offers child development and social services designed to assist the family in solving its personal problems. Through four supportive agencies, health care and day care are provided.

Project sponsor is Portland Parent-Child Services, Inc. Policy decisions are the responsibility of the advisory board, composed of current clients and several graduates of the program. Due to poor administration and lack of technical assistance, the board has relinquished policy functions to the project director.

The project director and the social services coordinator are directly responsible for obtaining supportive services. Currently the only integrating linkages are purchase of service arrangements and core service linkages, primarily referral and follow-up.

The Portland Parent-Child Center is financed through the Parent-Child Center Program of the Office of Child Development, HEW. The project began operations in fall 1968.

Jackson County Child Development Centers Project: Jackson County, Oregon

The project currently operates four centers serving 135 children and directly provides education, nutrition, social services, and screening for special problems. Six other service providers, along with private health practitioners and supportive volunteer groups, provide health and individual functional services.

The project sponsor is Jackson County Child Development Centers, Inc. Policy direction and financial decisions are the responsibility of a governing board composed of representatives of local private and public agencies, target-area residents, and parents of Head Start children. In addition, a Parent Advisory Council was established (to comply with federal regulations) to approve program priorities and budgets developed by the board and assist the director in implementing personnel policies and program evaluation.

The project director and her staff, especially the social services and health coordinators, are responsible for linking autonomous service providers in the process of voluntary coordination.

COMPARISON OF THE PROJECT INTEGRATORS

Three characteristics shared by the integrators affected the development of linked services and the impact of the project on service delivery to its clients. These were the lack of authority, either organizationally or through contract, of the integrator over the supportive service providers; the goals and objectives of the project; and the resources and incentives available to the integrator.

Lack of Authority over Supportive Service Providers

None of the five projects had any administrative authority over the agencies providing supporting services; the voluntary coordination was typically informal. Exceptions were some purchase of service contracts (discussed below in the section on Linkages) and letters of commitment from participating agencies stating concurrence with the project objectives, which services the agency would provide, and other intended cooperation.

Such letters of commitment were rare and were more expressions of good faith than binding documents. These letters generally defined responsibilities and conditions for service and were used in the first year; but subsequent lapse has contributed to the deterioration of the projects' supportive service delivery system.

Goals and Objectives of the Integrator

The objectives of the integrators were primarily to provide a group of clients with a range of services in order to achieve some goal, such as reducing student dropout rates; minimizing handicaps arising from economic, cultural, and linguistic factors that interfere with adjustment and achievement in school; or enhancing the intellectual, physical, and emotional development of the clients. These objectives were reinforced by the federal grant requirements in each case. In each project, the supporting services were clustered around the basic service provided by the integrator. Emphasis was on manipulation of the existing service delivery system, either on behalf of the client group or on a client-by-client basis, rather than development of an integrated service delivery system.

The objectives and philosophy of the integrator staff were an outgrowth of the project's objectives. For example, the director of the Oakland Parent-Child Center has key responsibility for developing working relationships with linked service providers. At the same time she is responsible for day-to-day administration and supervision of the prime services of the project, as well as program development, planning, obtaining funding, and meeting federal grant requirements.

In another case, the health coordinator of Jackson County Head Start is responsible for provision of health services in the four centers, supervision of the staff, and coordination between the centers. She took the initiative in persuading other agencies providing health services and private practitioners to donate their services to project clients.

The one exception to this dual responsibility was the client service coordinator in the Edison Drop-Out Project, whose main function was to obtain service agreements from providers. She was not, however, a full-time member of the project.

These continuing direct service responsibilities of the staff limited the time available for coordination of supportive services.

This time limitation factor resulted in staff generally confining their approach to seeking service providers already offering the additional services needed by clients and thus attempting to form linkages. The integrator staff frequently negotiated small procedural adjustments, such as adapting the location or timing of service delivery to better serve particular clients, or conducting some special orientation or training. There was no attempt to make basic changes in the service content or delivery procedures, or to stimulate an agency to develop new services.

Resources and Incentives Available to the Integrator

The major and almost sole resource available to the integrator in the projects studied was the power to persuade service providers to connect or to link their services with those of the prime service. The ways in which projects did this are described in the sections on linkages and techniques.

A few projects, however, had two additional resources. These were the availability of funds to pay for some services if necessary and, second, strong commitment and efforts of the project director and staff. The second proved critical given the lack of formal authority and the constant demands made on time and energy by direct service responsibilities.

Additional resources appeared in individual projects. In one, the staff member responsible for forming working arrangements with external providers had good relationships with them prior to the project. These personal connections were parlayed into agreements to provide service. In another, the local school district (the project sponsor) had existing ties with supportive service providers which it extended to the project. In this same project (Galveston Child Development Project), and uniquely among the projects studied, the stature of those associated with the project sponsor helped to develop linkages. Most important was the fact that the board of education was composed of many powerful individuals in the community. The project advisory board also included community leaders.

These resources produced three related incentives for autonomous agencies to participate in the project. First, they perceived the integrator as able to assist or allow them to achieve their own goals. In one case, the Oakland Parent-Child Center, the county Mental Health Department provided consultation to the staff of the project because of its interest in providing preventive mental health services to a minority client group it had failed to reach through its own programs. Similarly, a goal-attainment incentive motivated the Jackson County school district to furnish services such as speech therapy, audiological screenings, and exchange of media to the project in order to meet the needs of low-income children who would eventually enter the school system it operated.

A second incentive was the opportunity to expand clientele. These five projects provided access to a concentrated target population, as well as making individual clients requiring specialized services easily available to service providers. In some projects, for example, staff of linked hospitals or voluntary health organizations provided health information and education to project clients brought together by project staff.

Third, in some projects, the integrator's ability to be a bridge and buffer between established, traditional, and usually large service providers and the client population was an incentive to the supporting service providers. It was particularly important in instances where the client group or community involved was perceived as difficult or threatening by the supportive service provider's administration or staff.

An example of all three incentives occurred in the Oakland Parent-Child Center, in which the local Red Cross provided classes in home health nursing and infant care to mothers at the project's facility. The operative incentives were the Red Cross's desire to reach clients of minority groups and the Parent-Child Center's staff ability to assemble a stable group of such clients and to act as an intermediary between the clients and the Red Cross.

In effect, the projects made it easy for service providers to fulfill their institutional objectives and responsibilities without making any additional effort or changing its service delivery system in any significant way. Participation as a supporting service to the prime service did not necessitate new skills, roles, or risk, and required very little expenditure of resources. Yet such service support provided the agency an opportunity to fulfill its own service mission.

COMPARISON OF INTEGRATIVE LINKAGES AND TECHNIQUES USED BY THE INTEGRATOR

Linkages

The voluntary projects studied used a number of integrative linkages to connect their clients with the services provided by other agencies. The status of development of linkages is shown in Table 11.1. Most important by far were core services. The administrative linkages of staff outstationing and purchase of service were also significant.

186

TABLE 11.1

Linkage Development in Five Voluntary Coordination Projects

Linkages	Linkages in Planning or Initial Stages of Development (percent)	Linkages Partially or Fully Developed (percent)
I. Fiscal		
1. Joint budgeting	20	—
2. Joint funding	—	80
3. Fund transfer	—	—
4. Purchase of service	—	80
II. Personnel practices		
1. Consolidated personnel administration	20	60
2. Joint use of staff	—	40
3. Staff transfer	—	—
4. Staff outstationing	—	60
5. Colocation*	—	—
III. Planning and programing		
1. Joint planning	40	20
2. Information-sharing	—	60
3. Joint programing	20	60
4. Joint development of operating policies	—	60
5. Joint evaluation	20	20
IV. Administrative support services		
1. Record-keeping	20	60
2. Grants management	—	100
3. Central support services	60	20
V. Direct services; core services		
1. Outreach	—	100
2. Intake	—	100
3. Diagnosis	—	100
4. Referral	—	100
5. Follow-up	—	80
VI. Case coordination		
1. Case conference	—	80
2. Case coordinator	—	60
3. Case team	—	60
Percent of total possible linkages	8	56

*Linkage deemed inappropriate.

187

In all cases, core services were administered by the integrator's staff. In one project, and for periods to time in others, almost the entire integrative effort was core services.

Outreach consisted mainly of establishing relationships with agencies likely to come in contact with potential clients, and keeping them informed of the nature of the project's services and the availability of slots. One project carried out intensive and highly successful door-to-door recruitment. Participating service providers relied on the integrator's staff to perform outreach. Intake was carried out either at the project site or in a client's home, usually providing access to many but not all of the services linked to the project. In one project, intake admitted the family to all services provided by staff of the integrator and to services provided at the project's facilities by outstationed staff of participating agencies. In another case, the forms required by all the major service providers were completed at intake. Admission to the prime service automatically qualified each child for all the supporting services except one. With varying degrees of detail, integrator staff carried out diagnosis of each client's total needs to determine what services would be provided both directly and by referral. At its most comprehensive, this consisted of a thorough screening for medical and dental needs, speech and learning problems, and psychological and family difficulties, and resulted in a specific program or plan tailored to meet each client's needs.

A major activity of all five project staffs was referral of individual clients to supporting service providers for needed services. This referral process included contacting service providers to facilitate entry by relaying information, setting up appointments, or securing special terms of service (that is, at lower cost, sooner than usual), and providing support to the clients by means of counseling, escort, transportation, and/or child care as needed. In most cases, referral was limited by the lack of structured procedures administratively agreed upon by the integrator staff and supporting service providers. Follow-up to determine whether clients received services they were referred for was carried out in four of the projects, although in one case it was unsystematic and inadequate. Follow-up is extremely time-consuming but seems to be crucial for assuring that clients get services. Since staff generally perceived their first responsibility as the completion of services to individual clients, little time was spent developing and refining systematic procedures for handling all cases.

In connection with core services, various modes of case coordination were used to provide continuity. Three of the projects had case coordinators, specifically responsible for seeing that individual clients get needed services. In three projects, case teams (that is, a group of staff from different disciplines) work together to coordinate service delivery for individual clients. In some projects, case

conferences involving staff members of the prime and supporting
service providers are called irregularly, usually in response to a
special problem.

The integrator in each of these projects utilized record-keeping
as required by their responsibility for core services. Thus, although
client records were not standardized or consolidated throughout a
project, each integrator maintained (with varying degrees of detail)
records of all referrals, service provided, and progress made.

Purchase of service was used by four of the projects in order
to take advantage of existing resources and expertise that could or
would not be donated. These arrangements have been generally
effective; obviously, purchase of service provides some control over
the service provider not characteristic of voluntary coordination.

Staff outstationing by participating service providers was also
used at some time in four projects. For example, in one project,
staff of two nonprofit organizations provided specialized courses in
home nursing, infant care, and games and toys to groups of mothers
at the project facility. Staff outstationing, as well as other instances
where staff of autonomous services were regularly and frequently
involved in providing services to project clients, led to some joint
programing and joint training. Thus, in three projects joint programing was done with individual service providers for the particular
service they contributed. In addition, joint training was motivated
in one case by the need to sensitize service providers to a particularly difficult client group, and in another by common problems and
interests.

Joint development of operating policies occurred in three projects, but in a limited way. While there was potential significance for
involving participating agencies in overall planning and evaluation,
and for facilitating service delivery by increasing their understanding
of the project's objectives and program and of clients' needs, little
impact was discernible at the time of the field visits.

Other administrative linkages utilized in some of the projects
were joint funding, grants-management, joint use of staff, and
information-sharing. However, these were not significant in terms
of project operations or impact. Two linkages not implemented
would probably have been particularly helpful: These were joint
planning and joint evaluation.

Techniques

Persuasion was the major technique utilized to develop and
maintain integrative linkages in all five projects. The only differences were in the consistency and deliberateness of the persuasive
effort and the amount of time devoted to it. Only in the Edison

Drop-Out Project was there a staff member whose primary responsibility was to secure service agreements from other service providers. In the other four projects, staff having this responsibility were limited by their essentially full-time administrative and direct service tasks. The marked effects of staff changes revealed the crucial difference an individual can make in this role.

The involvement of supporting service providers on the project board is an integrative technique begun in two of the projects.

Other techniques utilized with varying degrees of success were found in individual projects. In the Edison Drop-Out Project, continuous communication between the client service coordinator and each external provider approximated the staff liaison technique utilized effectively in some mediated coordination projects. (See Chapter 18.) In the Galveston Child Development Project, the informal contacts with agency administrators possessed by certain members of the school board were used to obtain commitments for service. During its first operating year, the Portland Parent-Child Center established contracts with participating service providers that spelled out conditions to be met. Finally, the ability of these projects to act as a bridge and buffer between the client group and established service providers, and described above under Resources and Incentives, has the potential for being a valuable technique, if consciously exploited.

IMPACT ON ACCESSIBILITY, CONTINUITY, AND EFFICIENCY

Because the prime service provided by the five projects studied was not previously available in the locality, it is difficult to determine what difference in accessibility is attributable to the fact that services are integrated, as opposed to the mere fact that they are presently available. Outreach efforts clearly contributed to the accessibility of services; and it appears that where linkages have been developed, more clients receive more services, because the provider more readily make referrals.

Positive impact on continuity occurs because the specific group of clients recruited for the project is assured additional services by external providers through such linkages as purchase of service, staff outstationing, and joint programing.

Core services have also played the major role in increasing continuity of service delivery in these projects but mostly on an individual client basis. More systematic, administrative-level approaches have been infrequent. While this case-by-case coordination has been quite effective, manipulating existing structures and operations for the benefit of individuals is extremely time-consuming and inefficient.

Another factor contributing to increased continuity was capacity of the integrators in these projects to act as a bridge-buffer between the client group and supporting service providers. These voluntary projects provide a two-way street of heightened continuity through services integration. The clients' willingness and ability to utilize the services of several providers is increased at the same time as the providers increase their willingness and ability to serve new and different clients. In these cases, the clients' enhanced receptivity to needed services resulted from the confidence they placed in a prime service provider established expressly to meet particular needs of the particular population they exemplified. The autonomous providers were enabled to enlarge their receptivity to clients because the arrangement presented a safe, structured modus operandi for serving a "problem" clientele without administrative change and at minimal cost.

Some economies of scale accrue from the assembly of a group of clients for service by a given provider. In addition, there is some reduction of duplication since the project provides core services, thus eliminating the need for service providers to engage in similar activities. However, the greatest impact on efficiency of these types of projects is their impact on problem solution by the provision of multiple services. In this respect, both enhanced accessibility and increased continuity also produce greater efficiency.

FACILITATORS OF VOLUNTARY COORDINATION

The major factors facilitating development of linkages in voluntary projects derived from the federal funding sources. Federal guidelines requiring a range of program elements and specifying working relationships with certain types of agencies were important in three projects. Second, the allowability of in-kind matching for the required local match encouraged some types of linkages. Third, technical assistance provided by national or regional HEW Office of Child Development staff helped two projects develop linkages.

Professional dedication—sometimes of nonproject professionals working in the community—was significant in three projects, particularly in the early stages of two of them. Membership of service provider representatives on boards or advisory committees was identified as furthering some linkages in four projects. In two projects, community advisory board control over certain aspects of project operations encouraged linkage development. Physical proximity of the services providers and the fact that the project facility was well located within the service area were each helpful in two projects.

191

Factors facilitating development of cooperative working agreements in individual projects were the interest and sustained efforts of some community residents, the existence of a fund surplus that it was necessary to deplete so as to retain full entitlement for subsequent appropriations, and the project director's contacts with funding sources, or political figures, or other service providers.

Factors facilitating initial development of the projects were government, community, and/or service provider recognition of the need for a new service delivery system, and their support of project creation. Studies and task forces that identified needs added to this process in two cases.

INHIBITORS OF VOLUNTARY COORDINATION

Two kinds of goal displacement were critical inhibitors of linkage development in the voluntary coordination projects: first, the concentration on programing, service delivery, and internal operations; and second, the necessity of responding to immediate problems related to various factors such as funding, government requirements, community demands, and personnel administration. These factors were intrinsic to the nature and objectives of the projects and reflected the lack of staff having primary responsibility for linkage development. Inadequate quality and quantity of staff (due both to lack of funds and lack of training) contributed to the failure to pursue linkages in three projects, and internal administrative problems and chaos added to the difficulties in two.

Several inhibitors were derived from the federal funding sources of the projects. In one case, the process of transferring responsibility of the project from one federal agency to another, involving funding delays, conflicting directives, and much wasted effort, was extremely debilitating to the project. Conflicting or unclear guidelines were a problem in three projects and in one of them contributed to continuing differences in the objectives held by the federal agency, the project, and the clients, which resulted in conflict detracting from program development. National OCD's failure to provide technical assistance added to the problems in two cases. In one instance, the short-term demonstration nature of project funding caused autonomous agencies to perceive project functions—such as outreach—as temporary and made them somewhat reluctant to rely on them.

Insufficient or limited funds were a problem in four of the projects. The fact that some projects were funded for a fixed amount restricted expansion of programs and development of linkages. The limited resources (including funds, facilities, and staff) of some autonomous service providers inhibited cooperation in three projects.

Lack of formal contracts defining responsibilities and conditions for service inhibited integrative linkages in voluntary coordination projects. In two projects, providers would not sign formal contracts; in one case existing contracts were allowed to lapse; and in another no attempt was made to obtain formal agreements.

12

COMPARATIVE ANALYSIS OF NEIGHBORHOOD SERVICE CENTERS

DEFINITION OF NEIGHBORHOOD SERVICE CENTERS

Neighborhood service centers are designed to provide services (whether or not functionally related) required to meet the needs of all the residents in a defined geographic area. To the extent feasible, services of separate agencies are provided in a common facility.

SUMMARY DESCRIPTION OF THE NEIGHBORHOOD SERVICE CENTERS

Common Projects Characteristics

Several characteristics occur with regularity among the majority (though not all) of the projects. Obviously each center serves a target geographic area. The geographic areas vary from an actual neighborhood (HUB, Crossroads, JFK) to a complete urban entity (Kearns) to a county (Bacon County). With the exception of the JFK Neighborhood Service Center, the neighborhood centers provide core services—outreach, intake, diagnosis, referral, and follow-up—to clients. The six centers also provide direct service such as child care, financial counseling, parental guidance, and leisure-time counseling for senior citizens through their internal components. The centers attempted to supplement their own core and direct services with other linked or supportive services offered by independent service providers. Since the only prerequisite for service is a residency requirement, the integrator is concerned with the total needs of the family, which mandates a diversified array of service providers.

The characteristic mode of client entry into the delivery system (excluding the JFK Neighborhood Service Center) is through a central information and referral service. Depending upon the individual neighborhood service center's core services mix, the client is contacted by outreach workers and passes through a centralized intake unit prior to his referral to the linked and supportive services.

Four neighborhood service centers are under the auspices of a unit of general purpose government—state, county, or city. Two of the neighborhood service centers are private nonprofit corporations. The remaining center is operated by a special purpose public agency.

In terms of mode of organization, the neighborhood service centers were considered as examples of mediated coordination. That is, the primary mission of the integrator is the development of linkages between service providers rather than the provision of direct services. Therefore, the integrator focuses on improving the functioning of the service delivery system as it relates to a geographic area rather than obtaining specific services on behalf of an individual client. However, based on their various objectives, the extent to which coordination was pursued differed between centers.

Summary Description of Projects

Brief overviews of the seven neighborhood service centers are presented that focus on the following characteristics: initial actions resulting in project organization; the objectives of the centers; sponsorship of the projects; project integrator; the present funding sources; and current facilities.

Bacon County Community Development Center: Alma, Georgia

The initial actions resulting in the organization of the Community Development Center were in response to a report prepared by the Alma-Bacon County Health and Social Services Task Force in 1968. The task force (one of five) was charged with documenting the health and social service needs of the city and county with a population of 61,000 for presentation in a Model Cities application.

The objective of the center is the coordination of services housed in the facilities. To this end, the center's administration attempts to eliminate overlapping services and coordinates the services of outreach, intake, referral, and follow-up. At the time of the study, operating out of temporary facilities, two service providers deliver on-site services of training and education to unemployed citizens and technical assistance to employers, actual and potential, in identifying and meeting manpower needs. In addition, the center has working and contractual agreements with 13 off-site service providers to which referrals are made and by which specific functional services are provided.

The sponsor of the project is the Bacon County Board of Commissioners. Overall policy decisions are the responsibility of the Board of Commissioners, which has delegated the authority to the center advisory committee. Administrative responsibility for the day-to-day operation is delegated by the Board of Commissioners to the center coordinator, who is acting director of the Bacon County Division of Social Services. The Center Advisory Committee, operating through the center coordinator, functions as the integrator.

The local Model Cities program has funded the project under Section 105 of Title I of the Demonstration Cities and Metropolitan Development Act of 1965. Model Cities funds (supplemental) are also used as the matching share for Title IV-A and XVI funds of the Social Security Act of 1965 and Title III funds of the Older Americans Act of 1965. New facilities financed through a HUD Neighborhood Facilities grant were due to be completed in July 1972 and would house five additional service providers.

Community Social Services Center: Hamilton Township, New Jersey

The idea of the Hamilton Township Community Social Services Center was developed by the deputy director of the New Jersey Division of Public Welfare. The project was developed as a pilot in response to the 1970 amendments to the Social Security Act requiring the separation of income maintenance and social services.

The project was designed to test a case control system of integrating services through a multiservice center serving a population of 85,000. It required an integrated referral system that would involve caseworkers who could provide needed help and then withdraw, leaving the client more self-sufficient. The system involved physically locating service providers in a central facility, which currently houses six service providers. In addition, working arrangements exist with federal, state, and county agencies located in the community.

The sponsor of the project is the New Jersey State Department of Public Welfare. The department's governing board makes the appointments to the advisory committee on services to families and children for the center. The project director is responsible for the day-to-day administration and supervision of the center and functions as the integrator.

The project is funded by a Section 1115 grant from the U.S. Department of Health, Education, and Welfare, Social and Rehibilitation Services. The center is located in rented office space in a relatively isolated shopping center and has been operational since January 1971.

Crossroads Community Center: Dallas, Texas

Planning to improve the delivery of social services to the residents of South Dallas began in 1966 when, at the request of the City Manager, the director of the City Department of Urban Rehabilitation began to explore the feasibility of designing and building a multi-service center. In January 1967 the City of Dallas was advised by the Washington Interagency Review Committee that it had been selected as one of 14 cities to participate in the Neighborhood Center Pilot Program.

The Crossroads Community Center was designed to improve the delivery of social services to 70,000 target-area residents by bringing existing service providers into the center facility or transporting residents to off-site service providers. In addition, the center seeks to coordinate service delivery and develop additional needed services. To this end, 25 federal, state, city, and private service providers participate in providing a variety of services to clients. Sixteen service providers are located in the center; four are located within one block and five are outside the South Dallas area.

The sponsor of the project is the City of Dallas with overall policy decisions being the responsibility of the city manager as directed by the mayor and City Council. The mayor and City Council are, in turn, advised by the Crossroads Community Center Board. Administrative responsibility is delegated by the city manager to the center manager, who functions as the integrator.

Since 1970, the City of Dallas has provided matching funds and received funds under Titles IV-A, X, and XIV of the Social Security Act from the Texas State Department of Public Welfare. Current facilities (opened August 1, 1971) consist of a core services building and a health center.

HUB Service Center: Cincinnati, Ohio

Planning to improve the delivery of social services to the 37,730 residents of the Over-the-Rhine area of Cincinnati through a multi-service center began in the winter of 1967. A technical assistance committee composed of potential service providers, formed by the city manager, drafted a proposal for the city to participate in the Neighborhood Center Pilot Program. The application was approved by the Washington Interagency Review Committee in June 1967.

The HUB Service Center is designed to improve the delivery of social services by bringing existing service providers into the community, transporting residents to off-site services, and developing services that will meet the comprehensive needs of the area residents. To this end, 60 federal, state, city, and private service providers participate in providing a variety of services. Five service

197

providers are located on-site; 14 are located within the service area; and the others are located outside of the Over-the-Rhine area.

The sponsor of the project is HUB Services, Inc., a private nonprofit corporation. The Board of Managers is responsible for overall policy decisions. The board is composed of 18 community residents and 17 representatives of service providers or nonresident, at-large representatives. The Board of Managers and center director are advised by the Over-the-Rhine Council on community problems and service needs that are not being met. The Board of Managers, operating through the center director, functions as integrator.

HUB is funded by Model Cities supplemental funds for center administration, core services, credit union, education, library, transportation, legal, and recreation services. The parent and child center is funded by the Office of Child Development, Department of Health, Education, and Welfare. The senior citizens program is funded with Title III funds of the Older Americans Act.

From 1967 until the time of the study, HUB Service Center has made use of limited facilities. New facilities consisting of a community service center, Parent and Child Center, and a Senior Services Center had been designed, with construction to begin in mid-1972.

John F. Kennedy School and Community Center: Atlanta, Georgia

The idea for the John F. Kennedy School and Community Center to serve a population of 45,000 was developed by a task force established in 1965 by the Atlanta Board of Education to determine the best use of forthcoming funds of the Elementary and Secondary Education Act.

The concept of the center from its earliest stages was that of establishing a one-stop "shopping center" or "supermarket" for social services. It was to be a place where residents could conveniently gain access to various types of educational and social services. To that end, the center has informal working and referral relationships with state, city, and county service agencies. Currently, 11 service providers are located in the center.

The sponsor of the project is the Atlanta Board of Education. The center director is advised by an Executive Committee composed of the director of each agency located in the center. Charged with the responsibility for center policies, rules, and regulations, the committee lessens the school system's dominance and influence in the everyday operations of the facility. Administration of the center is charged to the center director, who is appointed by the School Board. The Executive Committee, operating through the center director, functions as the integrator.

The center staff is financed by the Atlanta Board of Education. Service providers share the operational costs of the center on a pro rata square footage basis.

198

The project operates out of a new facility that was designed as a result of cooperative planning by the on-site service providers. Construction was financed utilizing school board and private foundation funds and Neighborhood Facilities funds from the U.S. Department of Housing and Urban Development.

Kearns Family Life Center: Kearns, Utah

In response to acknowledged deficiencies in the delivery of services in Utah, the Division of Family Services of the State Department of Social Services designed a new social services delivery system to more effectively meet the needs of welfare recipients. The director of the State Department of Social Services appointed an interagency committee to draft a proposal to establish a Family Life Center in Kearns, Utah serving a population of 17,000.

Specifically, the center was designed to decentralize, expand, and develop a sound coordinated service delivery system involving public programs and, to the extent possible, voluntary programs. The center was also designed to determine whether persons needing services to improve employability and self-sufficiency would use such services voluntarily if not referred on a mandatory basis.

Ten federal, state, county, and private service providers participate in providing a range of services to the residents of the area. All of the service providers are located on-site.

The sponsor of the project is the Division of Family Services of the Utah Department of Social Services, with overall policy decisions the responsibility of the division. Administrative responsibility for day-to-day operation of the center is assumed by the center director who functions as the integrator.

Funding of the center is provided by a Section 1115 grant from the U.S. Department of Health, Education, and Welfare, Social and Rehabilitation Services, and the State of Utah. The center encountered problems in locating a facility due to state regulations restricting renting from private individuals. As a result of this six-month delay, the Kearns Family Life Center did not open until February 1971.

Yeatman District Community Corporation: St. Louis, Missouri

The Yeatman District Community Corporation, serving an area of 60,000 residents, is a result of intensive field work carried out by employees of the Human Development Corporation (HDC), the local community action agency. HDC outreach workers were assigned to the Yeatman neighborhood for the purpose of motivating residents in terms of community organization and identifying gaps in the delivery of social services. The goal of the organizational effort was the establishment of a multipurpose neighborhood service center.

The corporation was designed to integrate all service components and maintain strong client participation in program operation, which will induce the project to increase the general training, income, and resources of Yeatman neighborhood residents. Eight service components are internalized under the Yeatman umbrella—that is, they are financially and administratively controlled by the parent corporation. Several state and city providers share common facilities provided by the project.

The Corporation's Board of Directors is the policy-making body. Planning, budgeting, evaluation, personnel administration, and training are the centralized responsibilities of the board and its appointed executive director. Membership of the board consists entirely of clients, who are also shareholders in the corporation. The Board of Directors, operating through the executive director, functions as the integrator.

The Yeatman District Community Corporation is funded from the following sources: a Section 314(e) grant from the U.S. Department of Health, Education, and Welfare; HEW OCD; Office of Economic Opportunity; and Model Cities. The project operates out of a central facility, four satellite substations, and six neighborhood drop-in locations. The central facility is provided by the City of St. Louis for a token rent.

COMPARISON OF THE PROJECT INTEGRATORS

Three major characteristics, which affected the development of linked services, were generally shared by the neighborhood centers in their respective roles as integrators. These were the lack of authority of the center over service providers, the goals and objectives of the neighborhood center, and the resources and incentives available to the integrator.

Lack of Authority over Service Providers

None of the seven neighborhood centers had direct organizational or administrative authority over the agencies providing direct services. Center managers stressed the necessity of formal commitments from the social service providers, prior to their relocation in the centers. The service providers were of the opinion that direct authority of the center over their operations would destroy rather than nurture the close working relationship necessary for interagency activities.

In place of a formalized system of rules and regulations or contractual obligations, several of the projects developed agreements,
letters of commitment, and memoranda of understanding to compensate for agency autonomy and to equate the service providers'
objectives with those of the neighborhood service center. An integrated approach to service delivery was not the primary focus of
most of the agreements; they merely laid the groundwork for use of
a common facility including maintenance and utility cost rather than
participation in a total system. Specific agreements regarding
individual linkages are discussed later in this chapter.

Only in HUB Neighborhood Service Center did the integrator
possess the authority to review and jointly recommend personnel
changes in on-site service provider staff. The service providers in
the Crossroads Neighborhood Service Center agreed to participate
in the direct and support services provided by the center. However,
the extent of their involvement has been limited. For example, they
participate in central intake but at the same time retain their respective intake processes. While the integrator in the Yeatman Neighborhood Service Center exercises direct line authority over the eight
service components that are organizationally part of the corporation,
the project does not have direct authority over external service providers located in the center and satellite facilities.

Goals and Objectives of the Integrator

The goals and objectives of the seven neighborhood service centers involve two distinct service delivery approaches. The first is
the provision of their own core and/or direct services to be supplemented by services of colocated and off-site service providers.
This approach is service oriented to the client with a minimum of
emphasis on the system which provides the service. The second
approach incorporates the provision of core and direct services
while concurrently emphasizing the development of a jointly planned,
financed, and administered service delivery system. Data generated
during the field visits substantiate emphasis on the former with a
systems approach being of ancillary importance. The client-oriented
philosophy has developed due to the primary (short-run) objective of
merely bringing a variety of services into the neighborhood and creating additional services to fill gaps in the existing system. The role
of center-sponsored core services was, in general, to initiate,
monitor, and track the client within the service providers' respective
delivery systems rather than serve as a mechanism for development
of an improved system.

In effect, it has been the intent of the centers to view the service
providers as distinct operational entities not adaptive for a maximum

total impact on the client or in an integrative delivery system. Obviously, a systems approach to services integration involves more than the provision of core and administrative support services. This approach requires an overall philosophy that must accommodate the existing or anticipated operational policies of the service providers.

Several of the projects, through job description or structural organization, specify interagency planning, coordination, and program development to be ongoing functions. However, even where these functions have been delineated, they are generally implemented either in a pro forma manner by governing or advisory boards or in an informal, ad hoc manner by regular staff meetings primarily involving colocated service providers. The centers have not aggressively assumed a coordinative role and have not developed the types of integrating linkages that reflect an intent to focus on changing the service delivery system. For example, in only one project are integrative functions being addressed by a specific staff member. In the Crossroads Center, a staff member designated as interagency coordinator has as part of her responsibilities daily contact with the colocated service providers, but the scope of the duties was so diverse that this work task became of secondary importance.

Resources and Incentives Available to the Integrators

The factor with perhaps the most far-reaching implications is the lack of resources and incentives available to the integrators in the neighborhood service centers to develop integrating linkages. The importance of financial and/or other resources to encourage participation is the leverage to demand compliance with policies or regulations inherent in a center-sponsored delivery system.

The critical resource available to the integrator was the neighborhood service center facility itself, which enhanced the connection of the autonomous service providers with the clients. In each case, the center as a facility was not utilized as a bargaining device to develop a single coherent delivery system but rather just as a shelter for service providers. The various service providers were more than happy to respond to the "invitation" to relocate.

Use of center facilities, however, provided three incentives to the service providers for participation in the project. First, the location of the facility in the target area provided ready access to a concentrated population, as well as making individual clients requiring specialized services easily available to the service providers.

Second, the service providers were not bound by an organizational framework that altered their roles, objectives, or programmatic policies to any appreciable extent.

Third, in the Hamilton Neighborhood Service Center, the center staff served as a buffer between established, traditional, and usually large-service providers and the target-area population.

Several individual projects had other resources and incentives not common to all. Of these, control over funds is the most noteworthy. As previously described, the organization of Yeatman Neighborhood Service Center provides for an internal system of delivery of services. Each of the project component services is funded through a single administrative unit (Board of Directors). This single-point funding gave the board the capability to determine operational policy for service delivery for those components of the corporation. However, this power does not extend to the external service providers located in the center and satellites.

The Yeatman Neighborhood Service Center also utilized a natural resource, the community residents. The residents play three vital roles: first as clients, second as corporation stockholders, and third as policymakers. Therefore, the client-dominated Board of Directors not only makes policy regarding services provided by the corporation but also utilizes the component services.

Another valuable resource in both the HUB and Bacon County Neighborhood Service Centers was the support of the local elected officials. The City Manager and City Council of Cincinnati and the Mayor of Alma and Bacon County Board of Commissioners were instrumental in organizing the neighborhood centers. In Cincinnati, the elected officials appointed the directors of service providers to the HUB Board of Managers thus encouraging their participation. In Bacon County, the elected officials encouraged service provider participation through assignments on the five Model Cities planning and research task forces. The Bacon County Neighborhood Service Center is currently part of a division of the county government that is actively involved in long-range planning for social services delivery through the countywide Model Cities program. In both projects, the commitment of local elected officials to provide local funds, if necessary, to continue operations has given the centers a position of permanence among the community residents and service providers.

COMPARISON OF INTEGRATIVE LINKAGES USED BY THE NEIGHBORHOOD SERVICE CENTERS

This section of the report describes the extent to which the neighborhood centers have developed integrating linkages. Table 12.1 summarizes linkage development in each of the neighborhood

TABLE 12.1

Linkage Development in Six Neighborhood Service Centers

Linkages	Linkages in Planning or Initial Stages of Development (percent)	Linkages Partially or Fully Developed (percent)
I. Fiscal		
1. Joint budgeting	—	17
2. Joint funding	—	50
3. Fund transfer	—	—
4. Purchase of service	33	33
II. Personnel practices		
1. Consolidated personnel administration	—	17
2. Joint use of staff	17	17
3. Staff transfer	—	33
4. Staff outstationing	—	—
III. Planning and programing		
1. Joint planning	33	17
2. Information-sharing	17	83
3. Joint programing	17	83
4. Joint development of operating policies	33	33
5. Joint evaluation	33	50
IV. Administrative support services		
1. Record-keeping	17	83
2. Grants management	17	—
3. Central support services	17	17
V. Core services		
1. Outreach	17	50
2. Intake	17	83
3. Diagnosis	17	50
4. Referral	—	83
5. Follow-up	—	83
VI. Case coordination		
1. Case conference	17	67
2. Case coordinator	17	33
3. Case team	17	—
Percent of total possible linkages	13	43

service centers except Yeatman.[*] As the table illustrates, slightly more than half the linkages considered appropriate to services integration through neighborhood centers are at some stage of development in the projects.

Planning and Programing

Few of the centers had fully developed a joint process with service providers for planning, programing, and evaluation. For the most part, when joint activities in planning and programing occurred, the centers and service providers focused on narrow issues in programing for the center.

Organizational structures (boards and advisory committees) exist in each of the projects to address the issues of joint planning and programing; however, in only two instances has considerable progress accrued. In the HUB Neighborhood Service Center, the service providers as participants in joint staff meetings were successful in developing two new projects (job development and emergency assistance programs) for unemployed area residents. The service providers, through joint evaluation and staff meetings, enabled the Kearns Neighborhood Service Center to implement a drug crisis and financial aid program for deprived high school graduates.

Fiscal

Three of the projects, Crossroads, Kearns, and the Hamilton Neighborhood Service Centers, have not developed any of the identified fiscal arrangements to link service providers to the center. However, both Kearns and Hamilton are in the process of developing purchase of services plans for the centers through the state welfare agencies which are also the project sponsors.

In no instance have fund transfers been attempted among providers through the center.

Two neighborhood service centers, HUB and Bacon County, have attempted joint budgeting between the center and participating service providers. In Bacon County, joint determination of budget levels has involved only a limited number of providers and been concerned only with funding of outreach services and transportation.

---

[*]Yeatman was excluded because of its direct line authority and funding relationships with most of its components.

In HUB, a process of joint determination of budget levels for service providers was attempted but failed. A joint budget was developed for services in the initial planning of the project. However, budget requests for services were disapproved by the participating agencies.

Personnel Practices

Colocation is the rationale (physically speaking) for a neighborhood service center. This linkage relates to the "supermarket" or "shopping center" approach to social services delivery system. The relocated service providers in each center remained responsive to control from central or parent offices. Colocation as a device to fill service gaps was most effective when the service providers were selected by task forces or through independent research studies. The HUB and Bacon County Neighborhood Service Centers exemplify this approach.

With the exception of joint training, consolidated personnel administration has not taken place in any of the centers. These functions have been retained by the individual service providers. The failure to consolidate traditional personnel services reflects the unwillingness of service providers to relinquish authority over staff to the centers. In the HUB Neighborhood Service Center, original agreements gave the center an advisory role in the selection and dismissal of personnel by the service providers.

Joint use of staff has not met with great success in the neighborhood service centers. In fact, the linkage is operational in only the Bacon County Neighborhood Service Center. The center and the local community action agency utilize the outreach workers of both projects to provide for recruitment and follow-up for the participating supportive service providers.

A logical extension of the joint use of staff is the actual transfer of staff, that is, a case in which an employee is on the payroll of one agency but under the administrative control of another. The HUB Neighborhood Service center exemplifies this approach through the financing of community workers who are supervised by a local community improvement organization. As previously mentioned, the Bacon County Neighborhood Service Center funds six center outreach workers who are under the administrative control of the community action agency.

Administrative Support Services

In five of the neighborhood service centers (Hamilton excluded), centralized record-keeping parallels the existence and operational status of central intake systems in particular and core services in general.

In four centers (HUB, Kearns, Crossroads, Hamilton) record-keeping is maintained through central records sections or systems. The drawback (Crossroads excepted) is that only on-site agencies participate fully in the system.

In the four projects where the service providers participate in a unified core services system, record-keeping was viewed as a logical extension of coordinated activities in that the flow of client records complemented client movement through the system. The process involves two facets of operation: (a) standardized or centralized case information; and (b) procedures for flow of information and feedback.

However, while case information is standardized and a master record is utilized, the on-site agencies still use their own forms to maintain a record of client information (they transfer information from the intake forms to their own forms) because each agency requires records on "their own forms" on all clients served. The only positive impact of the central records system is the elimination of the client's undergoing sequential interviews describing his personal situation.

The capacity of the center to utilize a master record system for monitoring and follow-up is limited by the lack of regular and consistent feedback of client data from the individual service providers. This problem occurred in varying degrees in each project.

Core Services

The core services of outreach, intake, diagnosis, referral, and follow-up were at least partially implemented as a unit (all five services) in two neighborhood service centers (Crossroads and HUB) and selectively in three of the remaining four projects. The single exception was the JFK Neighborhood Service Center where core services were not designed during the project development. In all cases where implemented, core services were under the direct line authority of the neighborhood service center director.

Among the core services, outreach displayed the widest variance of implementation and operational efficiency. The Bacon County Neighborhood Service Center was successful in combining the outreach staff of the local community action agency with its own outreach workers to form a single staff. This led to a more equitable distribution of efforts throughout the county and reduced the number of supervisory personnel.

In each project, central intake was carried out by center staff at the Center. The process was most effective in the HUB and Crossroads Neighborhood Service Centers where information collected during the initial interviews was utilized to forgo repetitive interviews by service providers.

With varying degrees of detail and success, the neighborhood center staffs conducted diagnosis to determine the comprehensive needs and possible corrective actions for each client. Even though the service was in a partial state of implementation in all but JFK, its efficacy was confined by several factors. Generally, the service providers were reluctant to entrust diagnosis as it related to their specific programs to a second party. From their viewpoint there is a great deal of difference between a general assessment and a diagnosis of needs.

An integral part of each neighborhood service center was the referral of the clients to the supporting and linked service providers. The process was simplified by the clients' intake worker completing the necessary arrangements for his appointments with the service providers. All of the projects except JFK utilized a structured format including a variety of forms to assist the client in referral. Similarly, all of the projects, except JFK, provided transportation as a means to complete a referral to an off-site service provider. Follow-up to ensure the performance and adequacy of service was conducted in varying degrees by all but JFK. The approach was not uniform for all cases and considerably less sophisticated than the other core services. For example, follow-up in the Crossroads Neighborhood Service Center was assigned to outreach workers who were generally unfamiliar with the specifics of the client's case.

Modes of Case Coordination

Case conferences were utilized in four of the neighborhood centers: Crossroads, Bacon County, Kearns, and HUB. Conferences typically were called in response to a crisis situation for an individual client and were not part of a structured format for service delivery. This meant that the client's intake worker used his judgment to determine if the situation warranted a meeting of the various service providers.

Case coordinator functions were performed in Crossroads and Kearns Neighborhood Service Centers. Client intake workers performed case coordinator functions in Kearns.

IMPACT ON ACCESSIBILITY, CONTINUITY,
AND EFFICIENCY

The neighborhood service centers have had an impact on accessibility, continuity, and efficiency in the delivery of social services by linking service providers together in providing a range of services. Impact on service delivery to clients was examined from the viewpoint of the ease with which a client can initially enter the service delivery system (accessibility); the ability of a client to move through the service delivery system to receive the necessary range of services (continuity); and a reduction of duplication, economies of scale, and impact on problem solution (efficiency).

The seven neighborhood service centers examined have had varied degrees of impact on service delivery. Impact for the most part has been affected by the center's objectives and length of time they have been in operation.

Accessibility

The neighborhood service centers created, in a designated service area, a concentration of services that did not exist prior to their development. Since service providers are in close proximity (or colocated), and transportation is provided to others, access to a variety of services is convenient to clients.

The extended hours of operation by most neighborhood service centers into the night and weekend have also enhanced the accessibility of services. As a result residents who work during the hours of 8:00 a.m. and 5:00 p.m., Monday through Friday, can take advantage of services that they could not have prior to the establishment of the neighborhood service centers.

Neighborhood service centers are unique in their ability to increase the accessibility of a wide range of services to all residents of the designated service area. Colocation of service providers, creation of new services, and transportation to off-site service providers are utilized to increase accessibility.

Continuity

The neighborhood service centers provide a wide range of services and are responsive to the needs of multiproblem residents in their designated service areas.

The assessment of total client needs (diagnosis) is a prime tool used by neighborhood service centers to identify multiproblem needs of their clients. Once the client's needs have been identified, a service delivery plan is established and the client is referred to the appropriate service provider.

Five of the centers studied have had an impact on client movement through the service delivery system through the use of central records, follow-up, and modes of case coordination.

209

Central records have been utilized to record the client's needs that have been identified by intake and to record services as they are provided by internal and external service providers. Through the use of follow-up and a case coordinator, the centers are able to determine if clients receive the services to which they have been referred.

Through the use of central records, follow-up, and a case coordinator, clients are monitored as they move through the delivery system. As services are not delivered according to schedule, the case coordinator or keeper of the central records intervenes and initiates a special follow-up to correct this problem.

The centers that have had the greatest impact on continuity of service delivery have been those that have implemented the linkages of intake, diagnosis, referral, and follow-up.

Neighborhood service centers, through fiscal linkages, have been able to create new services or expand existing services in the service area. The colocation of service providers that exists in the neighborhood service centers, even without linkage agreements, has an impact on continuity of services. An example of this exists in the John F. Kennedy Neighborhood Service Center. Even without linkage agreements, service providers have coordinated service delivery for their clients. This has resulted in meeting multi-needs of clients. Informal information-sharing meetings between staff have resulted in the elimination of problems identified as being a deterrent to service delivery.

Efficiency

Neighborhood service centers have the capability of eliminating the duplication of efforts by the staff of service providers. Central intake in the neighborhood service centers permits the staff of service providers to devote more time to solving the clients' problems since they do not have to collect data for the determination of eligibility.

Neighborhood service centers' internal structure for the most part provides the framework for the elimination of the functions of core services by service providers.

The neighborhood service center has an advantage to be realized by its comprehensive orientation to family and neighborhood problems, including certain interactive efforts of programs and certain multiple effects. The combination of improved health and education can make employment possible that was previously impossible. A client's improved health combined with new skills jointly help him secure employment—impact on problem solution.

210

FACILITATORS OF NEIGHBORHOOD SERVICE CENTERS

Through neighborhood centers, several factors appear to facilitate the development of the characteristics of services integration. Foremost is the physical facility itself. Location within the target area community with space provided free or at a nominal cost provides the beginning point to obtain involvement of previously separate service providers in coordinating services for a defined geographic area.

Second is the presence of service providers on task forces and/or planning committees during project development. Participation prior to operational status led to a determination of a representative mix of service providers to be included in the system. Additionally, the participation also determined the operational policies of the direct services provided through the centers. In the JFK and Bacon County Neighborhood Service Centers the service providers participated in planning the actual physical layout of the centers.

Third, membership on boards and/or advisory committees provides a forum for discussion of the roles and objectives of each linked service provider in the system. Participants were also able to share information. Another aspect of committee investigation was the identification of service needs and inadequacies of the existing service delivery system.

Determination of congruent or complementary objectives of the service providers and the center in the initial discussions of providers' participation in the center-sponsored delivery system provides a framework to reduce the duplication of services, maximize services with existing funds, and expand services.

Support of the centers by local general purpose governments exemplified in the HUB, Kearns, and Bacon County Neighborhood Service Centers provides incentives for service providers to participate in the center and work with center staff. Technical assistance was provided in the three cases in the form of staff members to assist in the research and development of the project. While not affecting linkages per se, the technical assistance enabled the projects to approach the concept of services integration from a more rational perspective.

INHIBITORS OF NEIGHBORHOOD SERVICE CENTERS

The absence of integrated service delivery systems in the seven neighborhood service centers appears to be a function of several

211

interrelated variables. Their importance is not measured in a rank-order sequence but rather in a cause and effect relationship.

The initial inhibitor is the duration of operational status of the project. First, neighborhood service centers require an extended start-up period during which emphasis is placed on internal administrative and operational objectives rather than on linkage development with colocated service providers. Second, the demonstration nature of the projects detracts from the feeling of permanence within the community. The effect is a reticence on the part of the service providers to transfer authority to a project that may have an abbreviated life span. This variable with its concomitant effects in turn influences a third variable, service-provider attitudes.

The initial attitude of the service providers often bordered on hostility toward a new system of delivery of services sponsored by the centers. Part of the foundation for this negative attitude stemmed from the centers' inability to present a philosophy or a plan of action outlining participation and rationalizing an integrated service delivery system. Furthermore, in only one neighborhood service center, Crossroads, was a staff member assigned the responsibility of co-ordinating the efforts of the colocated and off-site service providers. Manifestation of this hostility occurred through (1) the service providers' refusal to relinquish administrative control over their respective staff members; (2) the failure to participate fully in the center-sponsored central intake, diagnosis, and record-keeping services; and (3) the reluctance to participate in joint planning, programing, and budgeting as a precondition for integrating the delivery of services.

The Kearns Neighborhood Service Center provides an example of the change of service provider attitudes with maturation of the project. Initially, the service providers felt that the center was attempting to control their service delivery by requiring them to participate in central intake, central records, and sharing of client information. Gradually during the first year, the service providers were convinced that the center was attempting to improve the delivery of services to clients rather than control their delivery systems. As a result of this change in attitude, the center was able to develop linkages in program operation, central intake, central records, and sharing of client information.

Another significant inhibitor was that the basic cooperative agreements between the centers and the on-site service providers generally lacked any substantive requirements for participation by providers in any other coordinative arrangements. For example, in one neighborhood center, the city attorney was charged with drawing up the agreements. Inevitably he lacked any idea of a larger services integration agenda and committed the center to provide facilities, central record-keeping, and core services in return only for attendance by agency representatives at center staff meetings.

As cited in an earlier section, the neighborhood service centers (Yeatman excluded) did not command the financial resources or other inducements to counter the basic operational and administrative difficulties perceived by the service providers. Hence, this bargaining position from which to promote an integrated system was severely limited.

13

CASE STUDIES

The Westside Community Mental Health Center, beginning its fourth year of operation with many important integrating linkages still being developed, illustrates that services integration is a slow, evolutionary process. The case also shows that grant administration policies and procedures can have a positive impact on integration by giving the integrator control over service provider access to funds. While Westside Community Mental Health Center presents a case for single-point funding and the efficacy of purchase of service agreements, it underscores the need for incentives to make linkages truly effective.

By contrast, the experience of the Community Council Child Care Project relative to grant administration policies and procedures is presented. In this case, the funding source, itself, became part of the hostile environment and an impediment to services integration, causing project staff to turn their attention to internal operations rather than coordination, and to survival rather than integration. Unclear guidelines and funding delays and uncertainties threatened the entire project, hindered the development of a planning component, and nearly closed one of its affiliated child care centers.

The Tri-County Project and the Vocational Incentives Program demonstrate how general purpose government can be an important facilitator of services integration, that negative service-provider attitudes can be overcome if the integrator has sufficient authority, and the significance of the project director's role in achieving integration objectives. In addition, the Tri-County Project, the most developed information and referral system studied, shows the favorable effect of support from key forces in the local environment (in this case the local United Fund), while the Vocational Incentives Program demonstrates that HEW itself can initiate changes in the environment to promote a services integration strategy.

Finally, the Greater Cleveland Mental Retardation Development Project and the Youth Advocacy Program are presented to show how services integration can be attained by a capable project staff whose mission is the coordination of service providers rather than service delivery. In both projects, a small staff whose major resources were expertise and time orchestrated their diverse techniques to assist service providers within the clear objective of integrating their respective service delivery systems. In Cleveland, project staff became the community's experts on the needs of the clients and the resources available or necessary to meet those needs. Either by necessity or desire, service providers were drawn to this expertise, which the staff then used to achieve their integration objectives.

In the Youth Advocacy Program, central staff provides (1) consultative and program development expertise to convene and support the programing activities of ad hoc coalitions of providers, (2) funds and/or administrative staff to demonstration programs, and (3) staff support to community planning groups dealing with problems of young people. In addition, field representatives are placed in community agencies to assist these agencies and, in so doing, advocate the needs of youth, lobby for increased program responsiveness, and develop programs to fill service gaps.

WESTSIDE COMMUNITY MENTAL HEALTH CENTER

The Westside Community Mental Health Center is a nonprofit corporation formed to secure funds and to operate a comprehensive mental health system for primarily low-income residents of the Westside catchment area of San Francisco, California. The center consists of a central office offering support services to and coordinating a consortium of 18 private agencies providing mental health services, including drug treatment, to residents of the area.

The concept for the Westside Center originated in 1966 with a group of psychiatrists at a large Westside hospital desirous of aligning the practice of psychiatry with the field of community mental health. The group wished to develop a mental health service delivery system among existing agencies to serve a new clientele.

The development of this system seems to have occurred in three stages, with each stage representing a shift in project focus. These stages included (1) the coalescing of traditional service providers in the catchment area into a service network accessible to the low-income, black, hippie, and Japanese populations not constituting their traditional clientele; (2) the expansion of services in the delivery system to this special clientele; and (3) the attempt to create continuity in service delivery through developing integrative linkages coordinating the activities of service providers.

The transition from one stage to the next occurred as a result of improvement in the relationships among service providers and between providers and the Westside core staff. Importantly, however, at each stage, the federal and/or county government, through funding, support, or administrative requirement had a beneficial role in promoting services integration.

Forming the Consortium

To implement and to fund the Westside Project, the psychiatrists took three major steps. First, they met with representatives of the primary funding sources for mental health services—the National Institutes of Mental Health, the California Department of Mental Hygiene, and the City-County Department of Public Health. Second, they prepared an application for an NIMH staffing grant to obtain the staff capacity necessary for project implementation. Third, they attempted to secure cooperative agreements for service provision with the hospitals serving the Westside area.

The cooperative agreements required careful negotiation to obtain since the hospitals would be serving a new clientele previously treated by distant state facilities, and the smaller hospitals feared that the larger would be favored in any distribution of project funds. The agreements were secured with the intervention of the Community Mental Health Service of the Department of Public Health, which saw the Westside cooperative attempt as complementing its own objectives. Westside, it was felt, could provide San Francisco with a demonstration program for delivery of mental health services, which might then serve as a national model at a time of federal interest in such models. Its consolidation of services and providers would enable the county department to work with one agency rather than many in administering mental health programs. Finally, the county was favorable to the project because of amendments to the state Short-Doyle Act governing mental health services and new federal legislation liberalizing funding for such services.

The Community Mental Health Service thus designated Westside the sole conduit of state and state-administered federal funds for mental health services in the Westside area. This decision was crucial to the formation of the consortium and later to project coherence. With control of funds, the project possessed the necessary incentive for enlisting the participation of service providers and the leverage to affect linkages integrating service delivery. Purchase of service contracts with each consortium member for stipulated services, such as the provision of a number of hospital beds for center clients, were a basic device promoting coordination.

Westside received a $500,000 NIMH staffing grant in 1968 and began operation early in 1969. As an example of mediated coordination, the project was implemented and developed largely through the leadership of the director and the core staff. They were aided in their efforts to achieve integration of services by project control of funds, persuasion, exchange of information and, later, a structure including overlapping community and agency membership on project boards.

Formation of the consortium was also abetted by a favorable environment. The mental health needs of the area's hippie population were recognized nationally as a result of the large interest of the media in the Haight-Ashbury "flower children," while the needs of the community's black population were equally well recognized locally. Some service providers whose participation the project had to enlist felt a strong measure of frustration and concern at their traditional failure to serve such urgent needs within their own community and so were receptive to a safely structured mechanism through which they could serve hitherto bypassed clientele. The project structure itself was designed to promote a favorable environment.

The primary contractor for all project funds is the Board of Directors, a 36-member body composed of an appointed representative from each of the provider agencies and an equal number of representatives elected by the Community Advisory Board (CAB). This citizen group consists of 40 members, themselves elected annually at a community forum open to all residents of the Westside catchment area. The CAB meets at least once each month in a continuing process of assessment of community needs and discussion of program priorities. The Board of Directors also meets monthly on a regular basis and often more frequently, when convened either by the board chairman or the Executive Committee of the board. Thus there is ongoing dialogue between the project and its target population, which can be promptly reflected in administrative policies and procedures. The community impact of the project may be appreciated by the unprecedented nature of the confrontation which occurs regularly in the Board of Directors meetings: Staff of prestigious private hospitals that have always served a middle-class clientele must respond directly to administrative proposals advanced by blacks, youths, Asians, and hippies from their surrounding neighborhood.

A major facilitator that made possible so innovative a structure was the professional stature and prestige of the initiators of the project and the fact that they themselves held executive positions at one of the major hospitals involved. The present executive director, appointed by the Board of Directors, had been the main instigator of the project and has since left his position at a consortium hospital to give full time to the position. He heads a multidisciplinary professional staff, which numbered about 25 at the time of the field work. These operated in five functional units: research, consultation (created in accordance with funding source requirements), drug program, office management, and comptroller. This staff is centrally located in the catchment area and provides no direct services to clients. Mental health services are provided through the existing facilities of the participating agencies, whose operating hours vary from 8 to 5 p.m., five days per week, to 24 hours daily. All facilities are located within the five square miles of the catchment area, and none is more than 10 minutes by automobile from any resident. No formal transportation system exists for client use.

Initial project focus was on creating this organizational structure, identifying priorities, and developing programs. Project staff had to meet two sets of priorities—the development of services to meet community needs and Short-Doyle Act requirements, and the development of administrative procedures emphasized by the federal and, to a lesser extent, county governments. At times these priorities conflicted, to the detriment of project administration and linkage development. A critical conflict concerned the initial resistance of some consortium members to share client information citing the supposed confidentiality of such information. This refusal inhibited implementation of a centralized follow-up and an evaluation system.

Expansion of Services

Despite internal conflicts, program expansion occurred rapidly. Providers established contact with new clientele with help from their nonwhite clinical and administrative staff newly hired at center urging. Service delivery to this clientele was further facilitated by the addition of minority-run provider agencies to the project delivery system and by the clientele-dominated Community Advisory Board and its representatives on the Board of Directors. A further NIMH grant, secured during 1971 to fund a drug treatment program scheduled to begin operation in November 1971, brought a sudden large expansion of services and, as will be seen, added a forceful external stimulus to the transition into the third stage of the project's development.

During this second phase, however, the whole thrust of project development was directed toward securing services and enhancing their accessibility to clients, while continuity of service was given scant attention. The integrator staff were most concerned with meeting urgent needs of the target population and with forestalling clients' institutionalization; the staffs of the provider agencies, while they all shared these objectives in some degree, were most concerned about establishing comfortable relations with their new clientele and about adjusting their relationship to the project staff itself. Thus, the linkages that were sought and effectuated during Stage Two were those that simply make services available to the client.

At the end of the period, and as a result of this focus of effort, Westside presented an excellent example of services integration through delivery-system provision of the range of quality services a client might require. These services include the following:

Client Services

Emergency services. Westside Crisis Clinic (Mount Zion Hospital) (Adult); San Francisco Suicide Prevention; Saint Mary's Hospital and Medical Center (Children); California Medical Clinic for Psychotherapy (City College Program).

Inpatient care. Mount Zion Hospital and Medical Center; Saint Mary's Hospital and Medical Center.

Outpatient care. California Medical Clinic for Psychotherapy; Catholic Social Services; Children's Hospital and Adult Medical Center; Family Service Agency of San Francisco; Jewish Family Service Agency; Mount Zion Hospital and Medical Center; Pacific-Presbyterian Medical Center; Saint Mary's Hospital and Medical Center; Pacific Psychotherapy Associates.

Partial hospitalization. Day Treatment Center (Pacific-Presbyterian Medical Center); Mount Zion Hospital and Medical Center; Saint Mary's Hospital and Medical Center; Westside Social Rehabilitation Center (Pacific-Presbyterian Medical Center).

Half-way house. Baker Place; Conard House; Progress House.

Drug treatment programs. Reality House; San Francisco Drug Treatment Program; Black Man's Free Medical Clinic; Westside Methadone Clinic.

Community Services

Consultation and education. California Medical Clinic for Psychotherapy; Children's Hospital and Adult Medical Center; Mount Zion Hospital and Adult Medical Center; Pacific Psychotherapy Associates; Saint Mary's Hospital and Medical Center; Westside Central Office.

The client was able to enter this linked system of six categories of service at any point, although the most common mode of entry was through an emergency facility (and most often at the 24-hour Westside Crisis Clinic at Mount Zion Hospital). There was no formal, centralized outreach despite the well-developed community participation. Eligibility requirements at intake were simple: The client established residence in the catchment area and was given service. Fees were determined by service given and the client was charged with whatever portion of the fee he was able to pay, from zero to the full amount. The center was then billed for the difference; in many cases, the center paid the full fee.

Diagnosis and disposition were determined at point of entry, and each consortium member was relied on to make referrals to whatever follow-on services appeared to be necessary. That is, it was assumed that client movement from service to service would be a normal clinical event if the needed services were available. Neither during this second stage of development nor subsequently were there any attempts to establish agency linkages beyond the consortium; referrals to external agencies have been entirely at the option of the individual consortium member with the exception of referrals to the State Hospital, which were reviewed by the Central Office.

In terms of linkages designed to assure continuity of needed services, then, the Westside project at the end of its second phase was undeveloped, but its achievement was nonetheless considerable. An entire class of population within the area that had previously had no community mental health services available to it and that had recourse only to the county hospital and state institutional care when its problems reached an acute stage, was able to receive a full spectrum of on-site quality services simply by establishing residence and degree of ability or inability to pay. The full thrust of project development had been on accessibility, and it was successful: The nonstop hours of the Crisis Clinic represented an enhancement of accessibility. Of particular importance was the emphasis placed on the racial and ethnic integration of agency staffs. A quantitative measure of the impact of this effort is seen in statistics regarding referrals from the Crisis Clinic. Between 1968 and 1969 the proportion of blacks among clients referred for outpatient care more than doubled— from 15.6 to 32 percent—while the black component of clients referred for inpatient care increased from 18.5 to 33.3 percent.

The project director and staff remained quite content with the simplified system of dispersed intake, diagnosis, and referral, which accelerated the reception process—that is, increased accessibility— and although they were administratively standardized, there was no effort to centralize these procedures. But without centralized record-keeping or follow-up, clients are lost to the system (or within the system), while evaluation of performance, programs, and procedures becomes almost impossible. The staff soon began to feel the need for development of linkages promoting better continuity simply through the exigencies of trying to provide better service to clients and improving administrative efficiency. These internal impulses, plus requirements of stated and federal grant programs, precipitated Stage 3 of the project development.

Achievement of Continuity Linkages

Most of the difficulties the Westside project has encountered have arisen in the course of trying to implement linkages that promote continuity, and in fact this effort was still under way in March 1972 when the project was studied at the beginning of its fourth year of operation. Wherever this effort confronted the traditional prerogatives of provider agencies, it ran into trouble. Thus, central reporting and record-keeping encountered stiff agency resistance on the score of client confidentiality (particularly sensitive in both mental health and drug addiction therapy), while consolidation of personnel practices and joint hiring ran head-on into the always sensitive area of autonomous staffing.

More generally, any effort by the center to replace traditionally informal procedures with a standard routine appeared "dictatorial" and was resisted by agency personnel. This resentment applied particularly to any procedure involving paperwork—reporting, record-keeping, monitoring, fiscal matters—since the provider agencies were unwilling (often unable) to relinquish their own long-standing internal forms for these procedures. The paperwork required by the center was thus an onerous additional task, consuming time the agency staffs felt was better devoted to clinical activity. The magnitude of the center's problems in this regard may be appreciated by reflecting that it had constant close working relationship with 18 separate agencies, several of which (the hospitals) had for decades been doing things "their way." It may be that the issue of confidentiality was in fact used in some instances as a cover to mask this underlying resistance to change.

The center began its campaign to improve continuity by implementing a "transaction report," by which a record of each administrative event involving a client was transmitted to central files. Agency compliance varied considerably. Once the system was computerized, however, it became possible to ascertain very quickly where transaction reportage was being neglected and to require compliance.

With a full-time computer staff now functioning at central administration, the process has become much more sophisticated and is now called a "transaction encounter report." The information conveyed identifies not simply the client and the service received but also the staff member administering the service and the exact amount of time (in minutes) spent in direct service. Thus, the computerized transaction reporting system provides both complete follow-up data and a large part of the information needed for program evaluation (and, incidentally, assessment of staff efficiency). The system makes it possible to tell at a glance what percentage of a staff member's 40-hour week is spent in direct services, the number of clients seen by a member agency during a week, the total hours spent with clients, and so on. Because of the number of agencies involved, the system provides a valuable tool for comparative evaluation of efficiency.

The ongoing follow-up provided by the system has become an integrative tool, since professional staff at member agencies have developed a much higher interest level. Previously, the final interview a staff psychiatrist had with a client was the last he heard of him, except for chance information. Now, professional staff are able to learn the disposition of a client six months after he was last seen. Clerical staff, who have the burden of the reporting system, do not necessarily share this professional enthusiasm.

While computerization of the transaction reports has solved the follow-up problem, the standardization of intake has not been so simply achieved and was, in fact, greatly complicated when the drug treatment program was added to the center services. One requirement of the federal drug program funding is completion of a 95-question data sheet on each client, much of which duplicates other required forms. After much experimentation, the center is now developing a single intake form for each type of member agency (depending on the programs involved) that will cover all data requirements, including those of the agency's own institution. Thus, center records may have to deal with as many as 10 types of intake forms but any individual agency will use but a single form, while the center assumes the burden of sorting out the data and reporting to the interested sources. Intake, then, remains dispersed throughout the service delivery system, but centralized administrative support removes much of its onus.

As operative at Westside, however, intake is closely tied to diagnosis and referral, and in these latter two linkages very serious gaps have been discovered in the drug treatment program as a result of which a centralized system of intake and referral is soon to be implemented for that particular program. The large problem is a breakdown in referral, to which several factors contribute. Because of their outreach activity, an increasing number of drug abuse clients enter through the drug halfway houses, and these facilities tend to exhibit both a narrow selectivity in clientele and a rigidity in clinical approach. The black halfway houses of the Fillmore district and the hippie halfway houses of the Haight-Ashbury are resistant to cross-referral: "Inappropriate" clients seeking entry are simply turned away. In the same way, most of the personnel in the halfway houses feel a disaffection for the methadone treatment program at the

Methadone Clinic and will make no referrals whatever to that facility. The center has for some time sought to implement a disinterested central intake, diagnosis, and referral facility, and such a single-point entry house is proposed. The other halfway houses will then be entirely relieved of the burden of intake paperwork, but whether this incentive will sufficiently compensate them for the fact that they will be merely receiving their clients instead of selecting them remains to be seen.

In implementing these continuity linkages, the center used a broad interpretation of its coercive powers under the purchase-of-service agreements to obtain compliance. While this fact again underscores the integrative value of single-conduit funding, it is worthy of note that, even so, compliance remained spotty so long as there was no incentive to the agency directly from the procedure itself. Data reporting became "very sloppy," as one director put it, in the period before the system was computerized and fully operative, during which time it seemed a pointless exercise in paperwork. The incentives that were later developed and that alone brought full compliance were the following: (1) the center became able to relieve the service providers of much interagency reporting, as described above; and (2) theoretically, agencies showing high performance efficiency in comparative evaluation made possible by the "transaction encounter" reports would be favored for continued or increased funding. The center was further aided in implementing central record-keeping when it was mandated by NIMH as a condition of the drug program grant; the administrative staff then had an external rationale for its internal procedural requirement.

In achieving consolidation of personnel practices and joint hiring, the NIMH drug program requirements were unequivocal, and the center used the necessity for compliance to standardize procedures for all agency programs funded through the project. Each agency does its own recruiting and draws up job descriptions, qualifications, salary range, fringe benefits, and so on. The Personnel Committee of the Board of Directors then reviews the candidate and all aspects of the job specifications, freely exercising its option to reject the applicant, adjust the salary, or revise the scope of the position. Questions of staff proficiency are similarly brought before the Personnel Committee, with the hiring agency in attendance. Thus, both hiring and firing for center-funded programs is done on a joint basis between the agency and the project as a whole, including its citizen component. This procedure has facilitated the hiring of nonwhite clinical and administrative staff, a key issue in center operation. In terms of service delivery, it ensures quality of service by maintaining professional standards, and it has impact on continuity by guaranteeing that new staff will share Westside project goals and objectives.

The center coupled these efforts to consolidate personnel practices with an attempt to develop an interdisciplinary approach to the delivery of mental health services. Thus it emphasized multidisciplinary staff recruitment by affiliated providers, so that a hospital, for example, would offer services provided by social workers in addition to physicians and psychiatrists. This emphasis was, in part, designed to enhance structural integration of the project and continuity in service delivery. Its effect on the latter, however, has not as yet been determined.

Westside Center has most successfully improved continuity, however, through its implementation of joint program planning, which followed naturally from the regular interaction between the CAB and the Board of Directors, and ongoing process of discovery of gaps in service, of informal program review, and of generation of new program concepts. All new programs are reviewed by the Program Planning Committee of the board and the CAB prior to submission to the Board of Directors for approval; budgets for new programs must be specifically approved by the Board's Finance Committee. A committee composed of clinical representatives of the provider agencies is the primary mechanism for coordination of program planning. Here new programs are subjected to a projectwide overview by the combined professional staffs. The process is highly effective but not entirely satisfactory to any of the participants. Agency staff complain about the long delay and the costly expenditure of time involved in the committee and CAB review, which frequently consists (from their point of view) of prolonged education of the community members in order to resolve their misapprehensions or misconceptions. Even the complainants, however, concede that the process often produces valuable insights and increases the sensitivity and efficacy of program planning. Center staff, for their part, feel that agency professionals participate too little in program planning (and in committee work generally) and are constantly prodding the clinicians to give more time to the process.

COMMUNITY COUNCIL CHILD CARE PROJECT

This child care project is a component program of the Maricopa County Community Council, the social planning organization serving Phoenix and its environs. It is the nascent mechanism for planning, developing, coordinating, and financing child care programs in the county and the potential 4-C for its service area. As the sole conduit of Title IV-A money for child care for former and potential AFDC recipients in the county, the project funds 19 child care facilities through purchase of service agreements for day care.

The project is an example of mediated coordination in which the project staff under the direction of the Community Council Board seeks the administrative integration of autonomous agencies providing child care and related health and social services. These agencies and parents of children enrolled in child care facilities serve on a variety of committees dealing with project operation and programing.

Project Development

The genesis of the Community Council Child Care Project was a May 1969 statewide campaign to prevent the closing of 10 Migrant Opportunity Program child care centers whose OEO funding was terminated. This campaign mobilized a variety of community organizations into a task force to locate and to obtain alternative funding for at least one center. Task force enquiries to the Arizona congressional delegation and HEW uncovered Title IV-A as a potential funding source.

Efforts to obtain Title IV-A funds spanned nearly a year, during which time task force focus shifted from funding one center to funding five, and finally, the entire project. These efforts were both helped and hindered by the Social and Rehabilitation Service (SRS) of HEW and the Arizona Department of Public Welfare, the federal and state IV-A administering agencies. They were particularly constrained by the federal formula grant planning and routing system, which necessitated working through the state to obtain federal funds.

Securing Title IV-A money was a complex process. It depended on acquisition of a local match, Department of Public Welfare approval of the proposal to use IV-A funds, and development of purchase of child care services provisions for the newly required IV-A state plan. The local share took nearly a year to obtain. It was raised from community donations solicited by a task force-created fund-raising organization and from the United Fund.

Department of Public Welfare approval of the task force proposal took an equally long time to secure since the department initially objected to the proposal. This objection was based, in part, on unfamiliarity with Title IV-A provisions. The department was also skeptical of using IV-A in a novel way—that is, to fund the entire operation of a child care center rather than to purchase child care slots in an existing center as was its practice. This skepticism was reinforced by the inability of SRS to provide a clear and accurate interpretation of IV-A provisions concerning eligible costs and statewideness. The latter was particularly problematic for the department since it feared statewideness necessitated immediate initiation of similar day-care activities throughout Arizona using scarce state revenue as the IV-A local match.

The department agreed to discuss the task force proposal and relevant IV-A plan provisions with task force representatives as a consequence of public pressure on state officials and congressional enquiries. These were primarily precipitated by task-force-generated publicity about the child care problem. In response to this meeting, community demand, HEW clarification of some IV-A provisions, and its Work Incentive Program (WIN) program child care requirements, the department approved the task force proposal. Thus, in December 1969, with task force and HEW assistance, the State Welfare Board amended its Family and Child Care Services Plan to provide for purchase of day care services using private contributions for the IV-A match.

By December also, the task force, Maricopa County Community Council, and several other organizations began consideration of 4-C as a means to coordinate the delivery of child care services in the county. By the time HEW approved the state plan purchase of services provisions in February 1971 and five centers were funded in March, a proposal for a 4-C project in Maricopa County was already being prepared.

Community acceptance of the project was readily attained. Many agencies concerned with child care participated in its development, viewing center coordination as a logical next step to center funding. Others felt it in their best interest to support a project that could help fulfill their own child care goals. Some United Fund agencies that were skeptical about the project with its tie to federal funding were won over by United Fund promises of continued support should IV-A money cease.

Department of Public Welfare approval was not as easily attained. The department was hesitant to permit a third party (the project) to administer IV-A child care funds for the county. By May, however, the department accepted the project plan for single-point funding. This acceptance was predicated on four factors: (1) project staff devised the project plan and assisted with the technical aspects of IV-A funding, alleviating the burden placed on the department; (2) the department considered it advantageous to work with one local umbrella agency responsible for IV-A funding rather than with many individual agencies; (3) it felt the project could raise the local match for, and create the facilities, needed to provide day care for children in WIN, Concentrated Employment Program (CEP), and AFDC enrollees; and (4) there was considerable community support for and involvement with the project.

Thus, on July 1, 1971, the contracts for the project were signed. On July 2, however, they were voided when Regional SRS questioned the statewideness and child care eligibility provisions of the Arizona IV-A plan. By this action, HEW revised its February authorization for the department to proceed with the purchase of child care services. The resultant delay in project implementation, however, was brief. Unified in support of the project, the welfare department and project staff collaborated to revise the state plan provisions. Immediate SRS acceptance of these provisions enabled the signing of new contracts on July 8.

Project Operation

Through the remainder of 1971, project priorities basically concerned survival: developing administrative procedures and a structure, securing funds for center operation, and undertaking planning to meet child care and related social service needs. Efforts to meet all three of these priorities were hindered by obstacles inherent in the IV-A routing system.

The development of administrative procedures was particularly constrained by the actions of the State Welfare Board, which did not share project support demonstrated by some welfare department staff. Consequently, there were department delays in relaying information about the project to and from HEW; new and changing procedures for project administration were devised; IV-A funds were reduced or withheld from some centers without explanation.

While these actions partially reflected opposition to the project, they also mirrored the department's unfamiliarity with Title IV-A and fear of illegally using funds that would have to be repaid by the state. In addition, they reflected SRS confusion about IV-A provisions.

In the end, it was this inability of HEW to clarify IV-A provisions that had the most debilitating effect on project operation since it precipitated a crisis in September 1971 that remained unsettled for nearly a year. This crisis not only hindered efforts to meet funding and planning priorities but also threatened the project with extinction. It occurred when some Department of Public Welfare and HEW staff questioned project, and state plan, compliance with IV-A provisions. At issue were whether (1) IV-A could finance 4-C planning costs; (2) IV-A could finance equipment for child care centers; (3) in-kind contributions could constitute part of the local IV-A share, and if so, how their cash value should be calculated; (4) the contract between the welfare department and the project was a third-party agreement as intended or a purchase of service agreement; and (5) IV-A could finance the administrative costs (project staff) of a third party.

Planning became an issue in late 1971 when project staff sought IV-A money to develop a capacity to assist affiliated members in planning efforts. The money was to support a day care needs and resources assessment, preparation of a child care and social services plan, planning staff, and a project evaluation system. Its allocation would enable the staff to develop joint planning and evaluation linkages with member agencies. The Department of Public Welfare, however, refused to provide IV-A for planning purposes until HEW clarified planning as an eligible IV-A cost.

The use of in-kind contributions for the IV-A local share similarly created a problem when the department contested (1) the donation of a school as a portion of the local share, and (2) the method of determining its cash value. Pending HEW interpretation of the relevant IV-A provisions, the department reduced the IV-A allocation for one center, compelling curtailment of many of its services.

Finally, the contract between the department and the project became an issue when HEW questioned whether it and the state plan complied with IV-A purchase-of-service regulations. The very existence of the project depended on the rapid, favorable resolution of this issue. If the contract were declared a purchase-of-service agreement, the 19 IV-A centers would lose enough IV-A money to make compliance with federal day-care standards impossible. Similarly, if IV-A could not be used for third-party administrative costs, the project would have lost its staff.

To resolve these issues, project staff and the Department of Public Welfare independently wrote to HEW in late 1971 requesting interpretation of the relevant IV-A provisions. Although their resolution depended on a prompt reply, months elapsed before HEW, prodded by congressional inquiries, began providing the necessary interpretations. In the interim, the Department of Public Welfare, fearing its liability for IV-A money allocated without written interpretations, disallowed all costs for purchase or repair of equipment by the 19 IV-A centers. Similarly, it ceased IV-A payment for the salary of the assistant project director who had a planning function.

HEW's delay in providing information resulted from the inability of its own staff to agree on guideline interpretation, and a breakdown in communication between the regional and national SRS offices. It occurred even though (1) all the issues, with the exception of in-kind contributions, arose during project development and were deemed settled by HEW approval, in February 1970, of the purchase-of-services portion of the state plan; and (2) several other IV-A-funded child care projects already had HEW approval to use IV-A for administrative, planning, and equipment costs.

In February 1972, SRS provided the Welfare Department and the project with the first of the written interpretations they sought. These guidelines have necessitated changes in project procedures and contracts, most of which are being made.

The planning issue, however, remains unsettled. HEW indicated that planning services were eligible for IV-A funding but that the Department of Public Welfare could not fund them under the existing contract with the project. Hence, another contract specifically for purchase of planning services had to be devised. The department will not negotiate this contract, largely because of the problems it encountered in purchasing child care services. As a consequence, project planning must be limited and the application for project designation as a 4-C has not been filed since without IV-A funding, project staff cannot perform the planning and coordinating functions of a 4-C agency. Thus, even with clarification of guidelines, the IV-A routing system in which the state controls federal funds, continues to inhibit the development and integration of the child care project.

THE TRI-COUNTY PROJECT

The Tri-County Project is an interagency, experimental project in the delivery of human services in Peoria, Tazewell, and Woodford counties, Illinois. The project is financed by and under the auspices of the Illinois Institute for Social Policy, a state agency established by Executive Order during July 1970 to research, demonstrate, and evaluate various social service programs. The project began operation on June 21, 1971 and is scheduled to continue until June 1973.

The Tri-County Project is a neutral coordinating body in which the funding sources for public and private service providers have invested the authority to move previously autonomous agencies toward integrative goals. Project staff includes the director and two administrative assistants, the deputy director and his administrative assistant, the director of research, and the supervisors of each of the respective County Service Access Centers. The office of the project director is the chief integrative agent. The authority and the tools of the office include the following:

- The governor endorses the project fully and has delegated to the director the status and the authority of his office to direct state agency cooperation with the project.
- The governor has given the director the authority to impose decisions on state agencies, whenever such decisions require no changes in law or written state policies. Matters requiring changes in basic agency policies or in law can be referred by the director to the governor's office to affect waivers or administrative change.
- Directors of state human service agencies operating in the tri-county area delegate substantial authority to the project director to facilitate the implementation of the project's goals and objectives.
- The local United Fund and the Human Resources Council of Peoria County have endorsed the project, the former urging participation by its member agencies. Because the United Fund represents their primary funding source, these private agencies comply with the project's goals and objectives. The

United Fund's and the Human Resources Council's interest in the project stems from the Service Access System's impact on making the services of private providers more accessible to clients, and from the Information System's potential for revealing aggregate data on client movement, which will help the fund to rationalize (1) priority determination, (2) the expansion or elimination of some services, and (3) budget allocations. The United Fund also sees that the combination of the project's coordinative functions and its Information System will reveal areas for interagency cooperation in the provision of services through purchase of service agreements. Project staff, supported by the fund and council staff, mediate solutions to private interagency problems.

The director's administrative leadership has been critical to the Tri-County Project's success. Because he participated in the project development and because of his experience working in bureaucracies, he understands the project's goals and objectives and is able to deal with the conflict and confusion inherent in affecting change in bureaucratic agencies. The direct's administrative style is based on an awareness of the limitations of his authority, so he claims and uses only as much authority as he actually holds. Consequently in the Tri-County situation, the director operates on the basis that it is easier to get results by the use of tact and diplomacy than it is from the use of force. However, he will exercise his authority when these procedures fail. The project does have considerable "nuisance power"—that is, the power to make organizational life difficult for noncooperative agencies by creating "static" from the United Fund or the state capital.

Background and Operation

The project implements several recommendations of a 1968 Peoria community self-survey and has been endorsed and supported by the local United Fund. In addition to the nine state human service agencies in the area, a total of 43 local public and voluntary agencies have elected to participate in the project. Virtually all staffed, direct-service agencies in the three counties are included. The only exceptions are the smaller township relief offices (the two largest are included) and juvenile court services in one of the counties.

The project is seeking to provide more efficient delivery of human services by operating an Information System, a Service Access System (SAS), and a Coordination Unit.

The project operates a twofold Information System to collect data on the movement of clients through the service system and to catalogue the range of community services. The first element of the system tracks all persons applying to or entering the system.

During project development, there was considerable discussion about how much client information should be collected and exchanged among agencies. In the interest of maintaining confidentiality for clients, it was decided to limit the collection of data basically to identifying information for the primary use of project personnel and to make client data available to participating agencies upon their formal request to the director of research. Information is kept on all applicants, on a name basis, including general identifying data such as age, race, income, and residential area. This information allows for follow-up on all applicants and facilitates client evaluation and feedback on a sample basis, permits the tracing of the "cycling" of some types of clients through the social service delivery system, and provides data on the number of persons receiving multiple services. Further, the system allows analysis of referral patterns and the identification of interagency problems, service gaps, and duplications, which may enhance community planning by the public and private sectors to rationalize the allocation of their available resources.

Specifically, the Information System keeps the following information on a client: (1) application, whether accepted or rejected; reasons for rejection; (2) services approved and provided, nature of services, and dates provided; (3) termination of services, date, reason; and (4) referral, to what services, dates, with what results.

The success of the Information System depends to a large extent upon the cooperation of agency personnel. Early feedback indicates that the system is working well and accurately. However, some agency line personnel have objected to it on the grounds that it represents additional paperwork for them. Obviously, gross refusal or some lesser degree of inefficiency to accurately report client information on the part of agency line personnel would seriously impede the Information System's operations.

The second element of the Information System involves cataloguing of program and eligibility information on all available services in the Tri-County area on a week-by-week basis. The project has published the SAS Resource Book, a 240-page document that describes in detail the service eligibility requirements of almost 100 public and private human service agencies in the Tri-County area.

The Service Access System is the project's primary operational component. Service Access specialists are knowledgeable of program content, eligibility standards, capacity limitations, and intake procedures of all public and private agencies in the Tri-County area. They perform preliminary diagnosis and refer clients to appropriate agencies. A formal contractual arrangement between the project and participating state and local public and private agencies empowers specialists to make service judgments that agencies must honor whenever legally or medically possible. When such service is impossible, the agency and the Service Access System are responsible for making immediate alternative arrangements for the client. In other words, participating agencies are bound to a "no-decline" policy. Other service arrangements detailed in the contract are as follows:

- Participating agencies must report to the Service Access System all persons seeking services regardless of whether or not the service is provided.
- Agencies who do not provide a service to an applicant must refer the person to the Service Access System for screening for other services.
- State agencies must make all referrals for other supportive services through the Service Access System, either by telephone or through personal referral of the individual or family.
- Private agencies must make all referrals to state agencies through the Service Access System. They make referrals to other private agencies through the Service Access System or directly. When private agencies make referrals directly, they must report them to the Service Access System.
- All agencies must report the disposition of service assignments or referrals to the Service Access System.
- When an agency provides more than one program service to an individual or family, the initiation of each service must be reported to the Service Access System. Agencies must also report the termination of each program service to an individual or family.

Project staff possesses authority to direct state agency compliance with the contract, and it relies heavily on its endoresement and support from the local United Fund and Human Resources Council to exact compliance from private agencies.

The contract between the project and the participating agencies embodies the resolution to a conflict that arose during the project's planning over whether or not the project should perform centralized intake and diagnosis. Many agencies objected to relinquishing their prerogative to perform these functions for a number of reasons. Some agencies believed that they would be turning over these functions to generalists who were less experienced and well trained than the personnel presently performing the tasks in the agencies, while others argued that generalists could not possibly perform adequate diagnosis services within their complex functional area. Some opposed the project's assuming these tasks on the basis that they did not care to relinquish the power inherent in an agency's ability to admit or deny service to a client. The settlement denied the project the authority to perform intake services and limited it to performing only enough diagnosis to link a client to an appropriate service provider. More precise diagnosis was left with the agency. However, the agencies did agree to conform to the reporting system stipulated in the contract.

Because SAS staff makes some decisions for agencies, there is some tension between the project and the agencies. Also, SAS serves as client advocates within the system and sometimes second-guesses agency actions. In varying degrees and fashions, this role is resented by agency staffs as interfering and meddlesome. Some agency staff, however, praise the SAS role in arranging services with other agencies, particularly in borderline, difficult cases. Several of the private agencies would probably like to withdraw from SAS and may do so. The main restraining force is the United Fund's endorsement of the project.

Specialists are stationed in Service Access Centers located in each county seat. Centers provide information concerning agencies to all persons who call or visit them, and function as access centers into the human services system for those persons. Although clients are not required to enter the service system through centers, persons not sure of what services they may need are encouraged to do so.

Persons who know what they need and where to go to get it can continue to enter the system through the agencies, although the agencies must report such clients to the system. Preliminary data gathered from the Information System over a five-month period showed that 90 percent of those entering the human service system were doing so through participating agencies, while only 10 percent were entering through the Service Access System.

Further, the data indicated that only 761 out of 8,413 persons, or 9 percent of those who sought aid, were getting it from more than one agency. Of those 761, a total of 568 persons were receiving aid from two agencies; 73, from four; four, from five; and one, from six places. This suggests that either a paucity of multiple-problem clients exist in the Tri-County area, or agency personnel are not screening clients for multiple problems. Project personnel have considered various possibilities to preclude the latter possibility. One solution is to invest project personnel with intake authority and to station these workers in a central intake center, or to outstation them in each agency. Another solution is to train present agency intake workers and to standardize the intake forms of all participating agencies to the extent that they alert workers to identify multiple-problem clients.

Another problem linked to the fact that so many clients initially enter the system through agencies is that it precludes the project from providing transportation for multiple-problem clients among various agencies.

Community workers stationed in Service Access Centers perform outreach and follow-up services. Workers conduct extensive public information campaigns to publicize the Service Access System.

Campaigns include such techniques as pamphlet drops and face-to-face contacts with all persons in the community to whom a client might turn for help, such as doctors, lawyers, school personnel, county employees, and clergy. There is evidence to suggest that campaigns are increasing the number of clients who enter the system. For certain, the outreach activity is discovering clients who probably would not have gotten any substantive assistance had it not been for the project. The project's outreach probably has not reduced outreach by participating agencies.

The Information System periodically provides computer printouts for community workers and other employees to conduct follow-up on clients. Follow-up is conducted by employee calls to agencies rather than to clients to determine if clients received services. Calls to clients, the project determined, violated some clients' notions that agencies delivered services in confidence. An impediment to follow-up is the time that lapses between the time a service is delivered and the availability of the computer printouts necessary for follow-up activities. If the time lapse is too long, follow-up efforts may be too late to benefit clients.

Some specialists are outstationed in high-volume agencies such as the Department of Public Aid, the Peoria State Hospital, Zeller Zone Mental Health Center, and the Peoria Public Schools to act as referral resources. These specialists interview and assess persons the agencies find ineligible for services and any persons needing additional services from the system. They do not interview other persons applying for and receiving the services of that agency on a regular basis, nor do they perform general information services. Outstationed specialists also serve as the contact point for the project's Coordination Unit.

Other specialists are circuit riders, who visit outlying rural communities in the Tri-County area on a rotating schedule. They are assisted in each community by community workers who are responsible for outreach and information functions. This aspect of the project has not proven particularly successful because of the limited amount of time that riders have been able to spend in each outlying area. This situation has essentially rendered the rider inaccessible to the client, and the project is considering discontinuation of this function. Generally, the project's approach to service delivery in rural areas has not been successful. Rural residents will use Service Access Centers and telephone services, but they resist arrangements with Peoria-based services.

A third component of the project is the Coordination Unit, which operates under the direction of the project director, whom the governor has designated as "coordinator of State Human Services." The unit functions to locate and confront policy and program problems, particularly problems of an interagency nature. Although originally specified in terms of state agencies, the unit function has tended to include problems involving voluntary and local public agencies as well. The techniques the unit employs in its coordinating function are those of research negotiation, acting as a catalytic agent, and efforts to clarify some policies and laws through the Springfield office of the Illinois Institute for Social Policy and the governor's office.

The project's early emphasis on operationalizing the Information System and the Service Access System preempted maximum utilization of the Coordination Unit's potential capabilities. However, during the project's early stages, the unit addressed a number of interagency problems including the clarification of policy confusion among county relief offices and between the local and state levels of DPA, and the negotiation and resolution of a jurisdictional dispute between Children and Family Services and the Zeller Zone Mental Health Center. Although the Coordination Unit has been able to resolve most disputes at the local level, it has found some difficulty in referring problems to the governor's office when it needs to defer to a higher authority. Presently the governor's authority over human services agencies is invested in a staff person who exercises it on an informal ad hoc basis when he has time to do so. The Coordination Unit could better utilize the governor's authority to resolve interagency disputes if it were invested in a more formal, dependable structure.

THE VOCATIONAL INCENTIVES PROGRAM

The Vocational Incentives Program (VIP) is a program in the same geographic area and with the same sponsorship as the Tri-County Project described above. The program was initiated on the expectation that the combination of a Division of Vocational Rehabilitation (DVR) Expansion Grant and WIN resources would be more efficient than operating separately two state programs in the Tri-County area to train and place employable welfare recipients. The merger was to result not only in reduction of duplication and various economies of scale but also in more effective and efficient service delivery.

VIP combines the efforts of five state agencies to train and place welfare recipients in gainful employment. Basically, the program merges the staff and program resources of the Peoria-Tazewell County WIN program with DVR resources funded with Vocational Rehabilitation monies. In addition to the merged efforts of these two state programs, the Illinois Bureau of Employment Security's offices in the Tri-County area augment VIP's employment resources; the Department of Public Aid (DPA) is VIP's referral resource and its outstationed caseworkers on VIP's teams to provide regular casework services to program clients. The Illinois Institute for

Social Policy administers and coordinates the program through its Peoria office.

The institute serves as an umbrella organization to facilitate the necessary interagency agreements and relates the direct service aspects of the program to other vocational services in the community. The director of the Tri-County Project is the executive officer of VIP. In this capacity, he is responsible to the administrator of the Bureau of Employment Security (BES) for the program and reporting requirements of the WIN program, to the director of the Division of Vocational Rehabilitation for the requirements of the Expansion Grant project, and to the director of the Department of Public Aid for DPA reports regarding WIN. In addition to these reporting responsibilities, the executive officer selects the Project Coordinator with the advice of DVR, BES, and DPA. Under the coordinator are two assistant coordinators, one from DVR and one from WIN, jointly selected by the institute and the merged programs.

All project staff, regardless of payroll status, with the exception of DPA outstationed caseworkers, are administratively responsible to the executive officer and the project coordinator. Presently, the project coordinator is on the institute payroll while former WIN and DVR employees continue on their respective agency payrolls. New positions created in connection with the project are charged against the expansion grant and are on the DVR payroll.

VIP's long-term service delivery objective is to train and place more employable public assistance clients in the Tri-County area than it was possible to do before the existence of the program. The project's target population is all public aid recipients and applicants who can be reasonably expected to profit from the provision of direct services to move them toward employment. Approximately 2,000 recipients will be screened into the program over a three-year period. VIP's sole source of referrals in the Department of Public Aid.

VIP's Service Delivery

All eligible clients are assigned to interagency teams, which work out an employment plan with each client. The plan may include basic education, physical restoration, mental health counseling, vocational training, on-the-job training, and so on. Each team consists of a counselor (WIN or DVR), a caseworker (DPA), a job development specialist, a job coach, and a clerk stenographer. The team sets an employment goal, works with, and strives to place the client in a job when he is prepared. Following placement the team maintains systematic follow-up contact for at least three months.

VIP's Impact on Service Delivery

VIP has implemented various processes that shorten the time it takes from the point of a client's initial contact to the time at which he receives VIP's services. When the WIN program operated separately, it took from two to three months to receive a medical report on a client. Under VIP, the DPA caseworker arranges for physical examinations during the client's initial screening. These physicals are performed by either of two community health clinics that have agreed to examine clients within a three-day period and report back to VIP within 10 to 14 days. Upon completion of screening in DPA offices, VIP personnel escort the client to VIP offices, where orientation processes begin. Each of these arrangements allows VIP to begin talking to a client about a program to gain employability and a job almost immediately after the client's initial contact with the DPA caseworker.

Other VIP processes are designed to identify and put multi-problem clients in contact with needed service providers. Each staff member of the team is attuned to identifying a client's needs for direct services beyond those that VIP offers. The caseworker on the team refers clients through the Service Access System (SAS) of the Tri-County project, an information and referral system operated by the Illinois Institute. SAS provides VIP immediate access to services and also supplies follow-up on supporting services. VIP provides a client with escort and transportation to support services and training sites if necessary. The project's contacts with job providing and developing organizations in the community (for example, the Illinois State Employment Service, the National Alliance of Businessmen, and the Urban League employment programs) provide a client immediate access to gainful employment upon completion of his program. Each of these processes brings a client closer to the array of services he needs to gain employability and, ultimately, employment.

Background

The State of Illinois was awarded $1.2 million for fiscal year 1972 from the $26 million appropriated nationally for Vocational Rehabilitation-Public Assistance Projects for the purpose of preparing and initiating special programs to expand vocational rehabilitation services to disabled public assistance recipients.

Upon announcement of the availability of expansion monies, the SRS Regional Commissioner met with the governor's assistant responsible for social services. Although no specific project details were discussed, the governor's representative offered the commissioner the assistance of his office to help integrate the efforts of the State Division of Vocational Rehabilitation, the legislated conduit for the expansion projects. A possible role for the institute in the expansion program was also discussed.

Involving the institute was considered desirable because (1) it had a branch in Peoria that was considered a suitable site for a demonstration program because of its manageable welfare case load and industrial base facilitating development of job training opportunities; (2) its Peoria office had demonstrated its skill in integrating autonomous state agencies in the Tri-County Project it operated; and (3) its objectives of developing, demonstrating, and evaluating ways to improve social services were consistent with those of the commissioner of SRS.

Following these initial conversations, the commissioner directed his office to prepare a preliminary proposal for an Illinois-Institute-administered expansion project integrating the efforts of the DVR and DPA in the Tri-County area. He then convened a meeting with representatives of both departments and the institute to discuss the project, Peoria as a possible location, and a role for the institute. The issue of project sponsorship, however, was not raised.

The DVR director, while preferring that his department design a project and select the site, tentatively accepted the commissioner's suggestion of a joint project with DPA and Peoria as the site. The director of Public Aid also agreed, indicating, however, that his department could not participate without additional staff for its Peoria office.

The commissioner subsequently held a meeting in Peoria at which representatives of the two state departments and the institute met with members of the business and industrial community to determine their receptivity to the project. It was followed by a Chicago meeting at which project sponsorship by the institute was broached. Its acceptance by all in attendance and by the governor's office compelled the DVR to accept also.

Following this meeting, the director of the Institute's Peoria office recommended that the project integrate the services of the Peoria-Tazewell County WIN program inasmuch as both were geared to the same clientele and had congruent objectives. The governor's office and the commissioner of SRS agreed to the proposal. However, it required a directive from the governor's office and a series of compromises to secure acceptance by the DVR, DPA, and the state and local offices of BES, the WIN administering agency.

DVR apprehension about loss of control over expansion program funds was mitigated by its involvement in project planning, desire to maintain its working relationship with SRS, and the directive from the governor's office. The directive similarly allayed BES reluctance. This reluctance was based on the fear that the exemplary Peoria-

Tazewell County WIN program would be submerged and weakened by the project. DPA cooperation was assured by an agreement to provide its Peoria office with more staff.

The Department of Labor provided the final obstacle to project planning. Its hesitancy to merge a WIN program with a project not administered by a traditional state agency, however, was overcome by requests from both BES and the governor's assistant.

While the question of WIN participation was being settled, HEW and the Department of Vocational Rehabilitation began preparing the project plan. This task eventually was assumed by a committee in Peoria consisting of representatives of HEW, DVR, and the director of the institute. Prior to plan approval, major problems arose about the use of WIN and DVR counselors interchangeably on the teams providing services to both WIN and DVR clients. DVR felt that WIN counselors initially would not have the expertise to approve vocational rehabilitation services for clients. Through the commissioner of SRS, a compromise was arranged providing for separate DVR and WIN-counselor-led teams for the first 6 to 12 months of project operation. During this time, all team members would receive training in the resources and technologies of both programs.

During this period also, a problem arose over the selection of a program coordinator to manage the project under the policy direction of the Institute's Tri-County office. The governor's office recommended that one person, jointly selected by all participating agencies, serve as the coordinator. When it became evident that DVR and WIN could not agree on a coordinator, the Institute's director asked the governor's office to intervene. Pending this intervention, he suspended further work on the project.

The governor's office, however, did not have the structure to respond to the request in a timely manner. For most purposes the governor's authority over state human resource agencies is delegated to a staff member who exercises it on an informal and ad hoc basis. Thus intervention from his office is dependent upon the ability of his staff to find the time and the resources to secure agency cooperation for ventures such as the Tri-County project. Consequently, intervention was delayed until several events made it inevitable.

The event precipitating intervention was HEW's decision to fund the project in October, which prompted the governor to announce and endorse the project publicly. Consequently, when the commissioner of SRS and DVR indicated that the project had not been implemented because of the impasse over selection of a coordinator, he directed his staff aide responsible for social services to settle the issue. The staff member then directed that the institute select the coordinator with the advice, but not necessarily the approval, of the participating agencies.

The selection was made shortly thereafter. On March 14, eight months after the initial conversation between the commissioner and the governor's assistant, VIP became operational.

GREATER CLEVELAND MENTAL RETARDATION DEVELOPMENT PROJECT

The Greater Cleveland Mental Retardation Development Project (sometimes called the Network Development Project) was a project carried out from 1966 to 1970 by the Welfare Federation of Cleveland. The object of the Cleveland Mental Retardation Project was to develop an effective system of interrelated, yet autonomous public and private agencies to serve the mentally retarded in the Cleveland area.

Ohio has long had an "exclusion law" providing that children with IQs below 50 be excluded from regular public school. Until the mid-1950s these children received service from no public agencies other than state hospitals. The exclusion law drove parents to form their own programs and ultimately to lobby for "county classes" and later for the formation of the Cuyahoga County Board of Mental Retardation, a major service provider.

The previous delivery system consisted of many small, dispersed parent-controlled classes for retarded children, poorly staffed and poorly housed. Most Welfare Federation agencies that provided other services (counseling for parents, dental service for retarded children, and so on) were reluctant to acknowledge that they occasionally accepted the retarded for fear they would be inundated by people seeking service.

The parent-controlled programs were fragmented and had to compete for the limited funds available for mental retardation from private sources. The public and voluntary agencies were busy denying that a need existed and covering up the fact that they were meeting that need only for a few.

Thus, conditions were ripe for a major thrust toward improved services for the mentally retarded. Active and demanding parent-groups were organizing into a loose association. The federal bureaucracy was responsive to the Kennedy Administration's interest in mental retardation. The Welfare Federation (through the effort of the Children's Council) was accepting the fact that it must give a higher priority to the needs of the retarded.

A first step in this direction was the recognition by the Welfare Federation of a serious problem and the assignment of a senior community development specialist to quarter-time work in the field. In slightly over 18 months this effort resulted in a significant integrative contribution and successful application for an HEW planning grant to design a five-year effort to build a network of services.

The initial one-year grant resulted in publication of a planning document that detailed the need and spelled out the resources required to be developed to meet the need. The "Directory of Services" (and a companion "Guide to Services for the Mentally Retarded" for laymen) were republished at intervals, and a "Fact Book," which documented needs and identified resources, was also prepared.

The Greater Cleveland Mental Retardation Development Project was financed for five years in yearly increments of $100,000 Vocational Rehabilitation research and demonstration funds and $25,000 local funds provided by three local foundations. Of this total, roughly $40,000 per year was set aside to finance demonstration programs, while the remainder was used for integrative tasks by a three-person staff consisting of a director, assistant director, and research assistant. During the five years of the project, there were further publications; committees and other groups were formed; two short-term demonstration projects were entered into; and generally a ferment of action on many fronts was created to organize existing agencies for a surge of increased service availability.

In 1970—at the end of the project—a profound change had taken place in Cleveland. Nine times more retarded adolescents and adults were receiving services through the Bureau of Vocational Rehabilitation. Four times more trainable mentally retarded students were receiving special schooling, and a 30 percent increase in enrollment of educable retarded children (IQ above 50) was recorded in public school programs.

These are statistical indices of a profound change in agency attitudes and interagency relations brought about during the project. These changes within and between agencies were brought about by a small staff working self-consciously and openly toward services integration, and without line authority, as mediators and facilitators.

Decentralization Strategy

Project staff elected a strategy that would strengthen all the viable service delivery agencies and redirect those whose goals had become obscure. This strategy was implemented in a variety of ways. In order to communicate this to the various agencies and the general public, the project adopted a graphic motif that visually conveyed its judgment that a decentralized yet interrelated system of agencies for the mentally retarded could be developed into a network of services. The logo consisted of dispersed centers (discs of varying size) linked to one another by bonds (lines) in clusters. Not every disc was tied to every other, yet every disc was tied to at least one other in the network.

The project organized a subset of the Welfare Federation's members into a coherent but informal system of related services. The "Guide" amd "Directory" served to define the set of agencies that would form the network. The planning documents and Fact Book helped to further define the connections implicit in the Guide and Directory. The agency forum (periodic meetings of representatives from each agency) provided occasion for affecting informal linkage of staffs.

Throughout the project, the theme of operational autonomy for agencies was coupled to the integrative theme of cooperation in the interest of clients. The Cleveland social service establishment was dominated by the Cleveland Foundation, the Welfare Foundation, and the United Appeal, which have close relationships. At the time of the project, the foundation was the major source of seed money and matching funds, while the federation made allocations of funds raised by the United Appeal. Although the agencies were technically autonomous, this interlocking establishment had significant power over the funding of special projects and continuing programs. Thus, the fact that the project operated under the auspices of the Welfare Federation and received funding from the Cleveland Foundation added an element of reflected power to augment the project staff's persuasive ability to attain cooperation. This power was based on an awareness that these connections with local funding sources would give the project influence over service providers' funds.

Full-Time Specialists: Resources for Coordination

The project employed community organization specialists whose central task was the mediation of services integration and linkage development among and between agencies. Thus, the integrator was neither a system administrator nor a service deliverer. The project director and staff took the position that delivery of services would impede their central interest, the building of a delivery network. They wanted to be seen as facilitators and information sources rather than as competing service providers.

One of the first efforts of project staff was to establish relations with provider and parent groups. During the life of the project, the staff offered a "fixed point of information" and operated as a "no-cost consultant" to these groups.

The fact that the staff provided by the project was "in addition to" existing staffing of mental retardation programs in the Cleveland area was an important factor. The presence of this small staff to plan and knit groups together made a profound difference in the coherence and relatedness of the overall system. Specialized staff skills made it possible (1) to augment the planning capabilities of the private voluntary agencies and the new public programs; (2) to prepare proposals and grant applications and to assist new public agencies to prepare planning documents during their developmental stages; (3) to serve as "free consultants" while simultaneously exerting subtle influence over program and funding by the Welfare Federation; and (4) to serve as "fixed point of information" (that is, to become the most knowledgeable center of information, which comprehends the system better than any of the component services) so that it can perform a routing (and controlling) function for interagency inquiries and perform ad hoc informal evaluations for federal, state, and private agencies.

It should be pointed out that this ad hoc informal evaluation function was strictly that, and no more. The project became known as a place where administrators could get the "straight scoop" on a program. With due regard to confidentiality of information, it responded to inquiries with value judgments based on its intimate knowledge of needs and resources and on its intuitive projection of the future pattern of the mental retardation system.

While the staff sought to devote their energies to planning, developmental, and integrative tasks, there was persistent expectation on the part of SRS that the project "do something." Instead of agreeing to offer direct services, staff used roughly one-third of their grant to fund programs to demonstrate the effectiveness of two integrating linkages—central support service and the core service of information and referral. To this end the project initially used about $40,000 to operate (through subcontract to the Vocational Guidance and Rehabilitation Service) a Mobile Analysis and Rehabilitation Team (MART). The three-man MART team operated as a traveling clinic to provide the central support services of assessment and technical assistance to the area's sheltered workshops. MART served as a demonstration until the County Board of Mental Retardation took over operation of sheltered workshops.

Then the "service" element of the grant budget was redirected from the MART project to provide increased funding for a mental retardation information and referral (I and R) service. This specialized I and R was housed in the Welfare Federation's Community Information Service, a general I and R for all public and private social services. This service then continued through to the end of the project and was later carried over as a semiautonomous I and R project under the county's Mental Health and Mental Retardation Board and CAR (the parent-citizen association) after the grant ended.

Coordination Techniques

The project explicitly spelled out the techniques used to strengthen the mental retardation service delivery system. Thus, it produced documented procedures with which to replicate the project in other communities. One of the important products of the project is its fully detailed Final Report, which describes the techniques used to build the network.

The project's principles for building a network of services are listed below. Some of these are underlying assumptions that have a profound effect on organizing methods, while others are procedures that lead toward development of integrated services. In capsule form, they include the following:

1. Develop a partnership of parents and professionals.

2. Wherever possible, adapt existing services to needs of the retarded (rather than establishing new services).

3. Neither ignore the state institutions nor let them dominate; admit them as working partners.

4. Centralize planning but decentralize development and operation of programs.

5. Develop local-area staff training capabilities.

6. Coordinate fund-seeking activities.

7. Develop written standards for service; insist on quality services.

8. Gather uniform, communitywide data and urge service providers to conduct self-evaluations based on this data.

9. Encourage research by service providers.

10. Foster communitywide cooperation and provide coordination.

11. Generate a citizen movement; play the advocacy role; be a lobby.

Consistent with these principles, the project used several strategies to build the network. Some of these were to develop a policy-making committee for the project composed of key representation from parents of the retarded, civic leaders, public officials, and professionals; to organize a group composed of service providers as a forum for systematic information-sharing; to cement staff contacts with public and private funding mechanisms to influence resource allocation within the system; and to use fact-gathering/publishing functions (Blueprints, Fact Books, Surveys, and so on) to influence the local environment and create a climate for coordination.

The project staff resources were also available to service providers in the form of consultation on administrative and policy problems of the agencies, technical assistance as they prepared their grant applications, and generally handling the bulk of the information-gatering and writing on mental retardation subjects for the whole system.

By offering these consultation and data-processing skills, it shaped the delivery system; by developing self-evaluation tools, it enabled providers to reassess their programs and redefine their identity; and by providing (as it did) preliminary planning services to the emerging Community Mental Health and Mental Retardation Board and the County Board of Mental Retardation, it had a profound effect on the thrust and program of these major service providers.

Finally, the publication of directories, guides, and checklists for self-evaluation tended to serve as "definers" of agency roles. The entries in the directory helped each agency to assume an identity and tended to clarify the perceptions of all other service providers about that agency's role.

YOUTH ADVOCACY PROGRAM

The Youth Advocacy Program (sometimes referred to as YAP) is a project designed to increase the capacity of youth to advocate their interests and to change the existing juvenile justice system in South Bend, Indiana. The program was funded in mid-1971 through the local Urban Coalition with a three-year research and demonstration grant from HEW's Youth Development and Delinquency Prevention Administration (YDDPA), and began operating in October of that year. Receiving policy direction from a committee of youth, the central administrative and coordinative staff is supplemented by field representatives stationed at established community agencies.

The broad base of the local Urban Coalition's leadership enabled it to act on behalf of youth in a variety of areas. The business community is represented on the Coalition Board, and their representatives reflect the broad reaches of the political spectrum. Among the most active are three of the major supporters of the Democratic Party, and two of the most prominent Republicans—one a National Committee member. The primary areas of concern were juvenile justice, jobs, and education. The Indiana corrections system is outmoded in its handling of youthful offenders. There are few jobs in the area for youth, and the generally high dropout rate in the city school system reaches 60 percent in the South Bend Model Neighborhood.

While these problems were recognized by the Urban Coalition at its formation, they were not immediately addressed. When a National Urban Coalition consultant offered assistance in forming a local Youth Coalition to deal with them, however, the president of the local group was receptive. Thus a network form of Youth Coalition, centered on the YMCA, was established as a task force of the Urban Coalition six months after the latter was formed.

During 1970 the Youth Coalition carried through a number of highly successful projects, in each case substantially aided by the influential connections and prestige of Urban Coalition members. For example, an inner-city gang belonging to the Youth Coalition was able to present a summer movie series because the films were provided free through business connections of a senior Coalition member. The same auspices and the same use of reflected associational prestige—clout, in short—made possible formation of the Youth Advocacy Program and the initial cooperation it received from provider agencies. Through the Urban Coalition, the project obtained technical assistance from the outset from the Institute for Urban Studies at Notre Dame University; and the YDDPA grant itself was made to the senior coalition, with the Youth Coalition as delegate agency. The chief of police and superintendent of high schools, through these auspices, sat in on development sessions, and the project was greatly assisted in making all its initial contacts by its prestigious sponsorship.

The project began with critical areas of ill will. Two serious errors were made in part due to the deadline for submission of the project funding application. In the first place, while many of the provider agencies participating in the project attached letters of endorsement to the grant application, they were not advised of project details until a month before the grant was announced; and then the approach lacked finesse. Each agency was visited and asked if it would be willing to have a project employee in its office, but several agencies had the impression they were being informed rather than consulted, an abruptness that partially resulted from overreliance on the Urban Coalition clout. In the second place, the mayor was informed of program details only a week before the grant was announced. While he agreed with project objectives, his Narcotics Commission had applied for a Law Enforcement Assistance Agency (LEAA) youth counseling and drug education grant, and he attacked the YAP program as "fragmenting" social services. Both problems were resolved with subsequent conciliation, and the experience was a timely lesson for the staff in the sensitiveness of their position.

The YAP has two central objectives—to increase the capacity of local youth to advocate their interests in established community institutions and to develop an alternative to the delinquency and criminal justice systems now in existence. Fulfillment of both objectives entails promoting change in existing agencies, rather than setting up another program structure, an approach determined by the Youth Coalition members who developed the original proposal. A major tool used is liaison between the Youth Advocacy Program and established institutions in the community so that individually they may become more responsive to the needs and concerns of youth and so that they can join with the program in the creation of an effective diversion system. Thus, major operational goals are (1) establishing communications between youth and the established service providers and (2) bringing service providers together to share resources and develop more effective programs.

A certain amount of conflict is implicit in these programmatic goals. Tension is created by the very effort to effect institutional change, and it takes both internal and external expression; differing concepts of strategy and emphasis provide a source of staff dissension, while service providers—although they may share the project goals— are reluctant to see themselves as "part of the problem." At the same time, by the very nature of its advocacy, the project and its staff are forced into a difficult and demanding role: they must operate in a multiracial, cross-cultural way, remaining open and credible both to the establishment and to the low-income minority community.

Although the Urban Coalition has overall fiscal responsibility for YAP, the Youth Coalition, as delegate agency, forms the project's executive board and has formal responsibility for policy and personnel. Besides its core administrative staff, YAP hires field workers who are located in established agencies and at-large workers providing various direct services.

Many independent service providers are connected with the project: county probation department, city police department, local Urban League, city School Corporation, city recreation commission, a voluntary agency serving children and families, Model Cities, and the city government through the Manpower Area Planning Commission. Additional service providers (including various neighborhood centers, the Legal Aid Society, the state employment office, and the YMCA) work with YAP on committees to plan, develop, and/or run specific programs; working relationships are developing with a few others such as Planned Parenthood and Notre Dame's Psychology Department. The only services provided directly through the project by these agencies are a youth employment program and some counseling. Other joint efforts are being developed, such as recreation services. However, all the services provided separately by each of these agencies are connected, at least potentially, as targets of concern to the project.

Coordination Techniques

The integrative mechanism of the YAP project is the staff itself. In YAP, each staff member—executive director, administrative assistant, technical assistance coordinator, field workers, program coordinator—is regularly involved in integrative functions in the form of administrative support service such as coordination, programing, and consultation. The major techniques used to provide these administrative support services are staff liaison and joint development of programs to demonstrate feasibility. Two kinds of liaison are involved—that of the field workers and the very different liaison provided by the technical assistance coordinator.

247

Staff Liaison

The project's primary device for identifying, assessing, and altering those features of key community institutions that obstruct favorable youth development has been the outstationing of staff appointed jointly by the Youth Coalition and the institution where each is to work. These field workers serve as liaison between youth and the agencies, each keeping abreast of the plans and programs of his agency as they relate to youth and serving as advocate to make them relevant to youth needs. They also play a key role in the development of a court diversion system by identifying and advocating ways in which their agency can help deflect nondangerous youth from the criminal justice system.

The YAP Technical Assistance Coordinator provides specific liaison with the Probation Department and the Juvenile Court. She gathers statistics from department files in order to determine the nexus of problems and of service impact; establishes relationships with probation officers in order to get referrals to YAP service components such as counseling and the Street Academy; and is the primary link for communication of needs and services, although other staff members contact individual probation officers about referred clients.

The method for joint hiring of the field workers is of great importance, since it served to facilitate the joint use of their services and so was a useful integrative technique. The field workers were first recruited by the Youth Coalition for an unspecified job. Each agency was then provided with the names of several recruits. The agency interviewed them independently and informed the Coalition which candidates it found acceptable. Final selection was then made by YAP as to which recruit would serve in which agency. This method served to legitimate the worker with the external service provider without prejudice to his ultimate independent responsibility to YAP, and at the same time it made him acceptable to the provider agency: They had chosen him.

This mutuality in hiring carried over operationally. Although the field workers were responsible to Youth Advocacy, they also received supervision in varying degrees from a staff member of the independent service provider. It is worthy of note that this flexibility on the part of the field workers contributed to their ability to function effectively. At the time the project was studied, specific functions of the field workers were still being developed at some provider agencies, and a few of the providers were still concerned about clarifying training and supervisory jurisdiction.

But this outstationing of field workers is one of the most important linkages developed by the project. It is a primary device for achieving the objectives of informing service providers of youth needs and, by advocacy, making the providers more responsive to youth. It led directly to joint programing and joint planning.

Joint programing is carried out both by the field workers in their respective agencies and by YAP counselors with several agencies, most notably the probation department and a recreation department center. In the case of the field workers, joint programing was a corollary of joint use of staff. While providing youth input to ongoing programs of their agencies, the field workers were able to refocus those programs and propose new ones for staff consideration. As for the counselors, they work closely with the probation and recreation departments developing services. In this way, joint programing is increasing both accessibility of service delivery (by creating new services and making old ones more relevant) and continuity.

Through development of a juvenile court diversion system (an activity designed by the YAP technical assistance coordinator), most of the project's field workers are engaged in long-range planning with their agency. The field workers are to provide current information on the role their agency might play in such a system. The Technical Coordinator is collecting and analyzing data on juvenile crime, referral, and disposition to be coordinated with a wide range of socioeconomic data being assembled by census tracts at the university's Institute of Urban Studies. The total informational input will be used to identify problem and impact areas as a basis for design of the court diversion system.

These linkages were not uniformly achieved in all agencies integrated by the project. The agencies varied in the degree to which they shared the goals of YAP or accepted YAP's role. As a consequence, they varied widely in the extent to which they saw YAP's administrative support services as meaningful or—in terms of their own operation—as either necessary or even useful. Some of the providers appeared to be merely tolerating the presence of the field worker, while others plainly saw the project as valuable and potentially useful both to clients and to their own operation. Although there was little measurable impact after six months of experience, the administrative support services—even when only partially implemented—clearly have large potential impact on accessibility and continuity. The use of outstationed field workers, under these conditions, appears to be an operable way of gaining recognition and access to autonomous agencies without relinquishing independence and effectiveness.

Joint Development of Program to Demonstrate Feasibility

YAP is active in several interagency efforts to develop and operate programs intended to demonstrate the feasibility and value of particular services and to stimulate existing agencies to provide them in the future. These include the Street Academy, which promotes learning by experience and student motivation and productive interaction with the environment. They also include an attempt to expand services in the recreation center bordering the Model Neighborhood, using Model Cities funds, and a Christmas employment program. This program was developed by a group of agencies assembled by the YAP to deal with the increased rate of juvenile theft usual before the holiday. Eighty high-risk youth were employed in small businesses and social service agencies for three weeks and were paid with funds contributed by Model Cities and private donors.

Also YAP is involving several agencies in an attempt to expand services in the recreation center bordering the Model Neighborhood, using Model Cities funds. These planning and programing responses to needs perceived by YAP staff were intended to demonstrate that such programs are feasible and effective, in the hope that existing service providers will pick them up.

Staff Structure

As noted, YAP must maintain a double posture of credibility to both the power structure of South Bend and its young and minority population. The composition of the staff, and their working inter-relationships are designed to achieve this. YAP staff members are chosen to represent differing life-styles and approaches, which allow them to relate to different parts of the community and then correlate these elements within the program. Thus the executive director, academically qualified and middle-class in style, is able to elicit cooperation from the city government, courts, school system, and so on. At the same time, the administrative assistant's more militant approach keeps the project directorate open and credible to clientele. The counseling staff, too, identifies primarily with the clientele, while field workers—depending on the agency for which they are chosen— relate in varying degrees to the agency itself. YAP is thus able both to negotiate with the power structure while maintaining live contact with its client group.

The staff operates in the same way horizontally. For example, field workers share information gained in working with their individual service providers, pull together resources, and collaborate on matters involving more than one external provider. They also share work and reassign tasks according to individual abilities. To some extent the program "senses out" agencies and then sends staff who seem appropriate to deal with them.

The project's provision of a direct service—counseling—and its effectiveness in doing so seems to enhance its legitimacy in the eyes of autonomous providers. The connection and experience of YAP staff with a difficult client group lends weight to their observations and suggestions regarding other agencies' programs and procedures.

True effectiveness of this integrative mechanism requires staff roles to be fully complementary and supportive, with easy internal exchange, but this cannot be achieved without stronger staff cohesion and better working relationships than obtained at the period of this study. The problem, as noted, would seem to be inherent in the design: that is, differing external roles imply differing internal approaches. The issue to be resolved is whether these alternative approaches must necessarily be divisive within the project. It was not clear in the spring of 1972, at the time of observation, how seriously these internal conflicts will affect the program if unresolved, of the willingness of the staff to resolve them. Equally unclear was the director's ability to forge his staff into a cohesive force.

An increasing rift with the Urban Coalition may also impede functioning. Several of those interviewed felt that the Urban Coalition wants the image of representing the interests of the disadvantaged but is unable to identify sufficiently to do so in fact. Other participants think the Urban Coalition desires to control the Youth Coalition and YAP in order to protect its own interests. The resolution of this situation will be crucial for the nature and role of the project since, aside from the reflected clout of the Urban Coalition, YAP has no powers either formal or informal.

Resources used to develop linkages are persuasion, negotiation, the collection of data for use in exerting pressure (not actually tried yet) and sharing of information on clients and program. A peripheral resource was the status of some individual participants and their contacts—for example, the director of the Institute for Urban Studies—which added legitimacy, encouraging some individuals and service providers to go along. Thus far, the techniques most extensively and inventively used have been the whole range of persuasion and negotiation, by individual staff and the total YAP. As the project advances into more concrete work, including direct service, programing and planning, service providers are beginning to perceive its constructive potentials. Also as the field representatives demonstrate their capability in providing substantive assistance to the agencies, they have attained legitimacy in the view of those agencies.

251

PART

II

**HUMAN RESOURCE
SERVICES IN THE STATES:
AN ANALYSIS OF
STATE HUMAN RESOURCE
AGENCIES AND THE ALLIED
SERVICES ACT OF 1972**

14

The newly created state human resource agencies[*] are one example of services integration in that they bring together two or more service providers (that is, state departments) into a single organizational entity for the purpose of improving service delivery. Accordingly, six states, five with a super-agency (Florida, Utah, Massachusetts, Maine, and Georgia) and one without a super-agency at the state level but with an interesting example of regional organization of state functions (Illinois), were included in the study, and their experience in integrating service delivery was evaluated.

During the course of the study, the Allied Services Act of 1972 was formulated and introduced in Congress. It too aims at services integration by bringing together in a comprehensive and coordinated planning effort a number of human services heretofore separately planned and implemented.

Since the field analysis undertaken in the six states had focused on many of the same issues to which the Allied Services Act was addressed, it was possible to consider the capacity of the state super-agencies to carry out the purposes and intent of the act. Part II focuses on that question.

The purpose of Part II is to provide a critique of the Allied Services Act based on the experiences of the six case states.

In particular, it examines (1) the extent to which states have consolidated human service functions in a single organizational

---

[*]In this report a state human resources agency (sometimes called a super-agency) refers to a single state agency responsible for four or more of the following social services: health, welfare-social services, mental health, mental retardation, vocational rehabilitation, crippled children's services, employment services, corrections, or youth services.

entity capable of fulfilling the purpose of the Allied Services Act;
(2) the extent to which states have developed a multifunctional planning and programing capacity, which will be necessary to carry out
the intent of the Allied Services Act; (3) the extent to which states
have decentralized the service delivery system to uniform substate
districts as contemplated by the Allied Services Act; and (4) the
extent to which states are structured to provide the coordinated
service delivery of programs covered by the Allied Services Act.

ORGANIZATION OF HUMAN RESOURCES AGENCIES
AND THE ALLIED SERVICES ACT

Provisions of the Allied Services Act build upon an existing
trend in state government to reorganize functions and rationalize
the service delivery systems.

Within the past decade, a significant number of states have
created human resource super-agencies that bring under a single
administrator most of the state human resource and service functions.
Such reorganizations have been typically based on a legislative intent
to reduce service fragmentation, achieve administrative economies,
and establish unitary policy control over state services in a broad
functional area. Thus, creation of super-agencies through reorganization efforts provides a basic organizational framework for development of state policies vis-a-vis each broad functional area.

Creation of state human resource super-agencies provides the
initial organizational framework for the development of a unified
service delivery system to meet the interrelated needs of individuals
in achieving a maximum degree of personal independence and self-
sufficiency. The creation of a super-agency, however, does not
automatically create a unified service delivery system. Subsequent
internal reorganizations of state agencies are necessary following
creation of the super-agency if a unified delivery system is to be
realized.

Where significant efforts have been made to coordinate the
state's service delivery, these efforts have corresponded to and
resulted from the state agency's development of capacity for comprehensive services planning.

HUMAN RESOURCES PLANNING CAPACITY
AND THE ALLIED SERVICES ACT

State super-agencies, for the most part, have emphasized development of a central office planning capacity. In instances where

planning staffs have been created or proposed on a local or regional basis, they are decentralized central office staffs of the super-agency. In only one instance was a state placing the nucleus of a regional human services planning staff under the direction of a body of local elected officials.

The role and function of human services planning staff differs among the case-study states from a strong central staff in Florida to a two-member coordination staff in Utah. In Illinois, the principal staff for planning coordinated human service delivery is located in an agency separate from any of the state service providers.

States have not yet developed the capacity within state government to prepare local allied services plans at the substate level. Each state is experimenting with substate delivery systems, and all of the states with super-agencies regard the experiments as possible prototypes of a statewide decentralization. However, these substate systems do not yet exist.

The extent to which the super-agencies in the case states have been working with local agencies that could be designated for local allied service planning is limited.

The capacity of local agencies to develop local allied services plans is limited:

1. Multifunctional regional planning agencies involving local elected officials have generally not been involved in human services planning due to the emphasis of their present federal and state funding sources on physical and economic planning.

2. Regional planning organizations that have been involved in human services planning have typically focused on only one service, program, or target population and have limited staff. These include 314(b) comprehensive health planning agencies, councils on aging, or area mental health boards. Importantly, though, they have brought together local elected officials (to a limited degree), public and private service providers, and consumer groups for purposes of planning.

3. Local agencies within general purpose government such as county health departments and welfare departments are typically service providers for a single function. Furthermore, the emphasis of such agencies has generally been on services administration rather than planning.

4. There are limited examples of a local human resources super-agency that parallel the state super-agency. However, an examination of such agencies in New York City and San Diego County, California, indicates that although development of a central planning capability is one of their organizational objectives, their present capacity for developing a local allied services plan is limited.

5. Except in a few major urban areas, private nonprofit organizations such as health and welfare planning councils, also eligible as a local agency under the act, have not generally developed extensive human services planning capacity.

It is likely that there will be few local allied services plans developed in a state in the first year or two of implementation of the Allied Services Act.

Most state agencies will probably seek to use the planning and capacity-building and the administrative cost grants to build staff of the state super-agencies as part of a statewide decentralized administrative structure that does not involve local elected officials, private service providers, and consumer groups in the planning of local services.

SUBSTATE DISTRICTS AND THE ALLIED SERVICES ACT

The mandate for state service agencies to realign their district boundaries to conform to a uniform system has resulted from the governors' implementation of OMB Circular A-95. While A-95 deals with uniform state planning and development districts and federal program review, the governors have extended the principle of uniform substate districts to include administration of state service programs.

Uniform substate districts for the administration of state service programs have not been widely achieved. Though executive orders for state agencies to bring their service regions into conformance with a uniform system have been issued in over forty states, realignment of state operations has been a slow process.

In the six case studies, all except Florida have promulgated executive orders designating a uniform system of substate districts for purposes of A-95 program review. Further, each has extended the coverage of the executive order to include conformance of substate districts for state services. In Florida, the state human resources agency is using districts that have been proposed as the A-95 districts. Thus, it is to be expected that these states will use these same districts as the service areas under the Allied Services Act.

COORDINATION OF SERVICE DELIVERY
AND THE ALLIED SERVICES ACT

The extent to which line divisions of super-agencies can coordinate and jointly plan, program, and deliver services depends primarily on the powers of the super-agency director, particularly his powers of reorganization, his budget authority, and the amount of his direct line authority over agency divisions. These powers vary from state to state. Some agencies go through successive stages of organization as in Utah, with the agency director being given more authority at each stage.

258

Even though substate districts are made uniform for all services, each service may continue to be administered separate and distinct from other services, with line authority over field staff exercised from the state central office for that service to the district office. However, the states with human resource super-agencies are at various stages of development of a more unified structure using the substate district as the geographic focus.

In order to develop a single administrative structure in a substate district, the super-agencies are attempting to define the role of a regional administrator and the degree of control needed over regional division heads. The roles vary from an exercise of direct line authority over field service staffs for all divisions of the super-agency to a coordinator using convenor powers or influence of the state department director or governor in obtaining cooperation of division field staffs.

In the design of a regional service delivery system, each state is attempting to develop a single system of core services (outreach, intake, information, referral, and follow-up) to be used for all services of the agency. Formal organizational powers will be used to obtain utilization of consolidated core services and coordination of service delivery.

With the exception of Utah, the state super-agencies generally are developing single substate administrative structures for the planning and delivery of state human services, which do not include involvement of local elected officials, private service providers, or consumer groups.

Human services functions are not uniformly assigned to super-agencies by state legislation. Thus attempts to coordinate service delivery may go beyond the organizational boundaries of the state agency and require the influence of the governor to obtain cooperation of other state departments in any unified service system. Coordination will be facilitated by establishment of uniform substate districts and reduction in the number of points of contact necessary for coordination of human resource services.

IMPLICATIONS FOR FEDERAL POLICY

The basic intent of the Allied Services Act is to assist states and localities in improving the coordination and delivery of human resource services. The six state case studies have yielded a number of findings about the states' ability to implement the act as intended. These findings are summarized below, and where action by HEW seems advisable, the recommended action is described.

The financial incentives specifically offered by the act are probably not great enough in themselves to induce states to reorganize their human resource systems. Beyond short-term planning and capacity-building grants and special grants for administrative costs, the only financial incentive under the act is the ability to transfer limited amounts of money from one grant program to another. The ability to make such a transfer would be likely to appeal only to a state that has already developed a desire to consolidate human resource services.

The extent of reorganization and consolidation of human resource services within states in recent years indicates that there already exist incentives strong enough to induce states to undertake reorganization. The Allied Services Act will build on those existing incentives and in that way accelerate state agency reorganization.

The impact of the act will depend in large part on the way it is administered. Those in HEW charged with implementation must recognize that they are involved in the evolutionary process of creating new institutions and that implementation requires an understanding of that process and how application of federal regulations can help or hinder it. Sensitive enforcement of regulations regarding reorganization and coordination can be very helpful in overcoming state inertia or resolving bureaucratic impasse. However, requiring "too much, too fast" can be counterproductive. As the cases illustrate, states are at different points in reorganization of human resource services. Consolidation of enough authority to effect the kinds of structural rearrangements necessary to realize the act's objectives is an evolutionary process. For example, Utah has been incrementally moving toward more centralized authority over a period of five years. Furthermore, the lead time needed to plan and implement the changes can be long. For example, Florida is just beginning the second level of internal restructuring the service delivery system three years after creation of the super-agency. These time lags and lead times must be accommodated.

On the other hand, there is a danger of requiring "too little, too slow." Taking into account the evolutionary nature of change and the stage of development in the individual state, HEW should insist on reasonable annual progress by the states in improving coordination, increasing the numbers of local plans, and so on. Due to the generality of eligible activities for Allied Services planning and capacity-building grants and special grants for administrative costs, HEW should pay particular attention to the scope and content of work to be performed. Without a specific work program for Allied Services planning and implementation, there will be few ways to judge the progress of the states in coordinating service delivery and achieving the intent of the Allied Services Act. Therefore, planning and capacity-building grants and administrative-cost grants should be made only on the basis of locally designed, measurable objectives and an explicit work program clearly related to the purposes of the act.

Involvement of local agencies in developing local allied service plans will in many cases encounter resistance at the state level. Such involvement means that state agency personnel must share with outside agencies, often for the first time, their authority. Few state agencies have an extensive history of local agency involvement, and only one of the case states is developing a decentralized statewide system that provides for local agency involvement. Most of the other states are attempting to decentralize state administration to a sub-state regional level and to consolidate common service functions and are expressing an intent to develop human resources planning staffs for the substate districts within the state regional staffs to plan for substate service areas. The clear implication is that HEW must be prepared to apply constant pressure to induce many of the states to include local allied services plans prepared by local agencies in the state plans.

Outside super-agency central office planning staff, there is little capacity to conduct allied services planning. In particular, there are extremely few substate regional or local planning organizations of any type that involve local elected officials, private service providers, and consumer groups concerned with human resource planning. Whichever of the local agencies eligible for designation under 201(b) of the act is selected to develop a local allied services plan, that capacity must for the most part be created. The magnitude of that task in terms of funds and manpower should not be underestimated.

In addition to providing funds, HEW should be prepared to provide technical assistance to state agencies and designated local agencies in carrying out allied services planning. Such assistance may include indirect as well as direct technical assistance in the conduct of population need assessments, inventories, and analyses of service resources, methods to coordinate or consolidate core services, service program analysis to determine appropriateness of waivers, involvement of service consumers, and public and private provider participation and coordination.

The legal creation of a state super-agency does not necessarily lead to coordination of state-provided human services in terms of redesign of separate service systems for each function assigned to the department. However, given the powers of direct line authority over service providers, the power of reorganization, and single departmental budgeting and planning powers, the stage can be set for the necessary second level of internal restructuring of the previously separate service systems of a newly created super-agency. In addition to possessing these powers, state super-agencies are better equipped to develop a new coordinated service system if there is sufficient staff available to the agency director to support a centralized budgeting and planning process. There should be continuing support for such a budgeting and planning process, beyond the two-year term of the planning and capacity-building grants and special grants for administrative costs.

In order to maximize the impact of the Allied Services Act, HEW should be prepared to provide technical assistance to the states on a broad scale. Such a program should include both direct and indirect technical assistance. The following points suggest how assistance may be provided.

1. Within HEW, an office or unit should be created that can cut across program lines of HEW for purposes of relating HEW operations to the Allied Services Act and to the states. This approach suggests placement of staff in the Office of the Secretary. Staff should work directly with counterparts under each commissioner, regional director, and regional commissioner.

2. Indirect technical assistance could be provided to states by HEW central office staff through an information clearinghouse relating state and demonstration-project experiences to the act. For example, state reorganization legislation such as Florida's could be utilized as examples of reorganizational methods and powers needed to facilitate coordination and integration of service delivery. Special attention should be given to the second-level reorganization. Similarly, the outcome and processes used in Section 1115 Demonstration, 1971 and 1972 Research and Demonstration Projects, and Targets of Opportunity projects could be selectively synthesized to provide information and examples to the states that relate to implementation of the act, coordinated service delivery systems, consolidated core service systems, and supporting management and administrative systems.

The approach using a technical assistance task force should be expanded and institutionalized to provide direct technical assistance to states. One approach could be the development of diagnostic field teams to work on-site at the request of the states. The HEW team could be composed of central-office or regional-office staffs or both.

Using materials generated for indirect technical assistance, the HEW field teams could conduct an extensive review of the organization, staffing, planning and evaluation system, budget process, program and services, and service delivery system of the states drawing on the experience of other states to identify successful approaches. In addition, the teams could determine what problems emanate from federal requirements and practices and what solutions would be appropriate. By viewing the coordination of program and review from the states' perspective, additional insights could be gained as to the relevant and critical waivers to program requirements necessary to bring about a coordinated service delivery system. In order to assure that technical assistance remains in fact advisory assistance and not federal directive, the task force should not have a role in the funding and plan review process.

The provision in the act that authorizes waivers of regulations should over time result in isolating those features of regulations that inhibit development and implementation of an Allied Services plan. However, HEW should not merely respond to waiver requests but should also effect needed changes on its own initiative. Administrative regulations for state plan requirements under human services programs included in the act should be thoroughly examined to determine where administrative requirements can be modified to facilitate their consolidation and incorporation within the State Allied Services Plan. Such a review should include an item-by-item comparative analysis of state plan requirements, including relevant handbooks, guides, instruction, and supporting documents for each program included in the act. Other factors that should be analyzed are statutory—that is, administrative requirements including those directly related to administrative criteria. Recommendations can then be developed to modify, consolidate, or eliminate duplicative or conflicting requirements.

The planning cycles of other HEW planning requirements, such as the Community Services Administration Program and Financial Plan cycle, should also be thoroughly examined to determine the extent to which these cycles conflict or duplicate the planning process described in the Allied Services Act. Conflicts should be resolved by HEW prior to full implementation of the act. In so doing, HEW should develop a logical process cycle, which may go thus: state-regional funding benchmarks, preparation of local allied services plans, state review of local plans, aggregation of local plans and preparation of the state allied services plan, and updating plans for individual programs.

In order to prepare itself for implementation of the act, HEW should develop an Allied Services research and demonstration strategy. To the extent that such projects are not already under way through fiscal year 1972 Targets of Opportunity or fiscal year 1971 R and D projects, a series of pilot projects should be conducted within the next year to provide several models for organization and conduct of Allied Services planning at the local, substate regional, and state agency levels. The purpose in developing models would be to describe the activities and products anticipated in state and local Allied Services plans to isolate the kinds of problems that can be anticipated and develop ways to deal with them. The selection of pilot projects should reflect the various organizational options available under the act as well as the different organizational settings for provision of state human services. The mix may be as follows:

- A state super-agency with legal responsibility for as many of the federal programs in the act as possible;
- A state in which three or more state agencies are responsible for providing state human services;
- A state where welfare-social services are state administered and a state where welfare-social services are state supervised but locally administered;

263

● A state designated substate regional service area in both a state-supervised and state-administered environment. This option may also include an office or agency designated by local elected officials to perform planning on behalf of a combination of local governments;

● A state where county government has major human service delivery responsibilities;

● An office or unit of local general purpose government; this option should probably be exercised in a highly urban area and include a case where local government is a provider of human services;

● A private nonprofit agency with staff and recognized planning capability operating in either a metropolitan or substate regional area.

The results of the pilot projects would provide a basis for developing the administrative guidelines relating to the planning requirements under the act and for developing a strategy for use of planning and capacity-building grants. The pilot projects would also identify the key problem areas in conducting human services planning and indicate the extent and type of technical assistance needed among state and local agencies. The experience and results of the pilot projects should be published and disseminated to state and local agencies as a form of indirect technical assistance.

ORGANIZATION OF PART II

Part II is composed of seven chapters. Chapter 15, Organization of Human Resources Agencies and the Allied Services Act, reviews provisions of the act that are designed to encourage reorganization of the planning and provision of human services. State reorganizations and the extent of creation of state super-agencies as well as their characteristics are discussed in light of the act.

Chapter 16, Human Resources Planning Capability and the Allied Services Act, reviews the extent of human resources planning capability in the six states in light of planning requirements of the act. Planning capacities at state, substate regional, and local levels are described in terms of the state super-agencies and other organizational units eligible to perform state and local allied services planning.

Chapter 17, Substate Districts and the Allied Services Act, describes the provisions of the Allied Services Act requiring substate districts for planning and service delivery in light of other federal incentives for use of substate districts in planning and administration. The extent of development of uniform statewide substate districts and their uses for human services planning and service delivery are described for each of the six case study states.

Chapter 18, Coordination of Service Delivery and the Allied Services Act, analyzes the powers and resources available to state super-agencies to bring about coordination of service delivery.

Chapter 19, on the Implications for Federal Policy, describes steps that the six case studies indicate should be taken by HEW to realize the purposes of the Allied Services Act.

Chapter 20, Case Studies, contains the experience of each state in services integration in historical perspective and fairly detailed accounts of the organizational structure and operating procedures of their ongoing undertakings in this field.

BACKGROUND

In a message to the 92d Congress, the president proposed the Allied Services Act of 1972 (Senate Bill 3643) to provide for improvement of the human services delivery system. Key features of the proposed bill include a number of legal, administrative, and fiscal tools to improve state and local government capacity to comprehensively plan, program, coordinate, and implement an array of services designed to serve the individual or the whole family.

The objective of the Allied Services Act of 1972 is to develop a more unified delivery system that coordinates complementary services at the state, substate, regional, and local level and reduces fragmentation in the delivery system.

The act's basic premises to achieve this objective are, first, that a unified service delivery system designed to free people from public dependency can be developed through a comprehensive planning process for geographic service areas with common goals; second, that state and local elected officials should be involved in service planning to address the particular problems and needs of the local area; and third, that local service plans should be developed by local elected officials involving public and private service providers and consumer groups.

There are eight key provisions of the Allied Services Act of 1972 that are designed to "encourage and assist state and local agencies to enter into new cooperative arrangements, and, where necessary, reorganize or reassign functions, at all levels in the system of the planning for and provision of services." These provisions are as follows:

1. Division of the state by the governor into substate districts ("service areas") for the purpose of administering local allied services plans.

2. Determination by the governor of the service areas in which local allied services plans will be developed.

3. Designation by the governor of which local agency in a service area for which its local plan is to be developed is to have primary responsibility for the preparation of the local plan and assuring its implementation. The act specifies organizational options for designation of a local agency focusing on local elected officials. The principal factor in designation of the local agency is a finding by the governor that there exists an agency with the capacity to prepare and carry out a local allied services plan.

4. Designation by the governor of a state agency to develop a state allied services plan that integrates local allied services plans prepared throughout the state. Further, the state agency has responsibility for the supervision and review of administration of local plans in each of the substate service areas.

5. Grants to states and local agencies for purposes of initial strengthening of state and local capacity to prepare and implement state and local allied service plans.

6. Special grants to states and local agencies for costs of coordination of planning and service delivery.

7. Authorization to consolidate planning grants under the various programs covered by the act into a single grant.

8. Authorization to transfer up to 25 percent of any program grant amount to another program included in the state or local allied services plan.

9. Authorization to waive requirements of statewideness, single or specified state or local agency, or technical or administrative requirements attached to any assistance program included in a state or local allied service plan in order to reduce legislative or administrative impediments to implementation of allied services plans.

In order to understand the setting in which the Allied Services Act would be implemented, several major trends should be considered. First, an increasing number of state governments are undergoing reorganization and state human resource super-agencies are being created.

Second, the creation of super-agencies is being paralleled by the decentralization of state service administration to substate district levels.

Third, under the aegis of OMB Circular A-95, states are designating uniform substate planning and development districts with which federal programs are expected to conform. The state chief executives are going one step beyond the requirements of A-95 by ordering that all state service functions conform to the designated uniform substate districts.

Fourth, the human resource super-agencies are beginning to use the substate districts as a focus for planning and implementing a coordinated service delivery system.

15

ORGANIZATION OF
HUMAN RESOURCE AGENCIES
AND THE ALLIED
SERVICES ACT

PROVISIONS OF THE ACT

The Allied Services Act is inteded to assist in the coordination of complementary services by currently separate agencies at the state and local levels. As stated in the act, it is designed to "encourage and assist state and local agencies to enter into new cooperative arrangements and, when necessary, reorganize or reassign function, at all levels in the system of the planning and provision of services."

The principal findings supporting this declaration of purpose are based on a recognition of obstacles to the effective provision of services. These include: (1) fragmentation among many agencies and organizations serving dependent individuals; (2) structured rigidity among state and local agencies and organizations; (3) inadequate coordination and communication among agencies providing human services; and (4) absence within states of a single locus of accountability for the effective provision of human services. These findings almost parallel the general pattern of reasons for the reorganization of state government advanced by the states that have reorganized.

STATE REORGANIZATION

While the Allied Services Act of 1972 expresses an intent to assist states in reorganization of human service functions, significant changes have already occurred in a majority of states.

Reorganization of state government has been a significant phenomenon of the past decade. One of the major characteristics in reorganization is establishment of constitutional limitations on the number of state departments. Of the five reorganizations in 1971-72, two, Montana and North Carolina, were guided by a constitutional limitation of 20 and 25 departments, respectively. A similar constitutional amendment was on the November 1972 ballot in Idaho, limiting the number of departments to 20. Florida had a constitutional limitation of 25 departments.

Another technique is the creation of departmental shells by state legislation. In this case, the legislature authorizes and establishes a framework of a limited number of departments. However, full operating powers are not yet given to the new departments. Rather, provisions are made for appointment of a department head who, in turn, is charged with the responsibility of preparing an organizational plan for the department for submission to the next session of the legislature. This approach was used in Maine and Massachusetts.

A third approach is to grant reorganization powers to the governor, who will, in turn, prepare a reorganization plan for the executive branch. The plan takes effect automatically, subject to the veto of the state legislature. This approach was used in reorganization of Georgia and North Carolina governments.

A typical outcome of state reorganization has been the creation of a human resources super-agency consisting of several previously separate departments performing human services functions. Since 1964, thirty-seven state governments have undertaken some form of reorganization of their executive branches. Thirteen states have undergone a total reorganization of the executive branch since 1965, and in the process have created state human resource super-agencies. Presently 26 states have a super-agency that combines at least four of the functions of welfare-social services, health, mental health, mental retardation, vocational rehabilitation, corrections, crippled children services, employment services, or youth services.

Creation of super-agencies for human resource services has been prompted by several organizational principles that are characteristic of state reorganization in general. These are (1) grouping of state agencies into broad functional areas; (2) establishment of relatively few functional departments; (3) determination of single lines of authority and explicit policy control by the governor and legislature; and (4) administration of state departments by single heads rather than by boards and commissions.

Legislative concerns in reorganization and reform of the state executive branch have been oriented toward clearly pinpointing for the chief executive and the legislature the responsibility for state services.

Two major currents are running through the state reorganization activities. While states are reorganizing their departments into super-agencies to centralize policy control, they are, at the same time, decentralizing the administrative structures of these super-agencies in order to improve delivery of state services. Thus, state structures are seen as being both "too little" and "too big."

TABLE 15.1

Service Functions: State Human Resource Super-Agencies

State	System Type	W-SS	MH	MR	AC	VR	ES	CCS	Public Health
California	S	X	X	X	X	X	X	X	X
Oregon	S	X	X	X	X	X	X	X	X
Massachusetts	A	X	X	X	X	X	–	X	X
Vermont	A	X	X	X	X	X	–	X	X
D. of Columbia	–	X	X	X	–	X	–	X	–
Alaska	A	X	X	X	X	–	X	X	X
Florida	A	X	X	X	X	X	–	X	X
Nevada	A	X	X	X	X	X	–	X	X
Washington	A	X	X	X	X	X	–	X	X
Arkansas	A	X	X	X	–	X	–	X	–
Delaware	A	X	X	X	X	–	–	X	X
Minnesota	S	X	X	X	–	X	–	X	–
New Jersey	S	X	X	X	X	X	–	–	–
Wisconsin	S	X	X	X	X	X	–	–	X
Wyoming	S	X	X	X	–	X	–	X	X
Iowa	S	X	X	X	X	–	–	–	–
Kansas	S	X	X	X	–	X	–	–	–
Maine	A	X	–	X	–	X	–	X	X
Missouri	A	X	X	X	–	X	–	–	X
New Hampshire	A	X	X	X	–	–	–	X	X
Oklahoma	A	X	–	X	–	X	–	X	–
Pennsylvania	A	X	X	X	–	X	–	–	–
Rhode Island	A	X	X	–	X	X	–	–	–
Utah	A	X	X	X	X	–	–	X	X
Georgia	S	X	X	X	–	X	–	X	X
North Carolina	S	X	X	X	X	X	–	X	X
Maryland	S	X	–	–	–	X	X	X	–

Note: W-SS: Welfare-Social Service; MH: Mental Health; MR: Mental Retardation; AC: Adult Corrections; VR: Vocational Rehabilitation; ES: Employment Services; CCS: Crippled Children's Service.

System Type: S: state supervised—locally administered; A: state administered.

The "too little" aspect is reflected in state reorganizations to group related departments under a single agency for a broad functional area. The rationale is that each existing department with limited programmatic concerns is "too little" to perform state policy planning for the functional area, resulting in operational programing for a narrowly defined area of service. Each separate department, in turn, lobbies for appropriations from the legislature in competition with departments performing related functions. As a consequence, little attention is given to broader state policies and priorities among different programs.

The response of state government is the aggregation of departments in a broad functional area into a single agency. Creation of such an agency, however, presents the problems of being "too big" for effective service delivery and responsiveness to local or regional needs. The centralization at the state level, with most of policy planning staff at the state capital, removes service delivery planning a long way from the person or family to be served.

In addition to administrative problems, public skepticism of large state bureaucratic structures provides incentives to develop alternative structures of administration and service delivery, which are close to the actual problem for which the service was intended. The response of state government is to develop substate structures for the administration of programs and service delivery. Most human resource super-agencies have not been developed with exactly the same pattern. Table 15.1 illustrates the functions assigned to the super-agency by state.

Another differentiating characteristic among state agencies is the type of welfare-social service system. Of the 54 states and territories where a welfare system is presently operating, 33 are state administered, while the remainder are locally administered under state supervision. Of the 26 states with a super-agency as the single state agency, 15 operate a state-administered welfare system.

While it can be argued that educational functions are logically part of the total network of human resource development functions of state government, in no instance is public education administered at the state level through the same department providing social and other related human services.

CHARACTERISTICS OF CASE-STUDY STATES

Of the six case-study states, all except Illinois have undergone a major state reorganization affecting human resource functions since 1965.

The Department of Health and Rehabilitative Services was created as one of 23 state departments in Florida in 1969.

TABLE 15.2

Service Functions: Case–Study State Human Resource Agencies

	W-SS	Health	MH	MR	VR	AC	CCS	Aging	Drugs and Alcoholism	Youth Services
Florida Department of Health and Rehabilitation Services	X	X	X	X	X	X	X	X	X	X
Georgia Deparment Human Resources	X	X	X	X	X	–	X	X	X	–
Maine Department of Health and Welfare	X	X	–	–	X	–	X	–	X	–
Massachusetts Executive Office of Human Resources	X	X	X	X	X	X	X	–	X	X
Utah Department of Social Services	X	X	X	X	–	X	X	X	X	–

Note: W-SS–Welfare–Social Service; MH–Mental Health; MR–Mental Retardation; AC–Adult Corrections; VR–Vocational Rehabilitation; ES–Employment Services; CCS–Crippled Children's Service.

271

Georgia created the Department of Human Resources in 1972.

Utah created the Department of Social Services in 1967 after a two-year little Hoover Commission study of the state executive branch.

Massachusetts created the Executive Office of Human Resources as one of 10 executive cabinet posts in 1969.

Maine established 13 major state departments and complete reorganization of all but human resource functions in 1972. Welfare and social services are presently the responsibility of the Department of Health and Welfare, which was created in 1936 as one of the first joint departments.

Illinois has not reorganized its human resources services; however, during the period 1965-72, it created major departments for environmental protection, transportation, corrections, law enforcement, and local government affairs.

Table 15.2 illustrates each of the service functions actually assigned to and performed by the human resource super-agencies in the case-study states.

MAJOR FINDINGS

Provisions of the Allied Services Act build upon an existing trend in state government to reorganize functions and rationalize the service delivery system in order to make state government more responsive to needs of its citizens.

Within the past decade, a significant number of states have created human resource super-agencies that bring under a single administrator most of the state human resource and service functions. Such reorganizations have been typically based on a legislative intent to reduce service fragmentation at both the state and local administrative levels, achieve administrative economies, and establish unitary policy control over state services in a broad functional area. Thus, creation of super-agencies through reorganization efforts provides a basic organizational framework for development of state policies vis-a-vis each broad functional area.

Creation of state human resource super-agencies provides the initial organizational framework for the development of a unified service delivery system to meet the interrelated needs of individuals in achieving a maximum degree of personal independence and self sufficiency. The creation of a super-agency, however, does not automatically create a unified service delivery system. Subsequent internal reorganizations of state agencies are necessary following creation of the super-agency if a unified delivery system is to be realized.

Where significant efforts have been made to coordinate the state's service delivery, these efforts have corresponded to and resulted from the state agency's development of capacity for comprehensive services planning.

CHAPTER

16

HUMAN RESOURCES
PLANNING CAPACITY
AND THE ALLIED
SERVICES ACT

COMPONENTS OF AN ALLIED SERVICES PLAN

The Allied Services Act of 1972 provided for the preparation of both local and state plans for the coordinated provision of human resource services. Plans are to address human needs and develop methods and strategies to (1) facilitate access to and use of services; (2) improve the effectiveness of the services; and (3) use service resources more efficiently and with minimal duplication.

In each case, plans must address the primary goal of the act, which is to lessen dependency through more effective service delivery. In particular, the state plan must include descriptions of (1) the current status of the coordinated provision of services in the state by summarizing the relevant portions of approved local plans; (2) steps to be taken both statewide and within selected geographic service areas to achieve a greater degree of coordination of service delivery; and (3) assurances that state plans under Titles I, IV, X, XIV, or XVI of the Social Security Act are coordinated with each other.

A local allied services plan must include the following elements: (1) a survey of needs and inventory of resources; (2) a listing of agencies and organizations agreeing to participate and an enumeration of human service programs to be coordinated; and (3) assurances of progress in coordinating services, expressed as descriptions of functions to be coordinated or consolidated, commonality of core services and how they will be coordinated or consolidated, benefits to individuals and families receiving services, administrative efficiencies of coordinated or consolidated service delivery, and a review and comment procedure with assurances that views of interested agencies, organizations, and individuals have been considered in preparation of the local plans.

274

State planning requirements indicate an objective to make local allied services plans the "building blocks" for the state plan. Then the state plan would be an aggregation of local plans synthesized to reflect a framework of state policies and priorities. However, it is left to the determination of the governor of the state whether and in which geographic service areas local allied service plans will be developed.

Three organizational options are available to a governor under the Allied Services Act for his designation of a local agency with primary responsibility for preparing and carrying out a local allied services plan:

1. An office or agency designated by the chief elected official or officials of a combination of units of general purpose local government to act on behalf of the member local governments in preparing a local allied services plan. In particular, this option provides for designation of a regional planning commission or council of governments to conduct allied services planning.

2. An office or agency of a unit of general purpose local government that is designated for purposes of preparing a local allied services plan by the chief elected official or officials of such a unit.

This option provides for designation of a city or county agency to conduct human services planning. These may include a city human resources agency, a county welfare deparment, or a city, county, or joint planning commission.

3. A public or nonprofit private agency that, for purposes of allied services planning, is under the supervision or direction of the designated state agency and that can engage in the planning or provision of a broad range of human services within a service area. This option may include a health and welfare planning council, a community action agency, or the district or regional office of the state agency. (The act restricts a governor in the selection of a public or nonprofit agency in that such an agency may be designated only if there is no office or agency of general purpose local government that will have the capacity to carry out a local allied services plan.)

At the substate district and local levels, there are a number of potential agencies for local allied services planning. They are of two types: (1) agencies whose primary mission is planning and (2) agencies that administer one or more service programs.

Planning Agencies

There are a variety of substate district and local planning organizations in addition to a subdistrict office of the state agency, which might be assigned the responsibility of developing local allied services plans. These include councils of government and regional planning and development commissions that may perform multi-functional long-range planning. The distinguishing characteristic of these agencies is the designation of the agency by local elected officials to perform particular planning functions. The governing body, particularly of a council of governments, is composed of the chief elected officials of the member governments. In increasing numbers, these agencies conform to the state-designated uniform substate districts and perform long-range planning, usually physical and economic development, upon which the state planning program is based. There are also a significant number of single-purpose planning agencies conforming to substate districts that involve local elected officials, public and private service providers, and consumer groups. Most notable of these are the 314(b) comprehensive health planning agencies. Also included are regional law enforcement planning agencies, councils on aging, comprehensive area manpower planning agencies, and area mental health boards. Also at the local level are the private nonprofit health and welfare planning councils that reflect the third option in the act for designation of a local agency for allied services planning.

Service Administration Agencies

The service administration agencies include agencies of local government as well as decentralized state offices.

In order to meet the planning objectives of the Allied Services Act, states must develop a capacity for human resources planning at both the state agency and local level. The following parts of this chapter briefly review the human resources planning capacity in the six case-study states. It is not intended as a detailed, definitive assessment of planning capacity. However, as a result of the case studies, judgments can be made of the general level of capacity and how that capacity fulfills the planning needs for the Allied Services Act. In addition, the case studies, although not designed to assess the capability of eligible local agencies, do indicate the extent to which the super-agencies are presently working with eligible local agencies.

Florida

Florida's Department of Health and Rehabilitative Services illustrates the maximum organizational development for planning among the six states. The Division of Planning and Evaluation is charged with the responsibility of designing the overall service delivery system for the network of services provided by the Department. With a 65-member staff, the division is organized into four bureaus: Comprehensive Health Planning, Comprehensive Rehabilitation Planning, Community Medical Facilities Planning, and Research and Evaluation. Within this organizational structure, departmental planning is conducted for services under the Social Security Act, Section 314(a) and (d) of the Public Health Services Act, the Older Americans Act, the Hill-Burton Act, the Community Mental Health Centers Act, the Developmental Disabilities Services and Facilities Construction Act, and the Juvenile Delinquency Prevention and Control Act. The division is, therefore, responsible for state-level planning and evaluation activities related to most of the human-services programs included in the Allied Services Act.

The Division of Planning and Evaluation's relationship with line divisions is twofold. First, the planning division develops an overall structure of departmental goals and objectives. Secondly, within this framework, planning division staff either directly plans the programs to address this goal structure or provides technical assistance to line division staff in program planning.

While the state department has developed a well-staffed planning operation, it is concentrated in the state central offices. The governor has not designated a uniform system of substate districts for all state departments and there are no uniform statewide development or organizational structures and staffs at the substate regional level.

A Section 1115 demonstration project in Palm Beach County is being used to test the role and functions of a single regional administrator for all the services of the department. At the same time, a centralized core services system with a computer-based records and information system is being developed encompassing all services of the department. The centralized core services system will be a key feature in development of a unified service delivery system administered on a regional basis within the 11 regions. Staff support for planning and evaluation, however, is being drawn from the department's central office staff.

Regional planning commissions and councils of government have not been established extensively in Florida. While there are 314(b) agencies, area mental health boards, and councils on aging, each has remained focused on a single function with limited staff. The welfare-social services system in Florida is state-administered, so for all practical purposes there are no county service agencies.

There are a few cases in which the state is involving local government and private agencies in human services planning. For example, the Department of Health and Rehabilitative Services has used task forces (which include local public and private agency representatives) as the coordinative mechanism in planning a demonstration of a comprehensive service delivery system.

Technical support staff has also been provided by central office personnel of both the Division of Planning and Evaluation and the line divisions of the department of the Metro County Government in planning a single system of core services in the county. In this instance, information generated out of a county-operated outreach, intake, information, referral, and follow-up system will be used for continuing planning for services.

In addition an advisory committee composed of elected and appointed officials of local government as well as representatives of local private service providers will be used to recommend service policy to the state with regard to services provided in Metro Dade. Preliminary discussions are also under way to utilize the same contractual arrangements with health and welfare planning councils in other parts of the state for both core services and planning.

Some of these examples are prototypes of a statewide organizational structure.

Utah

The Utah Department of Social Services is organizationally structured toward functional human services planning and programing within its line divisions. Though there is a central office of planning and evaluation within the office of the executive director, it has only two staff members. Therefore, the function of the central staff is restricted to a coordination of the planning efforts of line divisions.

Separate staffs in six of the seven line divisions (Indian Affairs excluded) are responsible for planning services under the Social Security Act, the Older Americans Act, Sections 314(a) and 314(d) of the Public Health Services Act, and portions of the Juvenile Delinquency Prevention and Control Act.

In Utah, the state is beginning to develop organizational structures for planning and delivery of human services on a substate district basis. A district human resource board involving elected officials of local general purpose government and the county school systems has been established in one test region that conforms to the governor's designated substate districts. A five-county council of governments was used as the base for development of the district board. Functions of the board will include planning and establishment of local policy for human services in the region. At present, however, the board will not have direct line authority over state agency field staffs in the district. Services include those provided by the Department of Social Services, the Department of Employment Security, the Juvenile Court System, the Department of Public Instruction, the Board of Higher Education, and the Utah Law Enforcement Planning Agency.

The board will offer a mechanism to coordinate planning and service delivery in a substate district when state human service functions are not concentrated in a single state agency. However, the initial staffing is seen as only one coordinator with no district planning staff support.

Operationally, the district plan envisions a central service facility and satellites throughout the region offering all of the services included in the regional service plan. Presently, services of various state departments are only available in separate facilities that do not uniformly cover the region.

The Utah Department of Community Affairs expects to utilize other councils of government as the base for development of district boards in the remaining substate districts.

Massachusetts

In Massachusetts, the Executive Office of Human Services tends to use interdepartmental staff committees as the structure for planning coordinated service delivery. This approach is reflected in interdepartmental committees for handicapped children, alcoholism services, correctional training programs and services, and comprehensive child care. Responsibility for overall program planning, however, is carried by an assistant secretary for Program Planning within the Executive Office.

As in Florida and Utah, planning efforts are being directed toward development of a rational service delivery system within a substate district. At the regional level there is an interdepartmental committee of regional directors. The committee is supported by an 11-member planning and programing staff, administratively under the assistant secretary.

Work of the staff is twofold. First, staff members are designing a coordinated core services system for outreach, intake, information, referral, and follow-up. Secondly, the staff is working closely with community groups within the region to determine gaps in the service system followed by programing efforts with departmental service providers to correct service deficiencies. The planning staff are state employees deployed to assist state service providers. Local elected officials are not included as part of any regional body for human services.

At present there are eight regional planning organizations funded under HUD's 701 program whose boundaries adhere closely to the state districts. Only 10 townships in the state are not included. These organizations do not have established ties to the Executive Office of Human Services.

Maine

In Maine, state human services planning of the Department of Health and Welfare is primarily conducted by staff of the line divisions. There is no central office designated the responsibility for state human service planning. A 15-member staff in the Office of the Commissioner is developing a state services management system, but this has not led to extensive interdivisional service programing.

Central to the reorganization is the creation of regional organizational structures for the planning and delivery of all services of the department. At present, only the bureau of social welfare has converted to a regional structure for service delivery. Regional planning and programing staffs have not been developed. Included in the reorganization is the creation of a centralized planning office and planning staffs attached to each of the regional directors' offices.

There are 10 regional planning commissions and one council of governments, staffed and funded to conduct planning for substate districts that include local elected officials on the policy boards. At present, however, these agencies are not involved in human services planning. The reorganization proposal for the Department of Health and Welfare includes a planning staff in the office of each regional director of community services. There are no plans to utilize existing staffs of regional planning organizations to conduct, or to involve local elected officials in, human services planning. Rather, a new staff will be added as part of the department's regional administrative structure.

Georgia

Final organizational structuring in Georgia's recently created Department of Human Resources has not been completed. However, it appears at this point that a single office of planning and evaluation with division status may be created. Staffs from the former commission of aging and state economic opportunity office, as well as key program staff from the line divisions, will be used to staff the division. A significant point in the potential organizational structure for planning is use of a central office staff that has been working with local agencies (the Community Action Agencies) across the state in human services planning and programing.

The present welfare-social services system is operated through 159 county agencies with local policy established by the county board of commissioners. Representatives of the board of commissioners also are members of area planning and development commissions (APDCs) in the 18 designated substate districts. Heretofore, staffs of the county welfare agencies have not been involved in human services planning encompassing the various programs included in the Allied Services Act. Similarly, the area planning and development commissions have not been involved in human services planning except for a three-year period in which the APDCs administered OEO program development grants and functioned as the community action agency for the substate district. However, the APDCs are widely accepted as the principal planning organizations in the state by local elected officials and are, therefore, being considered by the newly created Department of Human Resources as a primary organizational structure for human services planning in the state.

Illinois

In Illinois, while a state human resources super-agency has not been created, several events are significant in human services planning. The state through an executive order of the governor, created the Illinois Institute of Social Policy in 1970 to augment state agency efforts to plan and develop new methods of delivery of state human services. The institute was also charged with the responsibility for conducting demonstration projects and evaluating both new and old service delivery systems. Three demonstration projects have been designed and implemented. One of these projects, in the Tri-County area around Peoria, is testing a centralized information, referral, and follow-up service tying together the human services of state, local, and private service agencies. While the project is not exclusively local services planning, it includes an information system generating service data to be used on a regional basis to determine population need assessments and service resources. Project staff are acting as convenors of state and local service providers for planning improved service delivery with a common system of core services.

MAJOR FINDINGS

1. State super-agencies, for the most part, have emphasized development of a central office planning capacity. In instances where planning staffs have been created or proposed on a local or regional basis, they are decentralized central office staffs of the super-agency. In only one instance was a state placing the nucleus of a regional human services planning staff under the direction of a body of local elected officials.

2. The role and function of human services planning staff differs among the case-study states from a strong central staff in Florida to a two-member coordination staff in Utah. In Illinois, the principal staff for planning coordinated human service delivery is located in an agency separate from any of the state service providers.

3. States have not yet developed the capacity within state government to prepare local allied services plans at the substate level. Each state is experimenting with substate delivery systems and all of the states with super-agencies regard the experiments as possible prototypes of a statewide decentralization. However, these substate systems do not yet exist.

4. The extent to which the super-agencies in the case states have been working with local agencies that could be designated for local allied services planning is limited.

5. The capacity of local agencies to develop local allied services plans is limited.

(a) Multifunctional regional planning agencies involving local elected officials have generally not been involved in human services planning due to the emphasis of their present federal and state funding sources on physical and economic planning.

(b) Regional planning organizations that have been involved in human services planning have typically focused on only one service, program, or target population, and have limited staff. These include 314(b) comprehensive health planning agencies, councils on aging, or area mental health boards. Importantly, though, they have brought together local elected officials (to a limited degree), public and private service providers, and consumer groups for purposes of planning.

(c) Local agencies within general purpose government such as county health departments and welfare departments are typically service providers for a single function. Furthermore, the emphasis of such agencies has generally been on services administration rather than planning.

(d) There are limited examples of a local human resources super-agency that parallel the state super-agency. However, an examination of such agencies in New York City and San Diego County, California indicates that although development of a central planning capability is one of their organizational objectives, their present capacity for developing a local allied services plan is limited.

(e) Except in a few major urban areas, private nonprofit organizations such as health and welfare planning councils, also eligible as a local agency under the act, have not generally developed extensive human services planning capacity.

6. It is likely that there will be few local allied services plans developed in a state in the first year or two of implementation of the Allied Services Act.

7. Most state agencies will probably seek to use the planning and capacity-building and the administrative cost grants to build

staff of the state super-agencies as part of a statewide decentralized administrative structure that does not involve local elected officials, private service providers, and consumer groups in the planning of local services.

17

SUBSTATE DISTRICTS
AND THE ALLIED
SERVICES ACT

ALLIED SERVICES REQUIREMENTS
FOR SUBSTATE DISTRICTS

The Allied Services Act calls for the creation of a single system of substate districts for both the planning and administration of human services funded through programs included in the act. Specifically, the proposed act requires, in order to participate in the Allied Services Program, the governor to "divide the entire state into district areas for the purpose of administering local allied services plans."

As previously noted, the act gives priority for developing a local allied services plan to local public (nonstate) agencies designated by local officials. However, if the governor finds that no local public agency has the capacity to carry out a local plan, he may designate certain public or nonprofit private agencies including district offices of state departments.

This chapter examines the extent to which uniform substate district boundaries already exist and the state of development of substate districts with particular emphasis on developments within each of the six case-study states.

SUBSTATE STRUCTURES FOR PLANNING

More than 40 states have developed a set of substate regional organizations for purposes of conducting areawide physical and economic development planning and coordination of local planning. Under various forms of state enabling legislation and executive orders, these organizations have included regional councils of government and area planning and development commissions. Typical of the pattern is a form of voluntary membership of representation of local general purpose governments to form a policy-making board served by a small professional staff, heavily oriented toward physical planning.

At the local level, general purpose governments are joining area-wide planning organizations in order to deal with the problems of a substate region. While these organizations usually do not have functional operating responsibilities, they do provide a means to formulate policy and develop uniform approaches to regional problems. As noted earlier, voluntary associations of local governments are occurring within a framework of state-designated regions and under the authority of state enabling legislation.

In those instances where regional planning organizations developed capability in specific functional areas, states have utilized regional policy and plans as building blocks for state planning. For example, the state outdoor recreation plan is frequently an aggregation and synthesis of regional open space and recreation plans in the context of state policies and priorities.

In no instance, however, have federal and state funding sources encouraged in these organizations the development of human resources planning capability beyond a single service or function as a basis for state planning.

SUBSTATE STRUCTURES FOR ADMINISTRATION

Substate district systems have been developed over the past three decades for administration of specific state services. These district systems are essentially decentralized state departments with separate organizational structures focused on a narrowly defined problem or service and a single program with its own set of requirements.

Perhaps the oldest of these are the state highway department district offices for construction and maintenance of public roads. Service districts for areawide vocational and technical schools were also a forerunner of this now expanding organizational form.

Other district configurations for specific services include those for employment services, crippled children's services, vocational rehabilitation services, mental health programs, welfare and social services, and so on through almost every one of the various state-administered programs.

Typically, the districts for each program have been devised by different state agency staffs, at different times and under different criteria and program requirements. Rarely have any of the different substate districts of functional agencies had enabling legislation except a general grant of powers to the agency director to organize and administer his department.

FEDERAL INCENTIVES FOR SUBSTATE DISTRICTS

Federal approaches to regional solutions of problems vary widely in legislation and guidelines that require establishment and fostering of areawide organization. A recent review by the Advisory Commission on Intergovernmental Relations (ACIR) illustrates the point.

Forty-one states now have 129 regional comprehensive health planning agencies under the Partnership for Health Act.

Forty-five states have set up some 452 regional law enforcement districts under the Safe Streets Act.

In fifty states there are 957 single and multi-county Community Action Agencies.

In fifty states there are Comprehensive Areawide Manpower Programs organized on a substate area basis under the Department of Labor.*

Substate regions are also used in federally assisted development programs such as the economic development districts authorized under the Economic Development Act of 1965 and local development districts under the Appalachian Regional Commission.

Further, long-range physical planning for a substate district is performed by regional planning commissions and councils of government funded under Section 701 of the Housing and Urban Development Act.

Beginning in the mid-1960s, local elected officials, state executives, and officials of various federal agencies reflected concern with the plethora of federal categorical grant programs aimed at a wide variety of problems, administered by widely different state and local agencies. To reduce some of the problems stemming from a multiplicity of grant-in-aid programs and grant recipients, federal programs were directed to be carried out through an areawide organization or in conformance with an areawide plan. The recognition of the need for an areawide approach to multijurisdictional problems came, at the federal level, from both Congress and federal agencies. Both legislation and administrative regulations now require a regional approach to planning and delivery of federal assistance in

---

*ACIR, "Federalism in 1971" (Washington, D.C.: Government Printing Office, 1971).

the various functional areas of health, services for the poor, manpower, economic development, law enforcement, and community development.

Four federal enactments have focused attention on uniform alignments of federal programs within states. These are Section 204 of the Metropolitan Development Act of 1966, Intergovernmental Cooperation Act of 1968, and OMB Circulars A-80 and A-95.

One of the purposes of Circular A-80 was to encourage "a system of planning and development districts or regions in each state . . . for coordination of federal, state, and local development programs." Circular A-95, under authority of the Intergovernmental Cooperation Act and Section 204 of the Metropolitan Development Act (1) requires state, regional, and metropolitan clearinghouses for review and coordination of federal grant programs and (2) conformance of any planning and development district or region under any federal program to state districts, planning and development districts, or regions established in the state.

The magnitude of areawide or regional organization is indicated by the fact that a total of 381 substate clearinghouses have been designated for purposes of OMB Circular A-95. According to ACIR, the total consists of 211 metropolitan and 17 nonmetropolitan clearinghouses. About half of the metropolitan clearinghouses are councils of government, while the others are regional or metropolitan planning commissions. About 75 percent of the nonmetropolitan clearinghouses are multicounty development districts.

With respect to districting, OMB and the Federal Regional Councils are providing assistance to states by realigning federal programs to conform to substate districts, with priority given to states that reflect the following achievements:

1. A statewide system of substate planning and development districts has been established.

2. Substate districts have operational comprehensive planning and coordination agencies or organizations.

3. Substate districts are actively utilized by the state in its own planning and program administration.

4. Substate district planning and coordination organizations or agencies are supported by the state financially or in other ways to increase their capabilities and effectiveness.

5. The substate system has a statutory basis.

Chief executives in more than 40 states have thus far mandated the development of a statewide system of multipurpose substate districts for planning and development. The executive orders designating uniform substate districts have generally gone beyond the scope of Circular A-95 in that they have included directives to all state agencies to bring their decentralized offices into conformance with the designated districts. The states are in various stages of carrying out these mandates.

SUBSTATE DISTRICT DEVELOPMENT
IN SIX CASE-STUDY STATES

Florida

In Florida, the governor has not formally designated uniform substate districts in response to A-95. However, the Department of Health and Rehabilitative Services is adjusting the administrative structure of its line divisions to conform to a statewide system of 11 service regions, which reflect the recommended substate districts prepared by the State Planning Office. Thus far, only one of the line divisions has fully adjusted its administrative structure to conform to the 11 regions. Committees from various bureaus in other divisions are presently preparing plans to conform.

Utah

Utah designated a uniform system of substate districts through executive order in 1971, which is to apply to state services as well as federal programs. The state is using one of its designated substate districts as a pilot to develop a district human resources board composed of local elected officials for purposes of creating a single service system on a district basis. The board includes county commissioners, mayors, and school board chairmen.

The role and functions of the district board will be to assess needs and resources and to develop regional plans and policies for provision of state services in the region.

Massachusetts

Massachusetts has revised its system of substate regions in response to the OMB initiative. The new system to cover federal programs and state operations is expected to adhere closely to the eight regions delineated in the Department of Administration and Finance Bulletin A-65 adopted in 1968 and revised in 1970.

Only the five human resources agencies under the Executive Office of Human Services have attempted to conform to an earlier pattern of regions. However, each has its own regional director with different functions and staff levels.

Maine

In 1971, Maine formally established a uniform system of eight substate planning regions by executive order of the governor. The order specifically requires that state service agencies adjust their organizational structure to utilize the substate districts for planning and administration of services. The Department of Health and Welfare has been developing a regional structure for administration of services. Due to population densities, the department is considering combining the substate regions to result in four regions for the department. At this point, the department's Bureau of Social Welfare has six regional offices in operation. Regional directors, however, are not presently responsible for field staffs of the bureaus of health, medical care, or vocational rehabilitation.

Detailed proposals for reorganization of the department, including a merger with the state departments of mental health and corrections, contemplate development of a regional administrative structure for delivery of departmental services. Reorganization proposals for the Department of Health and Welfare will be reconsidered by the Maine Legislature in its next session.

Georgia

Georgia was one of the first states to develop a statewide system of substate districts. In the mid-1950s, multicounty regional organizations began to develop. Initially, these organizations could be characterized as privately stimulated, voluntary, quasi-governmental organizations with a self-described goal of overall economic and job development.

In 1957, the Georgia organizations were recognized by state enabling law as area planning and development commissions and began to receive state as well as federal funding. Their staffs became oriented to physical planning, as federal "701" program requirements had to be met to receive those program resources.

In 1969, the boundaries of the area planning and development commissions were adopted for the purposes of A-95. The executive order proved that the same boundaries were to be used for state services but implementation of that order has not been actively pursued. However, the recently created Department of Human Resources is examining the possible use of the substate districts for reorganization of the administrative structure for service delivery in the state. Further, the department is examining the use of the area planning and development commissions for human resources planning at the regional level. Details of the relationship of state central office or a regional administrator to any future human resources planning staff in the area planning and development commissions have not been spelled out.

Illinois

Illinois is taking a two-tier approach to a uniform system of substate districts for planning and program administration. In 1971, the governor issued an executive order designating a uniform system of seven substate regions. Further, the executive order directed state service agencies to revamp their substate districts to conform to the designated regions. The order, however, permits a second level of districts within the seven major regions. Not all state agencies have yet completed reorganization along substate districts.

MAJOR FINDINGS

1. The mandate for state service agencies to realign their district boundaries to conform to a uniform system has resulted from the governors' implementation of OMB Circular A-95. While A-95 deals with uniform state planning and development districts and program review, the governors have extended the principle of uniform substate districts to include administration of state service programs.

2. Uniform substate districts for the administration of state service programs have not been widely achieved. Though executive orders for state agencies to bring their service regions into conformance with a uniform system have been issued in over 40 states, realignment of state operations has been a slow process.

3. In the six case studies, all except Florida have promulgated executive orders designating a uniform system of substate districts for purposes of A-95 program review. Further, each has extended the coverage of the executive order to include conformance of substate procedures for state services. In Florida, the state human resources agency is using districts that have been proposed as the A-95 districts. Thus, it is to be expected that these states will use these same districts as the service areas under the Allied Services Act.

18

**COORDINATION OF
SERVICE DELIVERY
AND THE ALLIED
SERVICES ACT**

PROVISIONS OF THE ALLIED SERVICES ACT

The Allied Services Act finds an obstacle to effective provision of human services in "inadequate coordination and communication among agencies and organization providing human services." Thus, a declared purpose of the act is to assist states and localities to coordinate human service programs to improve provision and utilization of the services. Both state and local plan requirements include a section for describing the services and functions to be coordinated and the methods by which they will be coordinated.

There are a number of different methods by which human resources can be coordinated. State chief executives have increasingly been using executive office staff for program development and coordination in relatively broad functional areas that cut across program and departmental lines. Another frequently employed method of coordinating services is through a council or committee composed of the heads or representatives of the various departments to be coordinated. Unsatisfactory experience with these and similar approaches has been one of the major factors leading to the creation of human resource super-agencies. Given the fact that the most meaningful and lasting coordination is likely to be achieved through the super-agency structure, an analysis of how services are being coordinated through super-agencies should provide insight into the kinds of services coordination that can be anticipated under the Allied Services Act.

CHARACTERISTICS OF AND POWERS FOR
COORDINATING SERVICES AT THE STATE LEVEL

The first level of reorganization to occur in state human services super-agencies is administrative integration of the support functions of personnel, purchasing, accounting, budgeting, and planning. Typically, this level is established by state law and expresses the legislative intent to achieve administrative economies through reorganization. Offices or divisions of administrative services that perform all support functions but planning were created in Florida, Maine, and Georgia. Staff in the office of the director is also charged with overseeing the performance of these functions as they are carried out by the line divisions in Utah and Massachusetts. A reorganization study in Utah recommends further strengthening of central administrative services functions in the state agency.

A second level of reorganization within the state super-agencies, which generally occurs after the first level has taken effect, directly affects the coordination of service delivery. This level involves a redesign of the services delivery system of the various line divisions in which common activities are consolidated or coordinated. It is further reflected in state policies to broaden the base of community services and reduce institutionalization of service recipients.

Four types of powers are used by super-agency directors in coordinating services. These are as follows:

1. The power of single line authority over the line divisions of the agency. This includes the power to appoint and dismiss division heads and to direct the internal affairs of the various divisions.

2. The power to conduct internal reorganizations of the department. This includes the power to create and/or abolish divisions, to reassign functions to other divisions, and to create consolidated offices for departmental administrative services and planning.

3. The power of budgeting and allocation of resources to the line divisions. This may take the form of review and approval over all division budgets or establishment of a central departmental budget function.

4. The power to conduct comprehensive planning for the functional services provided by the department.

The extent to which these powers have been granted and the methods in which they have been used to achieve services coordination in the state human services super-agencies varies in each of the case states. The following discussion describes the powers granted to the agency director, the intent with which those powers have been utilized, and the factors that have either facilitated or inhibited coordination of services at the state level.

Florida

The powers of the secretary of the Department of Health and Rehabilitative Services have been used extensively in services integration efforts. They are direct line authority over divisions, the power of departmental budgeting and resource allocation, and the power of planning all departmental functions and services.

The director has formally exercised these powers in the appointment of four division heads (other division heads were inherited in the 1969 reorganization), in the creation of a Division of Planning and Evaluation, and in the assignment of staff to a departmental planning and evaluation program.

The intent of the super-agency was to develop a unified organizational structure from the previously separate departments, a departmental program budgeting system, and a strong planning and evaluation capacity as a means to weld together a cohesive state service delivery system. Direct line authority of the secretary has been used to emphasize among division directors a mandate to integrate departmental programing and services within the state.

Notably, Florida exemplifies efforts to redesign the department's service delivery system. Demonstration projects are under way testing methods and procedures for a common system of core services with different organizational arrangements. This approach is reflected in design of common intake information and case management systems. Further, each service program is being analyzed to determine commonality of service recipients and to develop interdivision service programs. For example, a system of joint diagnostic and evaluation centers for both vocational rehabilitation and mental retardation is being planned. Similarly, the corrections division is developing community correctional centers with program and services provided by other line divisions of the department.

Utah

The powers of the executive director of the Department of Social Services conferred in state legislation are (1) overall administration and supervision of the department; (2) effecting coordination of policies and program activities of the boards and divisions; and (3) approval of proposed budgets of each board and division.

The Utah super-agency consists of seven line divisions or service providers. When the agency was created, the boards that had administrative and policy control over the previously separate departments were retained in the new organizational structure as division boards.

The executive director does not have the power to appoint division directors. That power is reserved to the individual division board with the concurrence of the executive director. However, the director has the power to dismiss division heads with notification to the division board.

The executive director also has the power to consolidate personnel and administrative service functions in the divisions. Further, he has the administrative power to establish a division of other departmental service functions including budgeting, accounting, and planning. In fact, these functions have now been fully developed with a central departmental staff.

A reorganization study for the department was recently commissioned by the executive director. Clearly, the intent of the study was to determine methods for strengthening the organizational structure and move toward services integration. Recommendations included abolishing division boards in order to obtain direct line authority over divisions and restructuring the department with consolidated staffs for administrative services, budgeting, and planning and evaluation. The reorganization proposal also called for consolidation of field staffs into an operations division and central office program staff into a division of technical assistance.

Factors that have inhibited the development of a strong organizational structure with single line authority and development of a cohesive departmental service system have included (1) existence of boards between the executive director and division directors; (2) provisions in state law that delegate administrative authority over the divisions to both the division boards and the executive director; and (3) placement of the executive director in a role of coordinating policy-making functions of seven boards. These factors have made it difficult to realize the mandate to consolidate administrative services, budgeting, and planning staff of the line divisions in the office of executive director.

Issues of services integration were addressed in proposals to create a single departmental service system on a substate district basis. Preliminary work, including creation of district boards of local elected officials for each of the substate districts, is under way. Demonstration projects are being used to develop a common core services system, analyze the skill levels required for service delivery, and develop a master computerized system for management of case records. These elements are expected to be used in a test of a substate regional service system involving not only the Department of Social Services but other state agencies.

Not all human service functions are assigned by law to the department. In Utah's substate district experiment, the governor's support has been instrumental in obtaining the cooperation and participation of other state agencies responsible for service functions such as vocational rehabilitation, education, and employment services.

Massachusetts

The Executive Office of Human Services, as well as the other nine cabinet offices, are an outgrowth of a study that recommended that state government be reorganized by a two-step process. The first step was establishment of a number of functional secretariats under which all state agencies would be grouped. The agencies would continue their operations substantially unchanged during this step but would be subject to the general supervision of the appropriate secretary and his staff. The legislation did extend certain administrative powers to the secretary. These are (1) to review, approve, or amend budget requests of the agencies within his office; (2) to have access to all records and documents legally available to him within any agency in his office; (3) to conduct studies of the operations of said agencies to improve efficiency and manageability, and to recommend to the governor changes in the law affecting those operations; and (4) to conduct comprehensive planning with respect to the functional fields for which his office is responsible.

Directors of the constituent service agencies are still appointed by the governor and not the secretary. However, the governor has given the secretary responsibility to recruit and recommend candidates for directorship of the various service agencies.

While the secretary cannot merge or restructure functions within the service agencies, budgeting and planning powers have been key factors in state efforts to convert the state service system from an institutional base to one of community-based programs. An HEW demonstration grant has been used to provide planning staff in one substate region to begin development of a common core services system for state services. Interdepartmental committees have been used for planning comprehensive child care services, services for handicapped children, community-based correctional activities, and drug and alcohol services.

Maine

The powers of the commissioner of the Department of Health and Welfare include full responsibility and authority for planning, budgeting, and directing and administering the functions of the department. As such, he has the authority to organize, transfer, abolish, or create administrative units of the department. He has full appointive powers and direct line authority over all division heads. These powers have been also used to create a centralized administrative services staff and a regional organizational structure for welfare-social services.

A major reorganization proposal is before the next session of the state legislature that will include assigning the functions of mental health, mental retardation, corrections, and aging services to the department. At present only public health, welfare-social services, and vocational rehabilitation services are assigned to the department. Planning staff is presently limited to 314(a) comprehensive health planning and management system planning staff in the office of the commissioner and line division program staff within the central office. The reorganization proposal also provides for a consolidated planning staff at the central office and substate district levels.

The intent of the commissioner in exercising available power has been the development of planning and computer-based records and financial management systems for delivery of state services. To that end, emphasis has been placed on development of a computer-based system of administration of assistance payments and organization at a regional level for separation of social services from income maintenance. While services integration has been espoused as an intended goal of the department, the department has not developed a central staff for planning and evaluation of all departmental services.

Several factors influence the extent to which the department can achieve coordination. Field staff for all divisions are being colocated in regional service facilities. A central core services system of outreach, intake, information, referral, and follow-up is being developed along substate regional lines. The regional directors have direct line authority only over the department's bureau of social welfare staff in the regional offices; however, under the reorganization of the department now pending before the state legislature, regional directors would have line authority over all departmental field staff in a substate district.

Illinois

In Illinois, where there is no state human resources super-agency, the powers and influence of the governor are being used in the Tri-County Project to coordinate service delivery of public and private service providers in a single substate area. The organizational entity responsible for service coordination is the Illinois Institute for Social Policy, functioning with support from the governor's office as administrator of the Tri-County Project. Willingness of the 14 state service agencies operating in the three-county area to participate in the project was largely determined by the designation of the project director as the governor's coordinator of state human services.

A convenor power is being used to bring state and local service agencies together for planning improved service delivery through a common core services system. That power is also being used to obtain participation in the operation of the system and resolution of interagency disputes.

Within the project, the principal element for coordination of service delivery is a Coordination Unit, which functions to locate and confront policy and program problems, particularly problems of an interagency nature. Although originally specified in terms of state agencies, the unit function has tended to include problems involving voluntary and local public agencies as well. The techniques the unit employs in its coordinating functions are those of research, negotiation, catalytic agent, and efforts to clarify some policies and laws through the Springfield office of the Illinois Institute for Social Policy and the governor's office.

Supporting the Coordination Unit is an information system that collects data on the movement of clients through the service system, catalogues the range of services, and thereby allows analysis of referral patterns and discovery of interagency problems, service gaps, and duplications.

The information system data are being used by public and private sectors to rationalize the allocation of available resources.

Georgia

The Georgia Department of Human Resources was created early in 1972 and has not completed all facets of the reorganization. Therefore, Georgia is excluded from this discussion on the uses of delegated powers and resources in a state super-agency.

MAJOR FINDINGS

1. Reassignment of state functions organizationally intact to a single state agency does not necessarily yield coordination of state service delivery. A second level of internal reorganization is required, involving a consolidation and redesign of the previously separate services systems. The second level reorganization is generally preceded by development of a centralized or consolidated planning staff at the agency level.

2. The extent to which line divisions of super-agencies can coordinate and jointly plan, program, and deliver services depends primarily on the powers of the super-agency director, particularly his powers of reorganization, his budget authority, and the amount of his direct line authority over agency divisions. These powers vary from state to state. Some agencies go through successive

stages of organization as in Utah, with the agency director being given more authority at each stage.

3. Even though substate districts are made uniform for all services, each service may continue to be administered separate and distinct from other services, with line authority over field staff exercised from the state central office for that service to the district office. However, the states with human resource super-agencies are at various stages of development of a more unified structure using the substate district as the geographic focus.

4. In order to develop a single administrative structure in a substate district, the super-agencies are attempting to define the role of a regional administrator and the degree of control needed over regional division heads. The roles vary from an exercise of direct line authority over field service staffs for all divisions of the super-agency to a coordinator using convenor powers or influence of the state department director or governor in obtaining cooperation of division field staffs.

5. In the design of a regional service delivery system, each state is attempting to develop a single system of core services (outreach, intake, information, referral, and follow-up) to be used for all services of the agency. Formal organizational powers will be used to obtain utilization of consolidated core services and coordination in service delivery.

6. With the exception of Utah, the state super-agencies generally are developing single substate administrative structures for the delivery of state human services that do not include involvement of local elected officials, private service providers, or consumer groups. Planning structures, however, vary in the formal structure from a district board in Utah to expansion of the comprehensive health planning structure in Florida.

7. Human services functions are not uniformly assigned to super-agencies by state legislation. Thus, attempts to coordinate service delivery may go beyond the organizational boundaries to the state agency and require the influence of the governor to obtain cooperation of other state departments in any unified service system. Coordination will be facilitated by establishment of uniform substate districts the reduction in the number of points of contact necessary for coordination of human resource services.

The basic intent of the Allied Services Act is to assist states and localities in improving the coordination and delivery of human resource services. The six state case studies have yielded a number of findings about the states' ability to implement the act as intended. These findings, described in detail in the preceding chapters, are alluded to briefly in this chapter; and where action by HEW seems advisable, the recommended action is described.

The financial incentives specifically offered by the act are probably not great enough in themselves to induce states to reorganize their human resource systems. Beyond short-term planning and capacity-building grants and special grants for administrative costs, the only financial incentive under the act is the ability to transfer limited amounts of money from one grant program to another. The ability to make such a transfer would be likely to appeal only to a state that has already developed a desire to consolidate human resource services.

The extent of reorganization and consolidation of human resource services within states in recent years indicates that there already exist incentives strong enough to induce states to undertake reorganization. The Allied Services Act will build on those existing incentives and in that way accelerate state agency reorganization.

The impact of the act will depend in large part on the way it is administered. Those in HEW charged with implementation must recognize that they are involved in the evolutionary process of creating new institutions and that implementation requires an understanding of that process and how application of federal regulations can help or hinder it. Sensitive enforcement of regulations regarding reorganization and coordination can be very helpful in overcoming state inertia or resolving bureaucratic impasse. However, requiring "too much, too fast" can be counterproductive. As the cases illustrate, states are at different points in reorganization of human resource services. Consolidation of enough authority to affect the kinds of structural rearrangements necessary to realize the act's objectives is an evolutionary process. For example, Utah has been incrementally moving toward more centralized authority over a period of five years. Furthermore, the lead time needed to plan and implement the changes can be long. For example, Florida is just beginning the second level of internal restructuring of the service delivery system three years after creation of the super-agency. These time lags and lead times must be accommodated.

On the other hand, there is a danger of requiring ''too little, too slow.'' Taking into account the evolutionary nature of change and the stage of development in the individual state, HEW should insist on reasonable annual progress by the states in improving coordination, increasing the numbers of local plan, and so on. Due to the generality of eligible activities for Allied Services planning and capacity-building grants and special grants for administrative costs, HEW should pay particular attention to the scope and content of work to be performed. Without a specific work program for Allied Services planning and implementation, there will be few ways to judge the progress of the states in coordinating service delivery and achieving the intent of the Allied Services Act. Therefore, planning and capacity-building grants and administrative-cost grants should be made only on the basis of locally designed, measurable objectives and an explicit work program clearly related to the purposes of the act.

Involvement of local agencies in developing local allied services plans will in many cases encounter resistance at the state level. Such involvement means that state agency personnel must share their authority with outside agencies, often for the first time. Few state agencies have an extensive history of involvement of local agencies and local elected officials, and only one of the case states is developing a decentralized statewide system that provides for involvement of local agencies and local elected officials. Most of the other states are attempting to decentralize state administration to a substate regional level and to consolidate common service functions and are expressing an intent to develop human resources planning staffs for the substate districts within the state regional staffs to plan for substate service areas. The clear implication is that HEW must be prepared to apply constant pressure to induce many of the states to include local allied services plans prepared by local agencies in the state plans.

Outside super-agency central office planning staff, there is little capacity to conduct allied services planning. In particular, there are extremely few substate regional or local planning organizations of any type that involve local elected officials, private service providers, and consumer groups concerned with human resource planning. Whichever of the local agencies eligible for designation under 201(b) of the act is selected to develop a local allied services plan, that capacity must for the most part be created. The magnitude of that task in terms of funds and manpower should not be underestimated.

In addition to providing funds, HEW should be prepared to provide technical assistance to state agencies and designated local agencies in carrying out allied services planning. Such assistance may include indirect as well as direct technical assistance in the conduct of population need assessments, inventories, and analyses of service resources, methods to coordinate or consolidate core services, service program analysis to determine appropriateness of waivers, involvement of service consumers, and public and private provider participation and coordination.

The legal creation of a state super-agency does not necessarily lead to coordination of state-provided human services in terms of redesign of separate service systems for each function assigned to the department. However, given the powers of direct line authority over service providers, the power of reorganization, and single departmental budgeting and planning powers, the stage can be set for the necessary second level of internal restructuring of the previously separate service systems of a newly created super-agency. In addition to possessing these powers, state super-agencies are better equipped to develop a new coordinated service system if there is sufficient staff available to the agency director to support a centralized budgeting and planning process. There should be continuing support for such a budgeting and planning process, beyond the two-year term of the planning and capacity-building grants and special grants for administrative costs.

In order to maximize the impact of the Allied Services Act, HEW should be prepared to provide technical assistance to the states on a broad scale. Such a program should include both direct and indirect technical assistance. The following points suggest how assistance may be provided:

Within HEW, an office or unit should be created that can cut across program lines of HEW for purposes of relating HEW operations to the Allied Services Act and to the states. This approach suggests placement of staff in the office of the secretary. Staff should work directly with counterparts under each commissioner and all regional directors and regional commissioners.

Indirect technical assistance could be provided to states by HEW central office staff through an information clearinghouse relating state and demonstration-project experiences to the act. For example, state reorganization legislation such as Florida's could be utilized as examples of reorganizational methods and powers needed to facilitate coordination and integration of service delivery. Special attention should be given to the second level reorganization. Similarly, the outcome and processes used in Section 1115 Demonstration,

1971 and 1972 Research and Demonstration Projects, and Targets of Opportunity projects could be selectively synthesized to provide information and examples to the states that relate to implementation of the act, coordinated service delivery systems, consolidated core service systems, and supporting management and administrative systems.

The approach using a technical assistance task force should be expanded and institutionalized to provide direct technical assistance to states. One approach could be the development of diagnostic field teams to work on-site at the request of the states. Composition of the HEW team could be central-office or regional-office staffs or both.

Using materials generated for indirect technical assistance, the HEW field teams could conduct an extensive review of the organization, staffing, planning and evaluation system, budget process, program and services, and service delivery system of the states drawing on the experience of other states to identify successful approaches. In addition, the teams could determine what problems emanate from federal requirements and practices and what solutions would be appropriate. By viewing the coordination of program and review from the states' perspective, additional insights could be gained as to the relevant and critical waivers to program requirements necessary to bring about a coordinated service delivery system. In order to assure that technical assistance remains in fact advisory assistance and not federal directive, the task force should not have a role in the funding and plan review process.

The provision in the act that authorizes waivers of regulations should over time result in isolating those features of regulations that inhibit development and implementation of an Allied Services plan. However, HEW should not merely respond to waiver requests but should also effect needed changes on its own initiative. Administrative regulations for state plan requirements under human services programs included in the act should be thoroughly examined to determine where administrative requirements can be modified to facilitate their consolidation and incorporation within the State Allied Services Plan. Such a review should include an item-by-item comparative analysis of state plan requirements, including relevant handbooks, guides, instruction, and supporting documents for each program included in the act. Other factors that should be analyzed are statutory—that is, administrative requirements including those directly related to administrative criteria. Recommendations can then be developed to modify, consolidate, or eliminate duplicative or conflicting requirements.

The planning cycles of other HEW planning requirements, such as the Community Services Administrative Program and Financial Plan cycle, should also be thoroughly examined to determine the extent to which these cycles conflict or duplicate the planning process described in the Allied Services Act. Conflicts should be resolved by HEW prior to full implementation of the act. In so doing, HEW should develop a logical process cycle, which may go thus: state-regional funding benchmarks, preparation of local allied services plans, state review of local plans, aggregation of local plans and preparation of the state allied services plan, and updating plans for individual programs.

In order to prepare itself for implementation of the act, HEW should develop an Allied Services research and demonstration strategy. To the extent that such projects are not already under way through fiscal year 1972 Targets of Opportunity or fiscal year 1971 R and D projects, a series of pilot projects should be conducted within the next year to provide several models for organization and conduct of Allied Services planning at the local, substate regional, and state agency levels. The purpose in developing models would be to describe the activities and products anticipated in state and local Allied Services plans to isolate the kinds of problems that can be anticipated and develop ways to deal with them. The selection of pilot projects should reflect the various organizational options available under the act as well as the different organizational settings for provision of state human services. The mix may be as follows: a state super-agency with legal responsibility for as many of the federal programs in the act as possible; a state in which three or more state agencies are responsible for providing state human services; a state where welfare-social services are state administered and a state where welfare-social services are state supervised but locally administered; a state-designated substate regional service area in both a state-supervised and state-administered environment. This option may also include an office or agency designated by local elected officials to perform planning on behalf of a combination of local governments; a state where county government has major human service delivery responsibilities; an office or unit of local general purpose government—this option should probably be exercised in a highly urban area and include a case where local government is a provider of human services; a private nonprofit agency with staff and recognized planning capability operating in either a metropolitan or substate regional areas.

The results of the pilot projects would provide a basis for developing the administrative guidelines relating to the planning requirements under the act and for developing a strategy for use of planning and capacity-building grants. The pilot projects would also identify the key problem areas in conducting human services planning and indicate the extent and type of technical assistance needed among state and local agencies. The experience and results of the pilot projects should be published and disseminated to state and local agencies as a form of indirect technical assistance.

20

STATE OF FLORIDA DEPARTMENT OF
HEALTH AND REHABILITATION SERVICES

Background

Reorganization of state government was mandated in a new constitution in 1968, which specified that the executive branch shall consist of no more than 25 departments. The impetus to the new state constitution and reorganization was the influence of urban legislators following reapportionment. Reorganization was primarily legislative directed.

Generally, the rationale for reorganization was characterized by (1) reduction of state agencies and departments from a total of 220 to a new maximum of 25; (2) grouping of agencies into broad functional areas; (3) delineation of single lines of authority to the executives; (4) administration of departments by single heads rather than boards or commissions; (5) reduction in duplication or overlap of management and coordination of state services; and (6) clear lines of responsibility within the executive branch so that accountability for implementation of program and policies is clearly fixed. The Department of Health and Rehabilitative Services combined 20 agencies, boards, commissions, and program offices (see Figure 20.1).

Organizational Structure and Functions of the Department

Office of the Secretary

The administrative responsibility for operation of the department
rests with the Secretary of Health and Rehabilitative Services.
The explicit powers of the director of the department are to
(1) plan, direct, coordinate, and execute the power, duties, and functions vested in that department or vested in any division, bureau, or
section of that department; (2) compile annually a comprehensive
program budget for the department; and (3) promulgate rules and
regulations pursuant and limited to the powers, duties, and functions
vested in the department.
Within state law there are limitations on the director in the
internal organization of the department. State law requires that he
(1) shall not reallocate duties and functions specifically assigned to
a specific unit of the department; (2) may establish additional units
of the department where functions and agencies are assigned generally
to the department without specific designation to a unit.
Powers to direct, coordinate, and execute the powers, duties,
and functions vested in the division have been exercised informally
through regular division head staff meetings, Reappraisal of the
overall service delivery system and past philosophies by which state
institutions were operated have been encouraged by the secretary.
The capacity at the department director level has not been fully
developed to integrate administrative processes. However, Florida
is much further along than others examined in this study.

Administrative Services

A portion of the administrative functions have been decentralized
and delegated to operating divisions. Others have been centralized
at the staff division level. The following discussion describes the
extent of centralization and decentralization.
In practice, the administrative functions of accounting, fiscal
control, personnel, purchasing, and budgeting are decentralized.
The Division of Administrative Services operates with a skeleton
staff and functions more in a role of establishing departmental
administrative policy than providing administrative services to
operating departments.
The specific cases of centralization and decentralization of
administrative functions are mixed. First, all internal auditors of
operating divisions were transferred to the Division of Administrative
Services to form the present internal audit staff for the department.
Second, all legal staff of the operating divisions were transferred to
the division. Most of the professionals came from the Divisions of
Family Services and Health. All legal functions of the department

FIGURE 20.1

Florida Department of Health and Rehabilitative Purposes

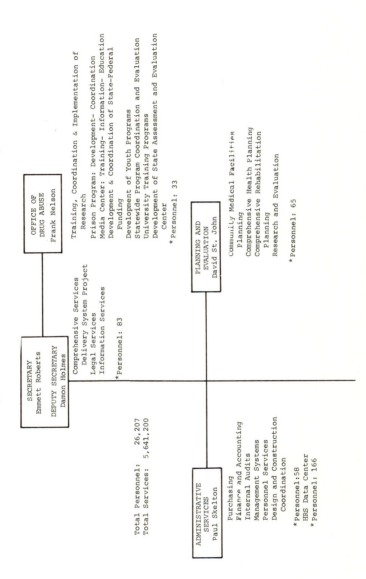

SECRETARY
Emmett Roberts

DEPUTY SECRETARY
Damon Holmes

Comprehensive Services
  Delivery System Project
Legal Services
Information Services

*Personnel: 83

OFFICE OF
DRUG ABUSE
Frank Nelson

Training, Coordination & Implementation of
  Research
Prison Program: Development- Coordination
Media Center: Training- Information- Education
Development & Coordination of State-Federal
  Funding
Development of Youth Programs
Statewide Program Coordination and Evaluation
University Training Programs
Development of State Assessment and Evaluation
  Center

*Personnel: 33

Total Personnel: 26,207
Total Services: 5,641,200

PLANNING AND
EVALUATION
David St. John

Community Medical Facilities
  Planning
Comprehensive Health Planning
Comprehensive Rehabilitation
  Planning
Research and Evaluation

*Personnel: 65

ADMINISTRATIVE
SERVICES
Paul Skelton

Purchasing
Finance and Accounting
Internal Audits
Management Systems
Personnel Services
Design and Construction
  Coordination

*Personnel:58
HRS Data Center
*Personnel: 166

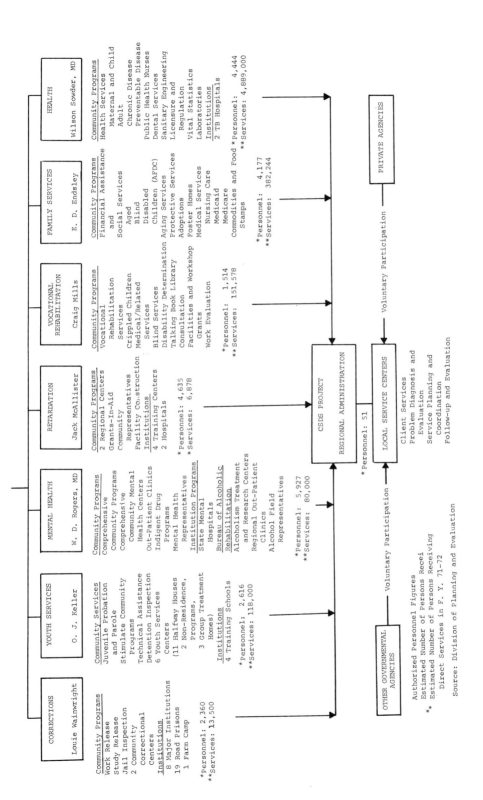

CORRECTIONS

Louie Wainwright

Community Programs
Work Release
Study Release
Jail Inspection
2 Community
  Correctional
  Centers
Institutions
8 Major Institutions
19 Road Prisons
1 Farm Camp

*Personnel: 2,360
**Services: 13,500

YOUTH SERVICES

O. J. Keller

Community Services
Juvenile Probation
  and Parole
Stimulate Community
  Programs
Technical Assistance
Detention Inspection
6 Youth Services
  Centers
(11 Halfway Houses
2 Non-Residence,
  Programs,
3 Group Treatment
  Homes)
Institutions
4 Training Schools

*Personnel: 2,616
**Services: 118,000

MENTAL HEALTH

W. D. Rogers, MD

Community Programs
Comprehensive
  Community Programs
Comprehensive
  Community Mental
  Health Centers
Out-Patient Clinics
Indigent Drug
  Programs
Mental Health
  Representatives
Institution Programs
State Mental
  Hospitals
Bureau of Alcoholic
  Rehabilitation
Alcoholism Treatment
  and Research Centers
Regional Out-Patient
  Clinics
Alcohol Field
  Representatives

*Personnel: 5,927
**Services: 80,000

RETARDATION

Jack McAllister

Community Programs
2 Regional Centers
Grants-In-Aid
Community
  Representatives
Facility Construction
Institutions
4 Training Centers
2 Hospitals

*Personnel: 4,635
**Services: 6,878

VOCATIONAL
REHABILITATION

Craig Mills

Community Programs
Vocational
  Rehabilitation
  Services
Crippled Children
Medical/Related
  Services
Blind Services
Disability Determination
Talking Book Library
Consultation
Facilities and Workshop
  Grants
Work Evaluation

*Personnel: 1,514
**Services: 151,578

FAMILY SERVICES

E. D. Endsley

Community Programs
Financial Assistance
  and
Social Services
  Aged
  Blind
  Disabled
  Children (AFDC)
Aging Services
Protective Services
Adoptions
Foster Homes
Medical Services
  Nursing Care
  Medicaid
  Medicare
Commodities and Food
  Stamps

*Personnel: 4,177
**Services: 382,244

HEALTH

Wilson Sowder, MD

Community Programs
Health Services
  Maternal and Child
  Adult
  Chronic Disease
  Preventable Disease
  Public Health Nurses
  Dental Services
Sanitary Engineering
Licensure and
  Regulation
Vital Statistics
Laboratories
Institutions
2 TB Hospitals

*Personnel: 4,444
**Services: 4,889,000

CSDS PROJECT

REGIONAL ADMINISTRATION

*Personnel: 51

LOCAL SERVICE CENTERS

Client Services
Problem Diagnosis and
  Evaluation
Service Planning and
  Coordination
Follow-up and Evaluation

PRIVATE AGENCIES

OTHER GOVERNMENTAL
AGENCIES ———— Voluntary Participation

Voluntary Participation

* Authorized Personnel Figures
Estimated Number of Persons Recei
** Estimated Number of Persons Receiving
Direct Services in F. Y. 71-72

Source: Division of Planning and Evaluation

are now centralized. Third, a departmental information services staff with five professionals was created. Data processing services are centralized in a departmental data processing center. This has obviated the necessity for operating divisions to have their own facility.

Though Family Services and Health are primary users, the data processing center provides services such as accounting, statistics, some client record-keeping, payroll preparation, assistance payments, and management information systems for all operating divisions.

Purchasing functions are decentralized throughout the department. In each operating division there is an office or section with this responsibility. Uniform purchasing policies and procedures are being developed; and the duties and functions of purchasing officers in line divisions, as well as the role of the Division of Administrative Services, are being articulated.

Florida is one of few states with a state program budgeting system. Responsibility for overall operation of the system is vested in the State Department of Administration, Division of Planning and Budgeting. Departmental organization for budget functions is decentralized. Budget offices are located in each line division. Budget requests are prepared on a divisional basis and synthesized at the department level.

Planning and Evaluation

Within the Division of Planning and Evaluation, there are four bureaus. These are comprehensive health planning, comprehensive rehabilitation planning, research and evaluation, and community medical facilities planning. Prior to reorganization, there was no clearly defined planning and evaluation function for what are now departmental services.

The Planning and Evaluation Division, with a 65-member staff, is responsible for rationalizing the overall delivery network of the services assigned to the department. The division staff works directly with line division staffs, particularly those in bureaus for planning and/or programing.

One of the first Planning and Evaluation tasks was the delineation of uniform service districts for each of the line divisions of the department. Eleven service regions were drawn in consultation with the state planning office to assure conformance to substate regions to be designated by the governor in the near future. These service regions are illustrated on Figure 20.2.

The major activity of the Planning and Evaluation Division during this fiscal year is the development of a "plan" for reducing and preventing public assistance dependency in Florida by providing social services that promote maximum self-sufficiency for

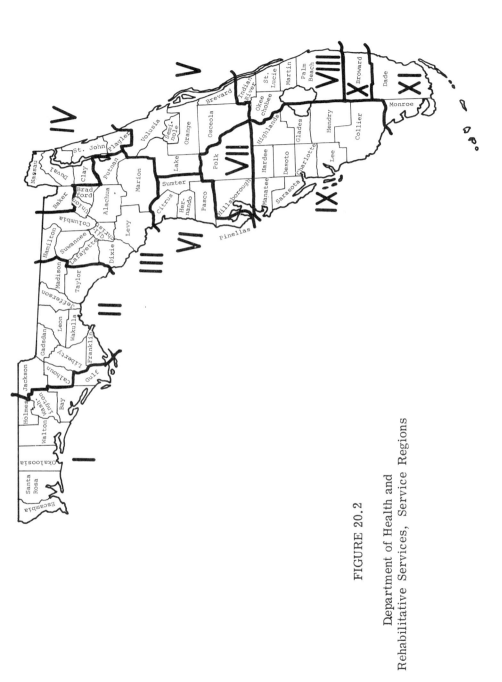

FIGURE 20.2

Department of Health and
Rehabilitative Services, Service Regions

309

individuals and their families and that enable persons to remain in or return to their own homes and communities. Specific tasks for the division have been development of a plan for regional service areas; analysis of all programs and service systems of line divisions; formulation of state definitions of former, current, and potential recipients; analysis of current program clientele for identification of eligible costs; analysis of systems to determine potential structures for community-based delivery; and analysis of restructuring of institutionally based services.

One bureau of the division is responsible for program planning and development of service linkages among line divisions. An example is a legislative package and operating plan prepared for state administration of juvenile predelinquent services, probation functions, and aftercare. The focus of this (assigned to the Division of Youth Services) is provision of community-based services for predelinquents and diversion of youth from the court system.

Four integrative planning activities of the departments are emerging: (1) adoption of a departmental policy of reduction of institutionally based services with a corresponding increase in community-based services for all divisions of the department; (2) a comprehensive analysis of each division's programs for carrying out the policy cited above, coupled with increased funding for services through Titles IV and XVI; (3) development of a single regional structure for delivery of all departmental services; and (4) consolidation and expansion of core services through purchase of services from local resources.

Organization and Service Delivery of Line Divisions

Division of Family Services

The Division of Family Services consists of 16 bureaus and sections with 11 regional administrative structures and a staff of more than 4,000. Estimated total of individuals receiving direct services of the division during fiscal year 1971/72 exceeded 380,000.

The Division of Family Services operates through district and unit offices in each of the 11 service regions. With the separation of assistance from social services, assistance payments are prepared out of a single data center located in Jacksonville.

Division of Youth Services

The Division of Youth Services performs the juvenile probation and parole functions for the state with a total staff of 2,600. Estimated number of individuals receiving direct services from the division during the last fiscal year exceeded 118,000. In 1971, the division began administration of a statewide juvenile probation system that relieved all juvenile court judges of administrative responsibility for probation.

An extensive plan for comprehensive services for youth in Florida includes intake, referral, and screening to determine alternative actions such as court action, nonjudicial supervision, nonresidential treatment, shelter-care, and individual group counseling. That plan, prepared by the Bureau of Comprehensive Rehabilitation Planning and Division of Youth Services staff, has formed the basis of statewide administration of the juvenile system by the division. It is worthy of note that this "comprehensive" program is not integrated with any educational or vocational component. As indicated below, however, cooperative agreements exist between Youth Services and Vocational Rehabilitation.

Division of Vocational Rehabilitation

The Division of Vocational Rehabilitation is presently organized into 16 district areas for service under the general vocational rehabilitation program, 13 districts for services of the Crippled Children's Bureau, and four state areas for services of the Bureau of Blind Services. Generally, the clientele breakdown is 230,000 in the general program, 27,000 for crippled children's services, and 10,000 for blind services.

Major concerns of the Division of Vocational Rehabilitation are steps necessary to realign the present 16 district organizations to conform to the 11 service region plan of the department. Within the division an interim committee has been created, reporting to the director problems encountered and alternatives of the division in conforming to regionalization. Presently, five of the 16 division districts for rehabilitation services are identical to the boundaries of the 11 region plan. The committee has conducted an extensive examination of present districts in terms of case-load, flow of clients, physical requirements, and changes required to conform to the reorganization plan.

In services, cooperative agreements and staff outstationing exists between the Vocational Rehabilitation Division and the Division of Corrections, Division of Youth Services, the Division of Retardation, and the Florida Probation and Parole Commission.

Division of Corrections

The Division of Corrections currently operates eight major correctional institutions, 19 road prisons, and three community correctional centers with a total staff of 3,400. Client population under the division exceeds 13,500.

A major thrust of the overall program in the division is in community-based correctional programs with a total of 14 centers in planning. Three are currently in operation. The centers are minimum-security centers with program components that include work release, furlough, community study, and educational release. The planning for additional centers envisions conversion of existing road prisons to community correctional centers.

Service components include Division of Family Services staff in its reception center and major institutions. The division has developed cooperative programs with the Division of Vocational Rehabilitation, the State Employment Service, and the State Department of Education. As previously described, vocational rehabilitation counselors are stationed in each of the eight major institutions on a full-time basis. A vocational education program is operated by the Department of Education, Division of Vocational Education.

Agreements are also being discussed with Retardation for the direct transfer of some inmates for retardation services in centers operated by the division.

Division of Retardation

The Division of Retardation is the designated state mental retardation agency with a total of 4,600 employees operating four training centers, two hospitals, two regional centers, and a community service program. The division is legislatively charged with responsibility for the planning, development, and coordination of a comprehensive statewide program for the mentally retarded and responsibility for administration and operation of all state facilities for the diagnosis, care, and training of mentally retarded. The division also has rule-making powers in establishing standards for day-care centers, rehabilitation centers, sheltered workshops, and boarding homes for mentally retarded.

Major organization changes in the Division of Retardation are projected to revamp the system of services on the basis of the department's regional service play. Similar to the concerns of other line divisions, the Division of Retardation is planning internal reorganization to break down the dichotomy of institutions and community services.

The division is reorganizing to adhere to the department's 11 regions. Current training centers are in six locations. The division is planning an additional three centers as focal points in service regions. Service capability will be expanded with additional satellite offices and mobile teams based on client load.

Discussions are also under way with the Mental Health Division to develop single comprehensive diagnostic and evaluation centers for both divisions.

Division of Mental Health

The Division of Mental Health is organized into five bureaus. Total staffing for the division is 6,000 employees. Estimated number of individuals receiving direct services from the division exceeds 80,000.

Under provisions of the state's Community Mental Health Act, the division is responsible for preparation of a statewide plan for community mental health services embodying regional plans prepared by area mental health boards.

The system of services of the Division of Mental Health is organized around four major institutions and 23 mental health districts. District services are provided through 23 mental health clinics and nine comprehensive mental health centers. An additional nine centers are in planning.

Reorganization of the Division of Mental Health projected in the next year will attempt to break down the separation of community and institutional services in the division—first steps in bringing the division into line with the department's regionalization plan. Four regions have been selected for decentralization in the first year. Operations of facilities and major consultive activity to centers and clinics will be shifted to a regional responsibility. Regional staff will provide a consultive liaison with the area mental health boards required by Florida law located within the region.

Division of Health

The Health Division is the most extensive of the department's organizational units in terms of structure and statewide services. With over 4,500 employees, this division provides direct and indirect services to the entire population of the state. Services of division include local health services, dental health, adult health and chronic diseases, entomology, maternal and child health, preventable diseases, tuberculosis, sanitary engineering, vital statistics, and health facilities and services.

Briefly, the division provides statewide consultative and supportive services to the 67 county health units, operates special programs such as migrant health services, establishes state health standards, performs state health inspection functions, and regulates health services through censure and regulation. Services such as home health services are provided in 37 of the 67 counties. Two tuberculosis institutions are operated by a bureau of the department. The state division also provides administrative support, including personnel and payroll preparation for all county health departments.

313

The state policy of increasing and promoting community based services in the context of a decentralized regional organizational structure is the key to increasing availability of services to the client in the Florida state system. Tests in Palm Beach and Metro Dade provide for mobile neighborhood outreach teams, standardization of eligibility criteria, and broadening of the information, intake, and referral functions. Both tests are being undertaken for the purposes of redesigning the state system of services.

The Comprehensive Service Delivery System project in the West Palm Beach and Metro Dade regions is intended to provide the department with a test of its decentralized regional organizational structure for the delivery of all of the department's services and coordination with community resources. The project is built around a central information, intake, and referral service.

Major investments are being made in the development of a management information and client records system in order to track clients through the delivery system. The project is also designed to develop new staffing patterns for service delivery embodying separation of services from payments and extension of outreach.

In terms of applicability to the geographically decentralized framework for the department, the Palm Beach service delivery system project has illustrated that a regional director needs line authority in order to operate any regional system. Preliminary experiences in a coordination role indicated insufficient clout to effect organizational change. Additional department clout has been obtained by placement of the project directly under the deputy director of the department, thus offering immediate access to the department director. Previously, the project director (then called a coordinator) reported to the director of the planning and evaluation division.

A contract between the Metro Dade government, which comprises a single substate region, and the department for a community-based information and referral system with an associated transportation component is providing a test of state utilization of local resources in linking state and local delivery systems.

STATE OF UTAH DEPARTMENT OF SOCIAL SERVICES

Background

Utah is a unique state in terms of population characteristics. Heavy urban concentrations are located along a 100-mile area that includes Ogden, Salt Lake City, and Provo. The remainder of the state is sparsely populated. Utah state government was reorganized in 1967 following a two-year study by a "little Hoover Commission" completed in 1966.

Organizing principles used in reorganization were as follows: (1) grouping of similar functions; (2) retention of existing boards for policy purposes and public participation in state government; and (3) development of umbrella departments for administration of similar functions.

The most significant change in the 1967 reorganization was the creation of three major umbrella departments. These were the departments of social services, development services, and natural resources. All of the major boards were retained through reorganization.

The Department of Social Services was initially created under provisions of the Health and Welfare Act of 1967 (Chapter 14, Sessions Laws of Utah, 1967). When created, the department was originally titled the Department of Health and Welfare. Existing organizational units placed in the department were the state boards of health, welfare, corrections, pardons, mental health, and Indian affairs. The act was passed March 9, 1967 and put into effect July 1, 1967. The Health and Welfare Act of 1967 and subsequent amendments specifically established an organizational structure for the Department of Social Services. Entities within the organizational structure included the following boards: (1) a seven-member Board and Division of Health; (2) a five-member Board and Division of Family Services; (3) a seven-member Board of Corrections and a three-member Board of Pardons in a Division of Corrections; (4) a five-member Board and Division of Mental Health; (5) a seven-member Board and Division of Indian Affairs; (6) a five-member Board and Division of Aging; and (7) a seven-member Board and Division of Alcoholism and Drugs.

The legislative intent of the organization as cited in the 1967 act was to coordinate and consolidate in a single department of state government the functions (previously) exercised by the health department, the board of corrections, the board of pardons, the Indian affairs commission, the committee on Indian affairs, and similar and affiliated agencies in order to establish lines of administrative responsibility, increase administrative efficiency, and decrease the cost of state government.

However, the intent and objectives of the department in the little Hoover Commission report were broader. The commission recommended overall responsibilities of a single department for social services to be:

1. To develop a directed consistent approach to health and welfare services, with emphasis on seeking out total

State requirements and providing services to treat and solve the range of problems affecting individuals and families.

2. To develop an information system to quickly identify the nature, extent, and status of all problem cases, and to permit an individualized approach to each.

3. To manage the group of agencies in such a way that a premium is placed on management . . . and continuous evaluation of progress.

4. To emphasize concrete planning, penetrating analyses of problems, and objectification of results.

5. To develop priorities for actions and resources.

6. To weld the department into a cohesive service group.

These objectives for the department suggest an emphasis on services integration prior to popularization of the term. The first objective further suggests development of a unified service delivery system for each of the functions assigned to the department. Further, the commission report emphasizes a significant planning role for the department and development of a central management team.

Organizational Structure and Functions of the Department

The Department of Social Services consists of seven line divisions. Figure 20.3 illustrates the general organization of the department.

The seven line divisions of the Utah Department of Social Services represent a mixture of divisions with discrete service systems and divisions that carry on staff functions of programing and technical assistance to local agencies. There are distinct service systems for the divisions of family services, health, corrections, and mental health. For the divisions of drugs and alcoholism, aging, and Indian affairs, however, the functions are planning and programing, with no distinct state-operated delivery system directly providing client services.

Office of the Executive Director

The executive director's powers are described legislatively in terms of his responsibility for overall administration and supervision of the department and for effecting coordination of policies and program activities conducted through the department's boards and divisions. Further, the director has approval powers over the proposed budget of each board and division.

The executive director does not have the power to appoint division directors. That power is reserved to the individual division

FIGURE 20.3

State of Utah Department of Social Services

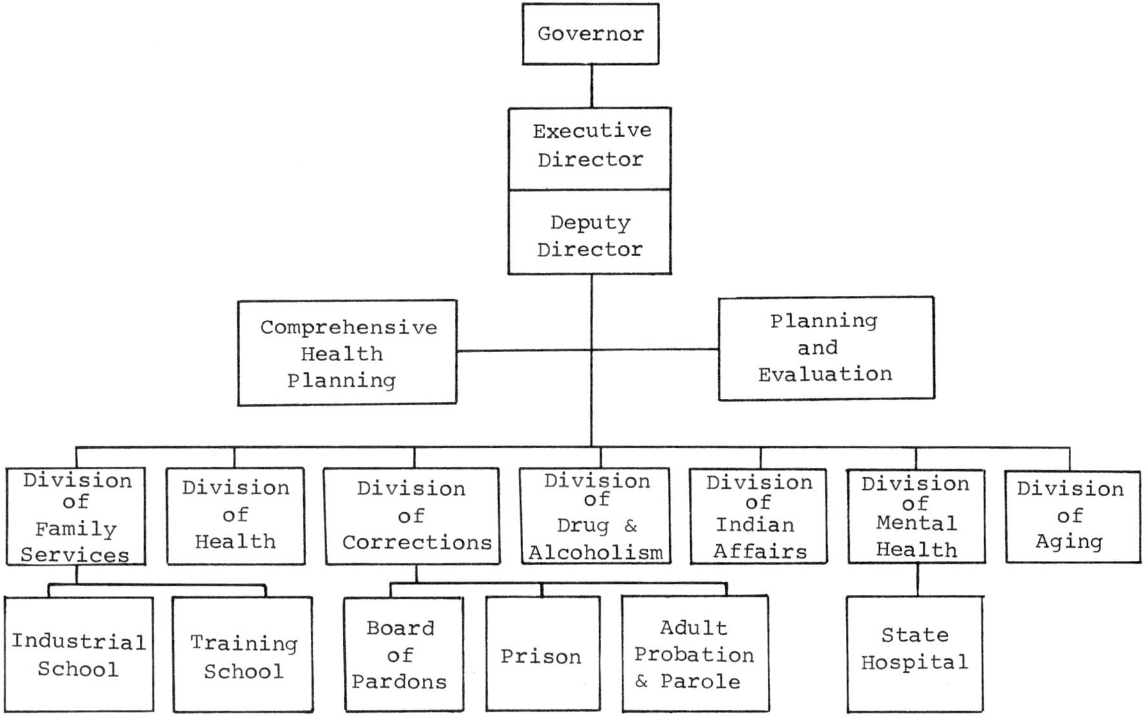

board with the concurrence of the executive director. Division directors may be removed at will by their boards. Removal of a division director by the executive director can only be done after consultation with the board.

While the executive director has administrative jurisdiction over division directors, the lack of full appointment powers seriously weakens his authority. While the boards are essentially policy boards, their administrative prerogatives tend to place division directors in the position of reporting to both the board and the executive director for administrative purposes. Therefore, the layer of boards between the executive director and division directors obscures the lines of administrative authority. Separate boards with policy and administrative powers within the department tend to more closely resemble separate agencies.

The executive director has the power to consolidate personnel and service functions in the divisions, including budgeting, accounting, and planning. In fact, these functions have not been fully developed with a central departmental staff.

For example, the departmental budgeting functions are decentralized. Typically, the fiscal officer of each division is responsible for the preparation of the division's budget. All division budgets are reviewed by the division boards. Responsibility for departmental review of division budgets is assigned to the deputy director.

Planning and evaluation staff within the office of the executive director is limited to two professionals. Principal activities have been to stimulate and encourage staff development of planning systems in line divisions, coordination of division planning efforts, and development of regional service concepts. Personnel and purchasing functions are administered separately by each line division.

Organization and Service Delivery of Line Divisions

Division of Family Services

Field operations of the Division of Family Services are organized into eight regions with county offices responsible to regional offices. Five regional offices offer both services and payments; three, services; and three, only eligibility determinations. There are 11 county offices offering both services and eligibility.

Case-load concept has been abolished in three of the eight state regions representing approximately 80 percent of the work-load of the division. Redesign of the services of the division is based on providing a functional episode of services.

The division operates under a five-member Board of Family Services. Other committees of the division include a medical advisory committee and a social service advisory committee. Under Utah law, provisions are also made for county boards of public welfare which function primarily as advisory groups to the state board. By law, county boards may hire the director of the county department "with the counsel of the Board (of Family Services)." However, in practice, directors are chosenbby the state.

Within the past year, an Office of Planning was established and staffed with one professional. During this year, staff has developed a planning cycle for the Division of Family Services. The focus of the document is a schedule of work tasks in order to prepare an annual operation plan, work program, appropriations request, program goals and objectives, and an overall program evaluation design. The planning cycle closely adheres to steps the division will need to take in preparation for the fiscal year 1973 Program and Financial Plan.

Several pilot projects in the state are being used by the division to revamp and upgrade the social services delivery system. Activities within the manpower utilization project have centered on an analysis of tasks in administration of assistance payments and delivery of services. Results have indicated task differentiation in professional and subprofessional work. Products of the study will provide a basis for staffing and training requirements for a cohesive service delivery system. The Kearns Family Life Center provides a local mode of linking nondivision services to a master service unit for intake, referral, and follow-up. The resystemization project is an effort funded through the division's administrative budget to revise the processing and information systems for administration of assistance payments.

Division of Health

The Division of Health performs the public health functions for the state with an annual budget of $4.6 million and 300 employees. The division is governed by a seven-member Board of Health. In addition, six statutory advisory bodies are attached to the division.

Services of the division include local health services, public health nursing, disease prevention, environmental health, special health services (crippled children, maternal and child care, and dental health), and medical care services.

In the 29 counties of the state, there are only five organized and operating local health departments. Four are county health departments for Weber, Salt Lake, Davis, and Utah counties. The local health department coverage areas constitute the urban population of the state. Recent changes in state legislation permit creation of district health departments. So far, one health department has been created serving a designated substate district.

The Division of Health administers a program of state aid to counties. The funding formula is a $2,000 base grant plus 17 cents per capita. The division also administers a medical facilities planning program that includes Hill Burton, mental retardation, and mental health facilities construction. Comprehensive health planning, however, is performed by a professional staff attached to the office of the executive director. Two 314(b) agencies in the state have been funded, while a third has an application pending. Due to urban-rural mix, the state will only qualify for one more 314(b) agency.

Activities of the comprehensive health planning staff during the past year include stimulation and assistance in development of local and regional health planning councils and agencies, conduct of long-range statewide health planning, areawide health planning development, conduct of a state health manpower survey, preliminary design of a rural health delivery system, development of procedures for placement of physicians in rural areas, and completion of a health education plan and a statewide environmental health study.

Division of Corrections

The Division of Corrections is responsible for operation of the state's correctional institution and the adult probation and parole system. The division operates one major institution with 600 inmates and a probation system with a case load of 1,800 on a $3.8 million budget and a total staff of 250.

The Division of Corrections is governed by the Board of Corrections with seven members responsible for overall policy of the division. The Board of Corrections also appoints a five-member constitutional body, the Board of Pardons, which is the decision-making body regarding all pardons and parole activities in the state.

The probation and parole function is administered through a central office and five regional offices. The projected regional structure is eight regions; however, only five are presently functioning.

One staff member in the office of the director is assigned responsibility for division research and planning. Shortly after placement of the division in the Department of Social Services, the division established an ad hoc interagency council for the purpose of coordinating services and programs in correctional institutions. During the past four years, the council has continued to meet on a monthly basis. The effort of this council has been to provide a structure for other state agency program planning as each relates to the state correctional system.

Coordination with the Division of Family Services has resulted in assignment of staff to the Utah State Prison and limited utilization of Family Services caseworkers in sparsely populated areas in the administration of the adult probation system. Similarly, coordination through the ad hoc group has resulted in extension of vocational rehabilitation and employment services in correctional institutions.

Division of Aging

The Division of Aging was the first new division added to the department following its creation in 1967. The division operates on a $500,000 budget with a total staff of 12 under a five-member policy board.

The primary function of division staff is the planning and programing of aging services in the state. As described earlier, planning activities are focused on staff support for continuing planning, technical review on Title III projects, assistance in formation of local councils on aging, and technical assistance to local councils in program planning.

Presently there are 19 county councils on aging in the state's 29 counties. Four of these have a full-time staff.

Major efforts in the next year will be directed toward formalizing planning for aging services on the basis of eight state regions. A regional council on aging would consist of representatives from each county council and serve as a focal point for development of regional yearly plans for services, training, and research. The state plan for aging would then consist of the aggregation of regional plans.

Division of Mental Health

The Division of Mental Health is responsible for operation of the state hospital and administration of the state's comprehensive mental health program. Total budget for the division is $5.5 million with a total personnel allocation of 370, most of what are assigned to the state hospital. The division is responsible to a seven-member policy board.

Programmatic areas of the division include community comprehensive mental health centers, community mental health clinics, a youth services program, local mental health services, the state hospital, and in-patient services.

Presently only three comprehensive mental health centers are operating in the state. Local mental health services are provided by a part-time staff of 14. Additionally, one mental health specialist is assigned to five of the eight state regions.

Division of Alcoholism and Drugs

The Division of Alcoholism and Drugs operates with a nine-member staff and a total budget of slightly less than $500,000. The division is the youngest of the seven in the department and was created in 1971. The division is responsible to a seven-member Board of Alcoholism and Drugs. Predecessors to the division were a Committee on Alcoholism attached to the Division of Health and a Division of Drugs created in 1970. The board is composed of four members from the alcoholism committee and three members from the previous board on drugs.

Major responsibilities of the division in the area of alcoholism include analyzing state facilities and private programs, serving as a clearinghouse for project review, and developing a comprehensive alcoholism plan and program for the state.

A state task force report on drugs completed in 1969 forms the basic foundation for program planning in the area of drug abuse. Major areas of concern are enforcement, education, and rehabilitation.

Programing activities include drug treatment and community consultation programs, drug education and prevention program, and institutes and workshops.

Division of Indian Affairs

The Division of Indian Affairs is the smallest of the divisions of the Department of Social Services. Present staffing is one full-time director and a secretarial position. Total state funds for the division last year were $7,500. Most of the operating funds of the division come from the administration of Navajo Oil Royalties. The division is responsible to a seven-member Board of Indian Affairs.

For the other tribes and urban Indians, the role of the division is primarily advocacy in trying to encourage development of programs and access to programs of other divisions and state departments to serve the Indian population.

Planning functions of the Division of Indian Affairs are extremely limited due to division resources. The director functions in a role of coordinator and resource mobilizer for planning and program development by individual Indian groups.

Substate Districts and Service System Redesign

Regional Administrative Structure

The framework for design of a regional service system is the state regionalization plan adopted by executive order under provisions of OMB Circular A-95.

The focus of departmental efforts has been one of the designated substate districts, comprising five counties in the southwest corner of the state. Coordination of state efforts is the responsibility of the State Planning Office and involves the Department of Social Services, Department of Employment Security, Utah Law Enforcement Planning Agency, the Board of Higher Education, the Department of Public Instruction, and the Juvenile Court System.

322

The rationale for selection of the southwestern region for pilot work and preliminary design of a regional system consists of the following points:

1. The district has the general characteristics common to most rural areas in Utah.
2. There presently exists in the district a suitable level and distribution of local resources upon which further development could be based.
3. There is initial receptivity to planning by local government officials and others in the district. An association of local general purpose governments has shown a long-time commitment to work together in solving common problems.
4. Twenty-two percent of the families in the substate district earn less than $3,000 per year.

Through a task force headed by the Department of Community Affairs, the state is moving slowly toward the formation of a regional service system.

To date, the design work has been drawn from an extensive study of the Department of Social Services and major proposals for reorganization.

The size of proposed district centers, the number of personnel and the specific programs will vary by district. It may be necessary to have subcenters within a particular district that has a large population base. The exact size and program structure should be based upon the needs for services of the district or community.

The philosophy upon which the proposed regional structure is based is to increase the responsiveness of the service delivery system to local needs. A District Human Resources Board is one of the mechanisms recommended to facilitate responsive, locally based programs. The board's role would be to ensure proper identification of needs and development of plans: to evaluate the needs and plans, to establish priorities, and to approve plans to meet those needs.

Under the proposed plan, the District Board would be appointed by the local county commissions in those districts where there is no areawide Council of Governments (COG) functioning. Where COGs are organized and recognized by the governor's office, the board would be appointed by the COG.

In the test region, articles of association and by-laws for a 15-member district board have been drawn by the Department of Social Services staff and subsequently adopted by the board. Membership of local elected officials on the board consists of chairman of the Boards of County Commissioners, the mayors of each municipality in the region, and the chairman of the county school boards.

Under the proposed District Board Plan, primary responsibility for planning, developing, and delivering services would be concentrated at the local level. Responsibility and authority would be decentralized not only for delivery of services, but also for identifying needs and objectives, developing programs, and allocating available resources. Local operations would function within previously established local objectives and statewide guidelines and goals. Similar to the provisions of the Allied Services Act, state plans would become an aggregation and synthesis of the district board plans for human services.

District or Areawide Planning agencies including the Manpower Planning Council, Health Council, Law Enforcement Planning and Council on Aging would be coordinated with and serve in an advisory capacity to the District Board.

Departmental Reorganization

In addition to the recommended district human resources centers and boards, the recent study has suggested major reorganization of the Department of Social Services. Among the extensive recommendations there are several key features. These are as follows:

1. That state-level functions and staff be minimized and be organized to augment, support, and assist regionally administered services.

2. That division boards within the Department of Social Services be eliminated. The conclusion in the study was that continuation of Division Boards within the department is likely to perpetuate division autonomy and will frustrate efforts to improve coordination and to reduce fragmentation and duplication of services. The study states that if the department is to assume its role of ensuring the development of a consolidated system, the executive director must be given necessary flexibility and authority to carry out that responsibility.

3. Internal reorganization was recommended to restructure the department into four primary functions—operations, technical services, planning and evaluation, and management services.

The finding of the study was that the state organization should be structured to support and service the regional delivery system. The recommended organization and its functions provide maximum support to the regional service structure and permit the state to serve in its role of funding, technical assistance, planning, evaluation, establishing priorities, and delivering those services that can be administered most effectively at the state level.

The department presently has the reorganization recommendations under in-house review for the purposes of evaluating the recommendations and determining which may be implemented administratively and which through the legislative process. It is evident that key recommendations, if implemented, must be through major revision to the state health and welfare law. While the executive director presently has the power to consolidate management services of the department, the legislature must decide on the abolishment of division boards and creation of key divisions due to the specificity of state law regarding the internal structure of the department.

STATE OF MASSACHUSETTS EXECUTIVE OFFICE OF HUMAN SERVICES

Background

The Massachusetts Legislature established the Executive Office of Human Services as well as nine other cabinet offices in 1969 to reorganize state activities into functional groupings. The secretary of Human Services presently supervises the existing departments and commissions responsible for drug addiction, rehabilitation, mental health, public welfare, programs for the blind, youth services, veteran services and soldiers' homes, state prisons, and parole boards.

The Executive Office of Human Services (as well as the other nine cabinet offices) are an outgrowth of a study of state government prepared by the state office of planning and program coordination in 1968. The report recommended that the state government should be modernized by a two-step process. The first step would be the establishment of a number of functional secretariats under which all of the many state agencies would be grouped. The agencies would continue their operations substantially unchanged during this step but would be subject to the general supervision of the appropriate secretary and his staff. During this time, each secretary would develop a plan and necessary legislation to reorganize further the units under his supervision and such other agencies or functions he felt should be under his office supervision. With the legislature's approval, the secretaries would then take over the management of their respective functions.

The governor then appointed an advisory committee to prepare more detailed recommendations and necessary legislation. The committee was composed of state officials, a number of state legislators, businessmen and representatives from such good-government organizations as the League of Women Voters. Recommendations were subsequently adopted in the reorganization legislation. The elderly lobby also succeeded during this time in convincing the legislature to establish an Executive Office of Elderly Service, removing that function from Human Services.

Organization of the Executive Office

The office is headed by a secretary appointed by the governor who serves as the executive officer of the governor in the area of Human Services. He is served by one undersecretary and five assistant secretaries. The assistant secretaries are responsible respectively for intergovernmental relations, program planning, project management, budget and administration, and legal affairs. These six officials and staff support comprise the official staff of the secretary.

Subordinate to the secretary and his staff are the existing departments and commissions that provide human services. Government services in Massachusetts have a unique structure: First, they are centralized in the state; then the next level is municipal. For all practical purposes, there is no county government.

Formal powers of the secretary to deal with his constituent agencies are limited. Specifically, he possesses the following powers: (1) to review, approve, or amend budget requests of the agencies within his office; (2) to have access to all records and documents legally available to him within any agency in his office; (3) to conduct studies of the operations of said agencies to improve efficiency and manageability and to recommend to the governor changes in the law affecting those operations; and (4) to conduct comprehensive planning with respect to the functional fields for which his office is responsible.

For the legislature, the creation of the cabinet secretaries was only a step in the reorganization of the state government. In their view, the cabinet secretaries were to study the operation of their constituent agencies and, within two years, make recommendations to the legislature for further reorganization. Consequently, the legislature made no changes in the status, title, or duty of any department or officer. State officials thus have no statutory reasons to pay any attention to the secretaries. However, with the support of the governor, the secretary of Human Services has viewed his role in much larger terms. As described above, he has assembled a staff larger than expected by the legislature. The governor has also given him the responsibility of recruiting and recommending candidates for executive positions in his constituent agencies. Since assuming his post in August 1971, the secretary has replaced the directors of Public Health and Corrections with men of his own choosing. The incumbent directors of Public Welfare and Commissioners of Mental Health and Youth Affairs were men who fortunately shared the secretary's views. Consequently, the secretary has close relationships with the directors of all of the operating departments.

However, because of restrictions set in the reorganization legislation, the secretary cannot unilaterally merge or restructure functions or positions.

Priorities and Major Activities of the Executive Office

Similar to departmental policy in Florida, the policy of the
Executive Office of Human Services is the conversion of the service
system from an institutional base to one of community-based programs. In light of this policy, the secretary has placed priority on
the following activities: (1) controlling cost in health services;
(2) development of comprehensive services for children; (3) development of community-based correctional activities; (4) creation of
a comprehensive program to deal with alcoholism; (5) more effective
use of drug control expenditure; and (6) to establish a financial
management control system in the Department of Public Welfare.
    Related to these priorities, the executive office staff has insti-
tuted the following coordinating or integrating activities:

    1. An interdepartmental committee on handicapped children.
Representatives from the various departments and bureaus that deal
with children participate in this committee to coordinate their various
activities dealing with handicapped children and to plan new activities.
    2. An interdepartmental committee on planning for alcohol serv-
ices. Presently most of the constituent human service agencies have
some programing for alcoholics but have never cooperated with each
other. Because of the committee, agency officials concerned with
alcoholism have met together for the first time. The secretary has
charged them with developing a comprehensive program for alcoholics.
    3. The secretary has directed the Vocational Rehabilitation Com-
mission to develop with corrections officials training programs for
prisoners.
    4. Likewise, the Health Department has been directed to review
medical care available in prisons and work with correctional officials
to improve it.
    5. Under the guidance of the assistant secretary for Intergovern-
mental Relations, new state plans have been written for Titles I,
IV-A, and XIV of the Social Security Act to expand social services
to former, current, and potential AFDC recipients.

    The priority activities call for comprehensive and coordinated
approaches to problems though services integration per se is not a
priority activity. Thus, the secretary is more concerned about
developing and maintaining the effectiveness of programs and ensuring that they serve the people they are intended to and that they
receive resources according to needs and priorities. In his view,
services integration would be a way to accomplish some of these
objectives but is not an objective in itself.
    The Executive Office has also received from HEW a staff capa-
bility grant for services integration. This grant has been used for

two purposes. First, department policy reflects a concern for the consumers of department services; thus, a portion of the funds are being used to hire a small group of consumer advocates to work out of the Executive Office. In some cases, these individuals will be actual consumers or former consumers of departmental services. They will review proposed regulations and programs for consumer interest and sit on departmental planning committees.

Second, the secretary has commissioned a services integration demonstration in the Northeast state administrative region. The regional human service directors in this region along the coast north of Boston established on their own initiative a regional coordinating committee. Provision of staff is seen as a method to expand upon regional interdepartmental efforts.

A team of 10 or 12 people will work with the regional staffs to attempt to improve the delivery of services. It is expected that this staff will undertake such activities as design of a standard intake system for all categories of services. Consumer interest will be strongly represented in the work of this team, which will work with community groups to determine gaps in the service system and with agencies to correct them. Primary emphasis will be given to welfare programs.

The staff expects also to organize training sessions of social workers and recipients to discuss attitudes as well as administrative bottlenecks. The project has been kept free-form to give staff the flexibility to deal with problems of program effectiveness.

Development of Substate Regions in Massachusetts

Administrative Bulletin No. 65, which set forth the "Uniform Geographic Areas for State Administration and Provision of Services," was issued in the summer of 1968 by the commissioner of Administration and Finance (A and F). It stated that "all departments and agencies of the Commonwealth should have the same field organization pattern of regions and their component areas." A map showing the boundaries of the seven uniform administrative regions and 37 service areas accompanied this bulletin. The rationale for the establishment of this new system was "to attain the most efficient and effective provision of services to the people of the Commonwealth, to improve coordination and to encourage cooperative activity between state agencies, to enable better planning for and utilization of federal funds in conjunction with new federal regulations, and to provide a common statistical base for planning and organization." The head of each state agency with a field organization was instructed to comply with the new administrative field setup by July 1, 1970 or to show cause why it was not applicable.

In 1970, an eighth region was created out of the northern parts of regions III and IV.

Bulletin A-65 merely set policy on state administrative boundaries for agencies with field organizations. It did not discuss structure or functions of the regional organizations nor stipulate the number of regional offices an agency should have. In addition, it contained no requirement that agencies plan by regions. Through the establishment of uniform regions alone, it was hoped that the many objectives of the bulletin would be met.

The state policy on substate districts has not been enforced by the Department of Administration and Finance. By the summer of 1969, the state department was swamped by the problems of the upcoming state reorganization and lacked time to work on developing uniform substate service districts. Thus, Massachusetts has agreed to the OMB assistance. If its work program progresses on schedule, a single substate system to strengthen the A-65 system should become operational by September 1, 1972.

Regional Administration of Human Services

Presently, only four state departments and one state commission, all of which are human-service agencies, are using A and F's regional and service-area boundaries. The Department of Mental Health (DMH) follows them almost exactly, but it required the least changes to conform. The Department of Public Health uses the state regions, but not the service areas. The Department of Public Welfare uses some of the service areas but has very different regional lines. The original 1968 regional lines are followed with a few slight variations because of court boundaries by the Department of Youth Services (DYS), which only decentralized its operations last November; however, DYS does not use the service areas. Finally, the Massachusetts Rehabilitation Commission follows its own three-region system, created in 1970 by combining groups of designated regions.

These five agencies have been working continually since 1968 to comply with the earlier designated substate district boundaries and their efforts have been largely self-motivated. Because all of these agencies were deeply involved in social service delivery and knew from early 1969 that they would be placed in the Executive Office of Human Services under the reorganization plan, a single regional system appealed in some degree to each of them.

Other state agencies with field organizations, such as the Departments of Education, Community Affairs, and Commerce and Development and the Division of Employment Security gave reasons (accepted by A and F) why they should not comply with A-65.

329

Except for Public Health, which remains committed to centralization, these five agencies that have partially complied with the state directive have done so within the last five years. In the decentralization and regionalization of human-service organizations, many roles in these agencies remain unclear. In each agency, staff said that there are great differences in power, staff size, and functions among its regional offices.

Mental Health became highly decentralized when it reorganized in 1967. It has seven regional offices, each with a director who supervises all state mental health activities in a region. Though the DMH admits the existence of Region VIII, it has no separate regional office for it. Mental health activities there are presently administered by the Region III and IV offices. Planning is done by region, and each year the directors submit to the central office their budgets and plans for approval. The hierarchy of a regional office includes the director, a retardation administrator, a specialist in legal medicine, and a business manager.

The DMH has also organized within service areas. Each one has or will have an associate area director, whose main function is to develop, together with the service-area board made up of area residents, a comprehensive mental health program. The associate area directors have no administrative control over state mental health centers or hospitals.

Conclusion

Since the substate district boundaries are to be changed, it is probably fortunate that state departments have done so little to comply with those set forth in A-65. At least there has been a minimum of wasted effort. A and F's assistant secretary for Planning and Inter-Governmental Coordination is in charge of planning the new uniform regional system. The state has recently organized a task force, consisting of a representative of the Federal Regional Council and an assistant secretary from each of the other nine executive offices, to assist in the delineation and formulation of policy for the regionalization of state services by uniform substate districts.

STATE OF GEORGIA DEPARTMENT OF HUMAN RESOURCES

Background

The Georgia Department of Human Resources was created in 1971 as part of an enactment reorganizing and decentralizing the multifunctional executive branch. The law went into effect following the 1972 session of the General Assembly.

The initial plan for the department included the functions of health, mental health, mental retardation, welfare-social services, vocational rehabilitation, adult corrections, youth services, and the state parole commission. The General Assembly modified the plan, however, consolidating adult corrections, youth services, and the state pardons and parole commission in a separate Department of Offender Rehabilitation.

Organizational Structure

Policy for the Georgia Department of Human Resources is determined by a 15-member board appointed by the governor. The board, in turn, appoints a commissioner of Human Resources with the approval of the governor.

Powers of the commissioner are broadly defined to the extent that he "shall supervise, direct, account for, organize, plan, administer, and execute the functions vested in the department . . . subject to the general policy established by the Board."

Boards of the previously separate departments were abolished. These included the state board for children and youth and the state board of health.

Figure 20.4 illustrates the initial organizational structure of the department. However, discussions are under way within the department that may modify the structure within the next year. Briefly, the functions of the four line divisions are as follows.

The Division of Vocational Rehabilitation provides services to persons 16 years or older. Rehabilitation services will be available to any person with substantial mental or physical handicap to employment.

The Division of Family and Children Services provides welfare assistance payments and social services. Related services will include the determination of Medicaid eligibility, the provision of food stamps or surplus commodities, family planning information, and referral to work-training programs.

FIGURE 20.4

State of Georgia Department
of Human Resources

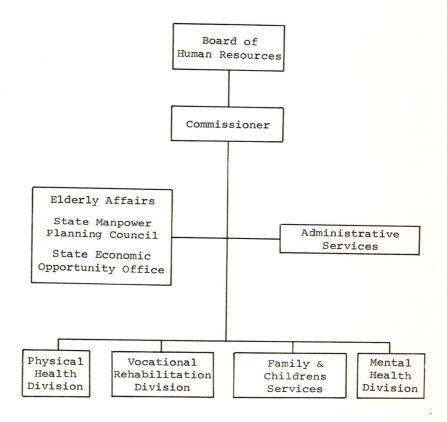

Other services provided by this division include the child welfare programs, the licensing of child-caring and child-placing agencies, and the court services and detention programs for juvenile offenders. Assistance payments and social services are administered through 159 county administration units.

The Division of Physical Health will have responsibility for the prevention and treatment of disease and the direct payment of claims for services to the poor under the medical assistance programs. This division will provide programs for family planning and will maintain all existing programs of occupational health and those programs of sanitation dealing with environmental sanitation and housing hygiene. Those functions in the previous Department of Public Health that were transferred to the Department of Natural Resources were water supply, solid waste management, air quality control, and water quality control.

The Division of Mental Health will have responsibility for all mental health programs. The state's mental institutions, as well as programs relating to the treatment of alcoholics, will be administered by this division.

The Department of Human Resources also includes the Council on Aging, the State Manpower Planning Council, and the State Economic Opportunity Office, which administers the federal OEO programs in the state.

Staffs attached to these organizational units, as well as selected central office staff from the line divisions may form the nucleus of a planning and evaluation division for the department. Actual creation of such a division has not been accomplished.

The department is currently examining its system for delivery of health and welfare services at the local level, which involves separate administrative procedures of 159 counties—a structure in which a client becomes eligible for varying amounts of benefits and social services depending upon the county in which he resides.

The department is examining the possibility of converting from this state-supervised county-administered welfare-social services system to a state-administered system. Further, the department is examining the use of uniform substate districts.

The following section briefly reviews the development of Georgia's system of substate districts indicating the type of regional organizational structures that have evolved and highlighting a brief period when human resources planning was performed at a substate district level. Further, this brief review conveys the setting in which the Department of Human Resources would develop a unified regional service delivery system and conduct human resource planning under the Allied Services Act.

Multicounty regional organizations in Georgia have a history that precedes the significant federal stimuli of the HUD (then HHFA) "701" planning grant assistance program, ARC- and EDA-funded[*] districts, and the regulations for nonmetropolitan regional clearing-houses required in Office of Management and Budget (then Bureau of the Budget) Circular A-95. Antecedents include voluntary groups to develop various watersheds, reclamation projects, and rural conservation and development committees.

A major event in Georgia was the evolution of multicounty, predominantly rural planning, and development commissions. Some of these organizations were directly descendant from the watershed and water resources development groups; others were created to seek industry for agriculturally based economies. The utilities (particularly the power companies), railroads, and other major economic interests were the motivating force behind the creation of these organizations. Also assisting was a strong academic impetus from the Institute of Community and Area Development and the Cooperative Extension Service of the land grant university. By 1965, seventeen such organizations were in existence throughout most of Georgia, all in predominantly rural areas.

Membership on the policy boards included business and economic representatives, "leading citizens," and elected officials from the county and larger city governments. More attention was given to public decisions in developments such as water supply, roads, and land acquisition by local government for industrial sites, as they might provide the needed infrastructure for industrial location. Through voluntary contributions and small local governmental appropriations, these organizations obtained their original staffing—characteristically persons whose skills ran to industrial solicitation and promotion.

In 1967, the Georgia organizations were recognized by state enabling law and began to receive state as well as federal funding. Their staff became more oriented to physical planning as federal "701" program requirements had to be met to receive those program resources. In the early 1960s, as EDA and ARC legislation moved through its formulative stages, the Georgia Area Planning and Development Commission's experience was used somewhat as a model for the establishment of local development district organizations under this new legislation. They were seen as a means of providing technical assistance to local governments, assisting through research

---

[*]ARC, Appalachian Regional Commission; EDA, Economic Development Administration.

and data in economic development, and conducting functional planning and grantsmanship necessary to obtain federal funds.

Almost concurrently, the Economic Opportunity Act of 1964 became law and organizations were established across the South to obtain the initial program development grants. Interestingly enough, in the nonurban areas many (if not most) of these agencies covered multicounty areas.

As such multicounty administrations already existed in Georgia, Office of Economic Opportunity/Community Action Program (OEO/CAP) development grants were made to all of the area planning and development commissions. Ideally, this combination of physical planning with "701" program funding, EDA or ARC support for economic development and infrastructure building, state financing for administration, and community action funds for human resources and social services delivery should have provided the type of multi-jurisdictional coordinated planning desperately needed in the rural South. As a matter of fact, the APDCs divested themselves of the community action function and OEO financing during the next three years until there were no such joint operations by 1967. This dissolution of a potentially valuable unification resulted largely from the citizen participation aspects of the CAP.

These organizations' significant characteristics are that they were created by local initiative (normally with county governmental leadership) in response to federal program stimulus to carry out a specific set of planning functions described in federal guidelines and to obtain federal grants. Little, if any, attention was given to a relationship with the state government or a joint planning of county human service programs. In fact, these agencies made significant efforts to isolate themselves from the traumas of school desegregation and the growing welfare load.

In 1969, the now famous Bureau of Budget (BOB) Circular A-95 was promulgated to implement the Intergovernmental Cooperation Act. Where the creation of regional agencies had been a local government activity occasioned by federal initiative, the state government entered the scene. BOB A-95 required that the governor establish regional clearinghouses for the review of a selected list of federal projects. Each of the 18 APDCs in Georgia have been so designated by the governor. State law, however, requires the APDCs to go further than A-95 in that plans under all federal programs operating within the substate district must be reviewed.

Conclusion

While Georgia's APDCs have only minimally been involved in human resources planning, their geographic coverage conforms to state established substate districts. Further, their organizational structure and staff capability have typically responded to federal initiatives and funding requirements. State planning in Georgia in other functional areas, principally physical and economic development, has been an aggregation of regional plans prepared by the APDCs with the involvement of local elected officials.

The choice of existing regional structures with local acceptance and acknowledged planning skills is being seriously considered as an appropriate mechanism for human resources planning among Georgia's 18 substate districts. Similarly, with the possibility of converting to a state-administered services delivery system, the substate districts present a reasonable alternative to a separate regionalization of human service functions.

STATE OF MAINE DEPARTMENT OF
HEALTH AND WELFARE

Background

Maine's Department of Health and Welfare is one of the oldest joint departments in the country, created in the last major state reorganization in 1931. The department presently performs the functions of public assistance, social services, public health, vocational rehabilitation, comprehensive health planning, and health facilities construction planning.

The department is currently organized in five major bureaus. These are health, medical care, rehabilitation, social welfare, and administration. The Bureau of Administration performs consolidated administrative functions for the line bureaus including accounting, auditing, personnel, office services, and data processing. Comprehensive health planning is performed by a five-member staff in the Office of the Commissioner, while health facilities construction planning is performed within the Bureau of Medical Care.

Powers of the commissioner include the powers of budgeting and planning department services, as well as direct line authority in administration of each of the department's service bureaus.

While the above presents a brief picture of the department, the State of Maine is undergoing another major reorganization of the executive branch. After a reorganization study in 1970, thirteen major state departments were authorized by 1971 legislation for reorganization of existing state agencies. These were Agriculture, Commerce and Industry, Consumer Protection, Education and Cultural Resources, Environmental Protection, Natural Resources, Public Safety, Military and Civil Defense, Finance and Administration,

FIGURE 20.5

State of Maine Governmental Reorganization

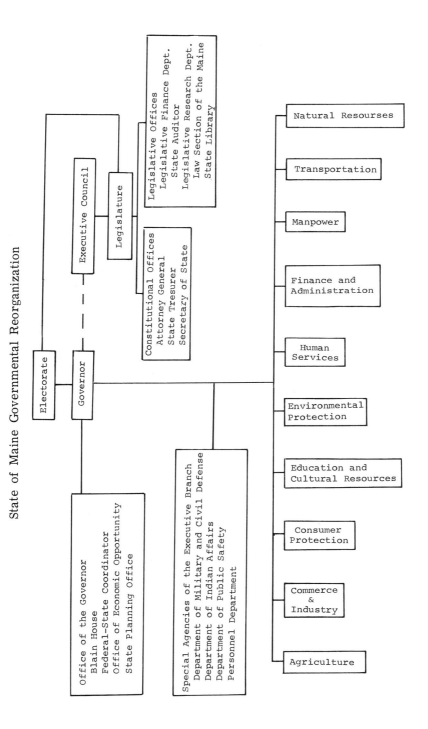

Human Services, Manpower Affairs, Transportation, and the Office of the Secretary of State. Figure 20.5 illustrates the new organizational structure.

Four principles characterize the Maine reorganization: (1) organization by broad functional areas and establishment of clear lines of authority and responsibility; (2) broadly establishing a department's mission to permit the development of a policy and resolution of conflict within a wide range of issues; (3) developmnnt of a single organizational location for similar and interrelated programs; and (4) reduction of the number of agency heads directly accountable to the governor.

Maine, like Massachusetts, used a two-phase approach to state organization. After legislation creating the major departments in 1971, plans of organization and legislation transferring the powers and functions of agencies were presented to the legislature in 1972. All reorganization bills, except for the departments of human services and natural resources, were passed in the 1972 session.

The reorganization related to natural resources brought intense opposition from public interest groups. In the case of human services, the legislature was reluctant to create what would become the largest state department, encompassing health, welfare, vocational rehabilitation, mental health, mental retardation, and corrections. Both reorganizations, however, were directed back to study groups for resubmission in the 1973 legislative session. There is a strong expectation for passage of both bills in the next session.

Substate Districts

At the same time, the state planning office in Maine was developing a uniform system of substate districts for statewide planning and administration of services. In January 1972, an executive order designated eight substate districts, for the most part adhering closely to the state's water basins and representing a fairly equal distribution of the state's population.

Within the executive order, the 10 regional planning commissions and one council of governments were assigned planning jurisdictions in each of the substate districts. In some cases, substate districts were assigned to two planning organizations with one-half of the district to each respectively.

State departments were also ordered to submit a report by October 1972 indicating steps taken to comply with the eight substate districts in administration of state programs. The order stated that "this report shall include a departmental review of field services and operations detailing the extent to which it would be desirable and possible to administer these services and operations on the basis of the districts."

Within the Department of Health and Welfare, steps have been taken to develop an organizational base for administration and delivery of human services in the context of substate districts. Typically the department has directed field staff from the central offices. Within the Bureau of Social Welfare, regional offices have been established in six of the eight substate districts. In each substate district, offices of the four service bureaus have been established in the same location. The authority of the regional director, however, has not been extended to include field staffs of other bureaus.

The plan of operation prepared in conjunction with reorganization legislation for a Department of Human Services calls for the creation of a bureau of community services for the delivery of community-based services related to public assistance, social services, vocational rehabilitation, public health, mental health, mental retardation, and corrections. Field staffs of currently separate bureaus and departments would be consolidated under a regional director with direct line authority over department service delivery within a substate district. At the same time, separate service systems would be consolidated where functions are identical or similar. In particular, the core service functions of outreach, intake, information, referral, and follow-up would be consolidated.

The plan also calls for development of staff capacity in administration and planning within the designated substate districts. Before building staff capacity, regional boundaries must be reworked. Presently, the services of the proposed department are administered along different substate districts. For example, probation and parole functions are administered through three substate districts, while community mental health is administered through eight substate districts. While proposals for administration of services in substate districts have not been completely fleshed out, it appears the department may propose combining substate districts in order to prevent creation of regional administrative staffs with an extremely small service population.

Redesign of the State Service Delivery System

The Department of Health and Welfare has been concentrating efforts to redesign the state service delivery system in order to meet the mandate for separation of public assistance and social services. Essential elements of the system are a core services staff and specialized service delivery staffs. Intake, referral, and service delivery are supported through a centralized case tracking system. Data generated is then used in a program budgeting process titled TOM, for Target, Objectives, and Mix of Services, to develop a regional mix of services and delivery system based on identified service needs.

As described earlier, the organizational base for planning and administration of state human services will conform to designated substate districts. Community-based services will be provided through regional offices, while institutional services will continue to be centralized at the state level. As reorganization is completed, other state services such as mental health and retardation services will be attached as specialized staffs using a common intake system.

Other facets in the redesign of the state service system in Maine included development of a computerized services case management system, a computerized public assistance payments management system, and conversion to a self-declaration system for public assistance payments.

STATE OF ILLINOIS, ILLINOIS INSTITUTE
OF SOCIAL POLICY

Background

Illinois has not undertaken a reorganization of state government as have the other case states, although the governor has committed himself publicly to reorganization. During November 1971, he appointed a coordinator for executive reorganization to operate with a small staff to review reorganization in other states, discuss national-state interfaces with federal agencies, search Illinois statutes for requirements regarding reorganization, and interview state agency personnel to obtain their preliminary ideas on reorganization. The vehicle for creating changes at the state level with regard to the delivery of human services has been an agency functioning as an arm of the governor's office.

Created by an executive order and funded through a state earmarking of 0.5 percent of public assistance appropriations for experimental programs, the Illinois Institute of Social Policy was charged with responsibility for developing, demonstrating, and evaluating ways to improve services relating to manpower, health, public assistance, and related state services. Further, the institute was authorized to operate demonstration projects "including joint programs for consolidation and restructuring of the state social service delivery systems."

The institute is currently operating three demonstration projects. These are (1) the Woodlawn Service Program, a multipurpose neighborhood center in a Chicago neighborhood; (2) the St. Charles Corrections Project, designed to provide basic and vocational education and vocational rehabilitation services in a state correctional institution; and (3) the Tri-County Project, the coordination of all state services within a three-county, predominantly rural area.

The Tri-County Project is the focal point of this case note in that state human services provided by a number of agencies are coordinated through an information and referral process to improve accessibility and continuity of services for recipients.

Substate Districts

In 1971, the governor of Illinois issued an executive order designating substate districts for planning and administration of state services.

The executive order followed a year of work by a state task force on regionalization. State departments were directed to adopt the regional boundaries by July 1971. All state agencies, however, have not yet completed modification of their organizational structures in order to meet these boundaries.

The Tri-County area is only one part of a 17-county substate region. Initially, in the design of the Tri-County Project, lack of uniformity of state service agency regions was identified as a problem in the coordination of services in all three counties. Minor adjustments were made in boundaries, which then included all project counties under the same administrative office of each agency. The larger question of coterminous service regions, however, was not dealt with.

Illinois expects to utilize a two-tier approach to substate regions, with major substate regions designated in the executive order. The order is permissive for a second level of substate districts within each major unit. The governor's task force on regionalization is serving as a continuing body to hear all state agency requests for modifications to the regionalization order.

While the Tri-County Project area does not encompass an entire substate region, the project illustrates how state human services may be coordinated with a single administrative staff at the second tier of substate districting.

Redesign of the State Service Delivery System

The Tri-County Project is seeking to provide more efficient delivery of human services by operating an Information System, a Service Access System, and a Coordination Unit.

The project's principal element for coordination of service delivery is a coordination unit that functions to locate and confront policy and program problems, particularly problems of an inter-agency nature. Although originally specified in terms of state

341

agencies, the unit function has tended to include problems involving voluntary and local public agencies as well. The techniques the unit employs in its coordinating function are those of research, negotiation, catalytic agent, and efforts to clarify some policies and laws through the Springfield office of the Illinois Institute for Social Policy and the governor's office.

Supporting the coordination unit is an information system that collects data on the movement of clients through the service system, catalogues the range of services, and thereby allows analysis of referral patterns and discovery of interagency problems, service gaps, and duplications. Data from the information system are being used by public and private sectors to rationalize their allocation of available resources.

The Tri-County Project also operates an information and referral system known as the "Service Access System." Through the use of service access specialists, who function as ombudsmen for clients, the recipient is brought into and guided through the system of state and local service providers. Staff also perform functions of outreach and follow-up.

Willingness of the nine state service agencies operating in the three-county area to participate in the Tri-County Project was enhanced by the designation of the project director as the governor's coordinator of state human services. This has lent additional clout to the ombudsman role of the staff members in obtaining services for recipients, service data, and follow-up.

The Illinois Institute for Social Policy's Peoria office also operates the Vocational Incentives Program, an effort which merges the staff and program resources of the Peoria-Tazewell County WIN program with Division of Vocational Rehabilitation resources funded with Vocational Rehabilitation-Public Assistance monies.

APPENDIX: LIST OF PROJECTS STUDIED

Sponsor	Location	Formal Title	Study Designation
Georgia Department of Vocational Rehabilitation Services	Atlanta, Georgia	Atlanta Employment Evaluation and Service Center	Atlanta Employment Evaluation and Service Center
Bacon County	Alma, Georgia	Bacon County Community Development Center	Bacon County Neighborhood Service Center
Maine Department of Health and Welfare	Bangor, Maine	Bangor Regional Office, Maine Department of Health and Welfare	Bangor Office, Maine Human Resource Agency
Maricopa County Community Council	Phoenix, Arizona	Community Council Child Care Project	Phoenix Child Care Project
City of Baltimore, Department of Social Services	Baltimore, Maryland	Community Organization and Services to Improve Family Living	Baltimore Family Living Project
Division of Public Welfare, New Jersey Department of Institutions and Agencies	Hamilton Township, New Jersey	Community Social Services Center	Hamilton Neighborhood Service Center
City of Dallas	Dallas, Texas	Crossroads Community Center	Crossroads Neighborhood Service Center
Delaware County Board of Assistance	Chester, Pennsylvania	Division of Social Services	Delaware County Division of Social Services
Philadelphia Board of Education	Philadelphia, Pennsylvania	Edison Drop-Out Prevention Project	Edison Drop-Out Project

Florida Department of Health and Rehabilitative Services	Tampa, Florida	Tampa Child Care Program	Tampa Child Care Program
Florida Department of Health and Rehabilitative Services	Tallahassee, Florida	Florida Department of Health and Rehabilitative Services	Florida Human Resource Agency
Galveston Board of Education	Galveston, Texas	Galveston Early Child Development Program	Galveston Child Development Project
Welfare Federation of Cleveland	Cleveland, Ohio	Greater Cleveland Mental Retardation Development Project	Cleveland Mental Retardation Project
HUB Services, Inc.	Cincinnati, Ohio	HUB Service Center	HUB Neighborhood Service Center
Jackson County Child Development Centers, Inc.	Jackson County, Oregon	Jackson County Child Development Centers Project	Jackson County Head Start
Atlanta Board of Education	Atlanta, Georgia	John F. Kennedy School and Community Center	JFK Neighborhood Service Center
Division of Family Services, Utah Department of Social Services	Kearns, Utah	Kearns Family Life Center	Kearns Neighborhood Service Center
City of New York	New York, New York	New York Neighborhood Government	—
Frederick Burke Foundation	Oakland, California	Parent-Child Center Project	Oakland Parent-Child Center
Parent-Child Services,	Portland, Oregon	Parent-Child Services Project	Portland Parent-Child Center

Sponsor	Location	Formal Title	Study Designation
San Diego County Human Resources Agency	San Diego, California	San Diego County Human Resources Agency	San Diego Human Resource Agency
Senior Centers, Inc.	Seattle, Washington	Senior Centers, Inc.	Seattle Senior Centers Project
United Family Services, Inc.	Pittsburgh, Pennsylvania	United Family Services, Inc.	United Family Services Project
Utah Department of Social Services	Salt Lake City, Utah	—	Utah Human Resources Agency
Illinois Institute for Social Policy	Peoria, Illinois	a. Vocational Incentives Program b. Tri-County Project	Vocational Incentives Program Tri-County Project
Westside Community Mental Health Center, Inc.	San Francisco, California	Westside Community Mental Health Center	Westside Mental Health Center
Yeatman District Community Corporation	St. Louis, Missouri	Yeatman District Community Corporation	Yeatman Neighborhood Service Center
Urban Coalition of St. Joseph County	South Bend, Indiana	Youth Advocacy Program	Youth Advocacy Program
Youth Service Bureau of Boise, Inc.	Boise, Idaho	Youth Service Bureau	Boise Youth Service Bureau

Also included in the study and discussed in Part II are the following: Georgia Department of Human Resources; Illinois Institute of Social Policy;* Massachusetts Executive Office of Human Services; Maine Department of Health and Welfare.*

---

*These services were studied in conjunction with the projects that they sponsor.

ABOUT THE AUTHORS

Sheldon P. Gans, the Senior Partner in Marshall Kaplan, Gans, and Kahn, has over ten years experience in social science research. He was the partner in charge of the HEW sponsored study of services integration projects from which this publication is drawn. Mr. Gans also has experience in working directly with local agencies and governments. At the local level, Mr. Gans has worked in cities such as Honolulu, Butte, San Francisco, Buffalo, Hartford, and San Antonio to directly prepare coordinated service approaches.

Mr. Gans holds a Master's Degree in Urban Planning from the Massachusetts Institute of Technology and has served as a Lecturer at San Diego State University and the University of California at Berkeley.

Gerald T. Horton is president and founder of The Research Group, Inc., a social science research firm based in Atlanta, Georgia. In his capacity as president of The Research Group, Inc. he has served the state governments of Connecticut, Kentucky, and Maryland as an advisor on human resources planning and human services delivery. He is a consultant to the Human Services Institute of Washington, D.C. where he is principal researcher on a case book on human services planning systems at the state, regional, and local governmental levels.

Mr. Horton's research efforts resulted in the publication of The Cities, The States and the HEW System by the National League of Cities. Mr. Horton is also a member of the Georgia House of Representatives where he has served for six years. He studied philosophy at Harvard University.

HEALTH CARE TEAMS: An Annotated
Bibliography
Monique K. Tichy

THE NEW HUMAN SERVICE WORKER:
Community College Education and the Social Services
Edward Allan Brawley

PARAPROFESSIONALS AND THEIR PERFORMANCE:
A Survey of Education, Health and Social Service
Programs
Alan Gartner

ORGANIZATION AND DELIVERY OF MENTAL
HEALTH SERVICES IN THE GHETTO: The
Lincoln Hospital Experience
Seymour R. Kaplan and
Melvin Roman

THE SOCIAL COSTS OF HUMAN
UNDERDEVELOPMENT: Case Study of Seven
New York City Neighborhoods
Marvin Berkowitz

WHERE HAVE ALL THE DOLLARS GONE? Public
Expenditures for Human Resource Development in
New York City 1961-71
Charles Brecher
foreword by Eli Ginzberg